CONTRARY COMMONWEALTH

RANDOLPH STARN

CONTRARY COMMONWEALTH

THE THEME OF EXILE IN MEDIEVAL AND RENAISSANCE ITALY

UNIVERSITY OF CALIFORNIA PRESS

BERKELEY   LOS ANGELES   LONDON

University of California Press
Berkeley and Los Angeles, California
University of California Press, Ltd.
London, England

© 1982 by
The Regents of the University of California

Library of Congress Cataloging in Publication Data
Starn, Randolph.
    Contrary commonwealth.
    Includes bibliographical references and index.
    1. Italy—History—1268-1492. 2. Italy—History
—1492-1559. 3. Exiles—Italy—History.
4. Refugees, Political—Italy—History. I. Title.
DG530.S7   945   81-21970
ISBN 0-520-04615-3   AACR2
    Printed in the United States of America

        1 2 3 4 5 6 7 8 9

Photographs are reproduced with the kind permission
of the Photographic Archive of the Department of the
History of Art, the Robbins Collection on Medieval
Canon Law, and the Bancroft Library at the Univer-
sity of California, Berkeley; the Humanities Research
Center, University of Texas at Austin; the Biblioteca
Apostolica Vaticana; The British Library, London;
and the Service de Documentation Photographique
de la Réunion des Musées Nationaux, Paris. The
drawings in Figure 14 were done by Janet Ecklund.
The index was prepared with the assistance of John
Brackett.

For Frances

*I' the commonwealth, I would
by contraries execute all
things....*

Gonzalo, a councillor on
Prospero's island of exile
in The Tempest, *II, i*

CONTENTS

LIST OF
ILLUSTRATIONS / MAPS / TABLES

ILLUSTRATIONS
(following pages 44 and 108)

1. The figure of the exile. Engraving by Enea Vico, mid-sixteenth century.
2. A medieval view of secular and spiritual bans. Miniature from the Heidelberg *Sachsenspiegel*, early thirteenth century. Universitätsbibliothek, Heidelberg, Ms. Pal. Germ. 164., fol. 37r.
3. Foreign intervention and exile in medieval Italy. The Ghibellines, allied with Emperor Frederick II, expel the Guelphs from Florence in 1248. Miniature from the *Cronica* of Giovanni Villani, mid-fourteenth century. Vatican Library, Chigi Ms. L. VIII, 296, fol. 80r.
4. The company of exiles in the thirteenth century.
   a. An army of Milanese exiles in the 1270s listens to a harangue by Ottone Visconti, archbishop of Milan. Fresco, Castle of Angera, early fourteenth century.
   b. Ottone Visconti enters Milan with his entourage in 1277 after fifteen years in exile. Fresco, Castle of Angera, early fourteenth century.
5. The "art of returning home" fails in Florence.
   a. Cardinal Niccolò of Prato abandons Florence in 1304 after unsuccessful negotiations for the return of the White Guelphs and the Ghibellines. Miniature from the *Cronica* of Giovanni Villani, mid-

MAPS

TABLES

PREFACE

According to some myths of origins, history began with an archetypal rebellion and the expulsion of the rebels from a state of innocence. I began thinking about this book when political protest and social discontent were leading many people to acts of defiance and some to real or imagined exile. During the troubles and then the anticlimactic calm of the past decade, it seemed especially important to look beyond the aura of inevitability that historians tend to give to established authority. It seemed clear at the same time that open or covert mechanisms of political domination and social control could not be easily or cheaply subverted. Exiles had challenged established orders since their earliest recorded appearance in ancient China and Egypt. I wondered what a study of exile would reveal about past and present boundaries to dissent and how such boundaries had changed over time.

Uncertain as I was about the answers, I could hardly avoid questions about exiles in that part of the past I had studied most closely. My first book had followed Machiavelli's republican successor Donato Giannotti through an involuntary absence of more than forty years from Florence after 1530. In the company of Messer Donato and his friends, I discovered that Italian exiles had the sweet revenge of appearing nearly everywhere in the historical record. Contemporary chroniclers and historians could not exclude them. Exiles in medieval and Renaissance Italy roused their supporters in town, raised the countryside, sought allies abroad, and, sometimes, made their way back home. Even when they were unable or unwilling to return, their presence across real and figurative frontiers was sure to be documented in the papers of legislative councils, executive offices, and judicial commissions. From the outcasts themselves a whole literature survived from the thirteenth century on. The Florentine writer Matteo Bandello, looking back from his vantage point in the sixteenth century, imagined that an entire city could be filled with exiles from the past. My historian's obligation, as I came to see it, was to populate that imaginary city, an Atlantis of exiles, with the histories of real people and the details of particular lives.

But how was an account of such a place, or what I began to think of as a "contrary commonwealth," a mirror image of the Italian city-state, to be constructed? There were no reliable foundations to build on. Like citizenship, exile could be defined in strictly legal terms; like citizenship, and much else besides, it could not be reduced to the formulas of the lawyers and the legal historians. Entering the world of the outsider through the archives of his enemies was bound to be difficult at best. To complicate matters further, the exiles of medieval and Renaissance Italy could be taken to prove that "the basic problem of Italian history is that before the nineteenth century there is no Italian history."[*] Exiles were witnesses to and victims of the profound contrasts in the Italian environment between the places from which they were expelled and the open countryside, mountain strongholds, and rival towns in which they took refuge. Deep-seated conflicts among corporate groups, factions, and families surfaced in their lives. Yet Dante stung the Florentines (he thought) with the irony that his banishment from Florence had made him a citizen of Italy, and other poets, the chroniclers, and the lawyers saw exile as a bond among people who had little else in common. Perhaps exile could be considered a theme of "Italian" history after all. But was there much difference between medieval and Renaissance exiles—or, for that matter, between their experience and the experience of exiles in other times and places? In short, the exiles of the Italian Middle Ages and Renaissance challenged, as exiles have always challenged, conventional boundaries and limits.

I responded in the first place with a flexible understanding of the contrary commonwealth, a large map of Italy, and a long view of time. There were exiles of various sorts in medieval and Renaissance Italy, and it was not easy for contemporaries to distinguish between the émigré, the

---

[*] Denys Hay, *The Italian Renaissance in Its Historical Background*, 2nd ed. (Cambridge, 1977), p. 29.

outlaw, the bandit, and the stranger. What contemporaries knew for a fact was that many people were compelled to live outside their home-land either because they had been driven away by force or the law or because they could not be reconciled with their enemies at home. I did not want to insist on narrow definitions where my sources did not. Nor did I wish to be confined to the history of a particular Italian state when the scope and significance of my theme extended by its very nature be-yond the borders of any single state or region. That the phenomenon of exile neither stopped where medievalists might nor began for the con-venience of Renaissance historians was obvious from the start.

Then again, practical limitations of some kind were called for. Political exiles were the most prominent and certainly the most articulate mem-bers of the contrary commonwealth. I decided for that reason to con-centrate on them, if not to isolate them from the company they kept with other troublemakers and innocents who prowled outside most towns in Italy most of the time. But this still left me without any way of ranging as widely as exiles. They were too numerous and too scattered to trace across the Alps and over the seas. I soon realized that I would have to confine myself to the Italian peninsula and even there to focus more often than not on those areas—northern and central Italy, especially Tuscany—where the figure of the outcast was notoriously familiar. As for chronol-ogy, there were the preconditions as well as the aftermath of the medi-eval and Renaissance experience to consider, but I found that my research could at least be centered on the long period from the thirteenth century to the end of the fifteenth century, from the Age of Dante to the foreign invasions of Italy beginning in 1494. The alternatives were either to write volumes or, like Lord Acton, who enjoined historians to study "prob-lems" rather than "periods," not to finish a book at all.

The book I did finish within a framework of deliberate and sometimes difficult choices is concerned with facts, rules, and voices of exile. By "facts of exile" I mean the circumstances contemporary sources record about exiles—their departures and their returns, their strategies, tactics, and forms of organization or of disorganization. Rules of legal definition and administrative routine do not necessarily stand apart from or follow the facts in the order of events. Even so, I have placed rules after facts not only because they can be seen more clearly in that position but also be-cause societies themselves transform actual forces into abstract formulas. As rules can be drawn from the papers of the lawyers and the bureau-crats, so can voices of and about exiles be recovered from poetry and prose, especially from the writings of exiles themselves. If I have given exiles the last word, it is so that they can be heard distinctly as a kind of commenting chorus.

The categories of fact, rule, and voice are only interpretative devices of course. I have used them to sort through and provisionally contain the randomness of the historical record and the contingencies, improvisations, and contradictions of countless particular histories. Such impositions on the past are unavoidable, given the distance that always separates us from "the way things really were." But I have tried to keep my own organizing and analytical distinctions open and elastic enough to accommodate and even to elicit the counterpressures of shifting textures of detail which are proper correctives to hardened historical categories. In this way I have passed on to the reader the task that I set for myself—to acknowledge the need for selectivity and interpretation without merely reducing particulars to paradigm, actions to plot, or evidence of the fullness of experience to a line of argument.

Still, we depend on historical "dramas" to convey a sense of passage through time. I have plotted the theme of exile accordingly through two major phases and so through long-standing but much-disputed claims for distinguishing between a medieval and a Renaissance world. The result is in effect (and perhaps inevitably) yet another gloss on Jacob Burckhardt's *Civilization of the Renaissance in Italy*. While seasons of praise or blame for that historical classic have come and gone in one of the more elaborate rituals of the tribe of historians, the notion of a transition from the Middle Ages to the Renaissance refuses to go away. I take it to be one of Burckhardt's central, though seldom fully appreciated, insights that what he called "Renaissance individualism" emerged with new forms of political, social, and cultural organization, which simultaneously promoted and militated against the free expression of individuality. In this context Burckhardt discerned the beginnings of a shift from a decentralized order of more or less private associations of community and authority toward a modern combination of concentrated political power and atomized self-interest. Many historians have gone on to see in the official spokesmen of Renaissance culture the early representatives of a brave new world. It seems to me that we should also learn to confront something of ourselves in those Renaissance outsiders whose powers of resistance were enclosed and disciplined within the orbit of the state. What I would like to show, among other things, in the history of the contrary commonwealth are the contrasting possibilities of dissent on either side of a historical transition that still seems significant—and deeply troubling.

I began working on this study as Fulbright Professor of American History at the University of Perugia and finished the Epilogue as a visiting member of the Institute for Advanced Study in Princeton. I am grateful for support and good company to both institutions and, in particular, to my hosts there, Sergio Bertelli and J. H. Elliott. In the time between Perugia and Princeton this has been a Berkeley book. The writing of it was bound up with living far from Italy in several distinct and demanding Berkeley communities of town, gown, and neighborhood—and so with some daily experience of the detachments and the engagements of exile. To Berkeley friends, colleagues, and students I am indebted for encouragement, help, and silences as I needed them. For their friendship and their example I think of William J. Bouwsma, Robert Brentano, and Gene Brucker as the magi I could not but try to follow in one way or another. My former student Ronald Weissman read and commented on chapters; Domenico Maffei took time during a brief stay in Berkeley to make helpful suggestions. Beth Berry, Loren Partridge, and Irwin Scheiner gave me the benefit of their reading and their advice at a crucial stage. The Department of History and the College of Letters and Science at Berkeley have been generous with leave time, and the Committee on Research and the Humanities Institute have provided welcome assistance. Dorothy Shannon typed the first draft with her usual concern and care; Peggy Van Sant and Ellen Campbell were especially resourceful in seeing through the typing of revisions. My wife Frances has been a close and always understanding companion on all the paths that this book has taken. I would never have been able to begin the journey, let alone complete it, without her sensitive criticism and her unfailing confidence that it could be done.

1

Premises and Vestiges

"O vestiges, ô prémisses,"
Dit l'Etranger parmi les sables, "toute
chose au monde m'est nouvelle!"

St.-John Perse, *Exil*, II, 20–21

"Infinite are the examples in every age of those . . . driven by exile
from a city or a state," wrote the Venetian political theorist and
historian Paolo Paruta in the 1580s. As in ancient Greece and Rome, so
again "for a long time in many parts of our Italy" exiles in many guises
"had succeeded in being instruments for keeping entire cities in perpetual
travail."[1] The thoughtful Renaissance observer did not hesitate to carry
his theme across particular limits of time and space. Countless instances
of exile as old and distant as they were recent and familiar came to his
mind. With a sure but sober sense of historical perspective, he compared
the Italy he knew with the ancient world. However unique the exile
might be in his own eyes, he was also caught, Paruta implied, in a web of
circumstances which were both inherent in his condition and inherited
from the past.

The Landscapes of Exile

In his book of etymologies Isidore of Seville traced the word *exsilium*
to deep and lasting roots. Exile was fundamentally a matter of location
and defined positions in space:

> Exile means, as it were, "outside the soil"—*extra solum*. For he who is
> "outside his own ground" is called an exile. So, for example, those who
> return from the space "beyond the threshold" to resume civic rights . . .
> which is to say, from beyond the boundaries of their homeland.[2]

Isidore's seventh-century definition was one of many connecting threads his work cast between the ancient and the medieval worlds. He may have found it in Cassiodorus's sixth-century manual on orthography. Cassiodorus had gone back for his own definition to contrasts between exile and home or native land in the language of Cicero, and under the Roman republic "to change soil" (*solum vertere*) had been practically synonymous with "exile" long before Cicero's time.[3] Centuries later medieval and Renaissance writers were repeating what was still, or had become again, the accepted etymological lore. Alberico da Rosciate did so in his fourteenth-century legal dictionary, and so did humanist scholars during the fifteenth and sixteenth centuries.[4]

By their time the old understanding of the exile as one who crossed over or lived outside some home boundary had branched out along a network of related terms. Vernacular words—the Italian *fuoruscito* or *estrinseco*, for example—denoted a person who had "exited outside" or occupied the space beyond the territory or the walls of his home country or city.[5] Similar meanings made their way into the technical jargon of the law. Some medieval lawyers thought the terms *bannitus* and *exbannitus* had originally been applied to the "outlaw" because he stood against or outside the area ruled under the *bannum*, the insignia of duly constituted authority. According to various commentators, "ejection" from a city best defined the *banniti* or *exbanniti* so often mentioned in the legislation of the Italian city-states.[6]

For all the corrections and refinements of modern scholarship, a study of the conditions of exile can still begin with the landscape. The claims of geography on historical explanation are of course very old, especially so in the Mediterranean world. Plato once described the human inhabitants of the region as frogs clustered around a rather small pond. More seriously, he plotted the development of civilization as he knew it along a line of gradual descent from the primitive cultures of the mountains to the civilizing—but ultimately corrupting—cities by the sea. Other classical writers, their Arab successors, and in our own time the historian Fernand Braudel have looked upon the Mediterranean environment as a greater historical force than any of the human actors who have attempted to master it.[7] This much is clear: that the phenomenon of exile in Italy was closely related to the character of the land and its surrounding sea.

The geology of the Italian peninsula provides the landscape of continual contrasts which figures in the terminology and in the experience of exile.[8] Old in terms of human habitation, the peninsula is physically young in its "sea of surprises," at once "the seat of wisdom and poetry" and "of

eruption, torrent, and tornado."[9] Some two million years ago, only yester-
day in geological time, the post-Pliocene uplifting in the western Mediterranean basin perfected the "boot" that Icarus and astronauts could not
have failed to recognize. The process of uplifting has continued, rejuve-
nating physical irregularities that might otherwise have worn away, and
fire and water have gone on to work abrupt transitions in the landscape.
The oldest historical record and the scientific vocabulary of vulcanism
are Italian; Vesuvius, Stromboli, Etna, and the jagged Tyrrhenian coastline are only the most spectacular Italian effects of volcanic activity.
Rivers from the Alps cut their way through the mazes of valleys and steep
gullies that mark the courses of the Tiber, the Arno, the tributaries of the
Po, and the ten parallel streams, from the Taro to the Biferno, of the
eastern Apennine slope. In the plains, water has piled up silt in fertile
places or seeped through trackless lowland stretches, like those reclaimed
only in recent times on the delta of the Po or in the Maremma or in what
were once the Pontine Marshes of Lazio.

Physical connections are limited and fragile within such an environment.[10] The length of the peninsula and the island satellite of Sicily ex-
tends through distinct climatic zones, from the Alps to the continental
climates of the Po valley, from the Mediterranean climates of the center
to the subtropical regions of the south. But in the winter flowers of
Liguria or the cooling breeze of Perugia in July or the snows on Etna
above orange groves, any apparent uniformity within each zone breaks
down, and to move from Tyrrhenian to Adriatic shores at almost any
point is to pass through very different ecologies. Mountains loom like
islands over the plain of the Po, the western coast, the Campagna, the
straits between "the continent" and Sicily. Wetlands interrupt the illusory openness of a plain, and rivers and torrential streams rise to flood in
wintertime or in summer showers. The most direct path between two
points is seldom straight in Italy. Even the surrounding seas pull at the
periphery with centrifugal force. The eastern coastline of the Adriatic
is closer to Venice or to Apulia than Venice to its own hinterland. Apulia
is farther than Tuscany from its medieval and early modern capital at
Naples, and from Tyrrhenian ports the Balearic Islands and Africa are
more accessible than Turin or Milan.

In Italy, then, there was always a material refuge for exiles—the ever-
present mountains, the valley over the ridge or up some river course, the
notch of a sheltered spot on the coast and the sea beyond, the lowlands
with all their hiding places and dangers. The material setting contributed
in turn to a human geography characterized by frequent movement across

physical frontiers. For planting or grazing people moved back and forth with seasonal changes from the classic centers of Mediterranean settlement on mountain slopes which were neither too high nor too exposed for regular habitation. Pockets of rich land lay scattered in vast tracts of mediocre or hostile ground, and the divisions of labor generated by distinct ecologies and discrete communities stimulated economic exchange along networks of trade.[11] As creatures of such an environment, Italian exiles were one class among many classes of migrants made noticeable and necessary by physical contrasts and the limits to self-sufficiency geographical differentiation imposed. Another name for the exiles of ancient Rome or of medieval and Renaissance Italy seems especially apt.[12] As *peregrini*—"wanderers" or "pilgrims"—they were pushed and pulled across a world as changeable as their own condition. (See Figure 1.) Exiles shared the rootlessness of mountain people passing with their sheep, labor, and hunger between highcountry and plain. They joined the human ebb and flow of traveling merchants and artisans, of peasants drawn to town, of the urban rich seeking investments, protection, and leisure in the countryside.

Man-made boundaries of a particularly Italian—and Mediterranean—type confirmed and complicated the physical divisions and so the possibilities for exile in the landscape. It was the city that usually defined the exile's loss and the *patria* to which he bent his efforts to return. Though his hometown might be far away, there were other towns in which he was sure to find aid and comfort. In this sense the phenomenon of exile fits that ideal urban framework without which, as Carlo Cattaneo admitted in an influential essay, Italian history seems to wander "in the labyrinth of conquests, factions, civil wars, and the endless composition and decomposition of states."[13] Outside home soil, as in Isidore of Seville's definition, exiles in medieval and Renaissance Italy were also characteristically *extra solum civitatis*—"outside the soil of their city."

To the northern and imperial eye of Otto of Freising in the middle of the twelfth century, towns already seemed a peculiar feature, and scandal, of the Italian scene. "Practically the entire land is divided among the cities," observed the German bishop and historian. He went on to report that "scarcely any noble or great man can be found in all the surrounding territory who does not acknowledge the authority of his city." So "desirous of liberty" were the towns of Italy that they had become independent republics, ready to contest the authority of the emperor and "receive with hostility him whom they ought to accept as their gentle prince."[14]

This picture of flourishing cities is all the more striking because it suggests a remarkable recovery from the long trauma of barbarian invasion. The devastation still seemed clear enough in the eighth century and has come to seem so again after a hard-fought scholarly debate over continuity and discontinuity in the history of early medieval Italy.[15] But towns nearly abandoned during the Lombard onslaught of the sixth century had sprung up again. New settlements had appeared. Fugitives from the barbarians colonized Venice and Ferrara, and many other towns were founded after the tenth century by the Byzantine, Norman, and Hohenstaufen rulers of the south or in the Po valley to the north. There were also migrations to different sites, as from Roman Ticinum to the Lombard capital of Pavia or, in central Italy, from valleys to more sheltered places where there had been Etruscan towns—Orvieto, Civita Castellana, Cortona, and Perugia, for example. Through the worst times of trouble during the early Middle Ages, Lombard dukes, Carolingian counts, and Italian bishops clung to their urban bases and their civic titles.[16] Leandro Alberti noted in a geographical treatise composed around the middle of the sixteenth century that some older authorities had counted nearly twelve hundred Italian towns. Even after limiting his own calculations to episcopal seats alone, Alberti believed that there were as many as three hundred.[17]

Although definitions changed with time and the point of view, the city was always understood to be a community circumscribed within its own physical and institutional space.[18] To be in exile beyond one's hometown was thus to be beyond the pale of fortification which served to define, defend, and contain it not only in times of siege but also in the rhythms of everyday life. Since the city was a fortress against both the internal and the external enemy, movement across the perimeter was closely controlled. The gates were shut and streets turned dark at the signal of curfew, and civic statutes prescribed punishments for entry at unauthorized periods or points of access. A few tricksters in Franco Sacchetti's fourteenth-century tales enjoyed themselves at the expense of such regulations. When Gonella the Buffoon was ordered never again to set foot inside Ferrara, he came back in a cart he had borrowed at Bologna. The hypocritical "apostle" Giovanni dell'Innamorato lingered outside Todi after curfew so that he could prey on the tender mercies of three pious virgins living in a hermitage nearby.[19] Most real exiles were not so fortunate.

But city walls were more than a material boundary. Effigies, altars, and relics of the patron saint were located at the gates so as to ward off the intruder with spiritual powers.[20] The walls could also embody "the will of the consuls and of all the people," as an inscription declared of the fortifications built at Viterbo in 1099. When Frederick Barbarossa commanded his men in 1162 to pull down the walls of Milan, he meant to extinguish the very identity of the city, and the surest sign of his failure was their reconstruction a few years later. By the fourteenth century the de facto independence of many Italian towns to elect their own officials and exercise jurisdiction within and around a circuit of walls became the attribute de jure of a true *civitas*.[21] The special characteristics which modern sociologists usually ascribe to urban life—its supposed cosmopolitanism, rationalism, individualism, and so on—have often been foisted by anachronism on Italian history.[22] What is clear is the fact that city dwellers in medieval and Renaissance Italy felt their uniqueness and flaunted it to the outside world. If the miniature or mural paintings of Italian towns in profile or in the round which began to appear in the fourteenth century were not as a rule very accurate in detail, they do picture a historical experience and historical aspirations only too familiar to exiles— the image of the city enclosed and vigilant within its own real and ideal boundaries.[23]

Such images, landscapes of mind and imagination, had their important part in the ecology of exile. As surely as mountains or plains, settings of perception give experience a local habitation and a name. The view through a window changes with the beholder; a piece of ground does not look the same to farmers, hunters, or city people. We colonize the landscape with memories, hopes, and anxieties. In the cognitive patterns, subjective desires, and cultural conditioning we bring to our reading of the physical world, some modern geographers have found good reasons for challenging traditions of material determinism or naïve empiricism in their discipline.[24] The terminology of exile in medieval and Renaissance Italy presents a challenge of this sort.

The meaning of *exsul* or, in the vernacular, of *fuoruscito* and *estrinseco* depended, after all, on the landscape being perceived in terms of "inside" and "outside" or "home" and "alien" spaces. While these distinctions conform well enough to the physical and the human geography of the Italian peninsula, they also seem to betray the categorical neatness of the *faits accomplis* that the play of perception, desire, and language intrudes onto the continuum of nature. One of the wisest students of attitudes toward the environment concludes that "people everywhere tend to structure space—geographical and cosmological—with themselves at the center and with concentric zones (more or less well defined) of decreasing value beyond."[25] The empirically minded may well insist that we orient ourselves in space as a matter of fact through everyday experience and observation. But this kind of mental mapping can also be attributed to deep-seated structures of the mind—as, for example, the outcome of those "binary oppositions" which we think into all our perceptions of the world according to the anthropologist Claude Lévi-Strauss and his followers. Then again, our readiness to distinguish centers from peripheries may ultimately derive from fundamental biological contrasts (life/death) or from the primary divisions and conflicts of social life (I–we/they).[26] However the borderlands and otherwheres of exile may be perceived or plotted on a map, it is clear that they occupy cognitive as well as physical space.

They also constitute moral and political ground.[27] When established institutions and values are identified as the regulating "center" of society, the criticisms and protests of the disaffected are likely to be seen as coming from the "margins." (Parties of the right and the left, upper and lower classes, high-minded or fallen virtue—we obviously convert many other political categories or ethical distinctions into positions in space.) In a society of center and margins, exiles are classic victims of campaigns of self-justification and self-defense waged against a shifting fringe of traitors, rebels, heretics, and deviants. Labeled and located in what can be regarded from the center as illegitimate and literally outlandish circumstances, the figure of the exile bears the scapegoat's burden. The regime at home may come to need its outcasts as much as it fears them, for by pointing to them, the regime can define itself, rally the faithful, and concentrate its power within a circle of native soil, familiar symbols, and traditional routines. Like Antaeus, the intimate enemy who loses a footing on home ground also loses his potency in the eyes of established authority.

But if the exile decides to resist, he will have psychological and moral defenses. On the inner map of memory he can possess the image of home territory and dwell in remembered places to keep his powers of resistance alive. Tactical inversions may turn moral contrasts between home and elsewhere to good account. If the outcast seems menacing from the center, the established order may appear intolerably stifling and repressive when seen from a distance. What seems like savage territory from one side of the border may seem only free and uncorrupted from the other; what looks like alien country and much worse to the insider's sight may become cosmopolitan and civilized in the exile's wider view of the world. Cut loose from institutionalized restraints, the exile may cry out for justice, purity, and humanity against the false consciences (and consciousness) at home. No arms need be lifted for wars of revenge to be fought on the landscape of exile.

Such figurative terrain was already staked out in the aboriginal texts of the Western tradition.[28] The theme of return from exile in the earliest Greek epics has been shown to chart an archetypal passage from lands of darkness to lands of light or, ultimately, from the world of the dead to the world of the living. To return home to Ithaca, Odysseus traversed the islands, caves, and underworlds which gave geographical expression to darkened understanding and death. Hearing the voice of the crane, an exiled Greek poet of the sixth century, his heart (as he said) beating black in the wilds, saw the pulsing life of his fields at home, ready to plough, with all their flowers. "Bridal bowers" and "city towers" represented Agave's loss by banishment in Euripides's *Bacchae*, just as "the shores and havens" of Troy were remembered more intensely for the "distant places of exile in waste lands" in the *Aeneid*. Since Ovid portrayed his place of exile on the Black Sea as everything that Rome was not, Pontus seemed to him all the darker, colder, and more barbarous. But such contrasts did not always work to the exile's disadvantage. Odysseus or Aeneas would have been lesser heroes at Penelope's side or in Ilium, and in a classical *topos* the exile gains citizenship of the world, with all its wonders, for being deprived of some small angle of space.

Symbolic contrasts between home territory and the lands of exile were also adapted to what has been called "a tendency in Hebrew thought to dissolve physical into moral states in contrast to the Greek tendency to do the reverse."[29] The wanderings of a nomadic existence and the experience of exile in the history of the Jews charged specific settings with moral functions and religious values. The Garden of Eden and the hard, hostile world after the Fall represented the oasis and the desert as metaphors of the godlike potential of the Israelites and then their desolation on turning away from God. Banished to the Land of Nod, Cain found the earth barren east of Eden (Gen. 4:12), and when, under the Covenant, individuals or the entire people of Israel lost the blessings of the Lord, they were thrust into the unholy cities and punishing lands of exile. To return to blessedness was to come home as from the plagues, the dust, the heat, and the preternatural darkness of Egypt, through the wilderness, and into the Promised Land of fine cities, rock-hewn cisterns, sheepfolds, vineyards, and olive groves. From the exile in Babylon the prophets foresaw a homecoming as though to another Eden, while the city of their captivity under Nebuchadnezzar lay waste in the distance behind them. The paradox of the prophetic vision was that the wilderness and the cities where the people of Israel suffered could also be looked upon as places of purification, renewal, and reconsecration. "And you shall remember," declares the Deuteronomist (8:2–5), "all the way which the Lord your God has led you those forty years in the wilderness, that he might humble you to know what was in your heart and whether you would keep his commandments or not." The writers of the New Testament and the early Christian fathers were drawing on a long tradition when they spoke of man's earthly life as a kind of punishment and preparation in "exile" for the heavenly Jerusalem to come (Heb. 11:13–16).[30]

But exiles need not depend on any specific inheritance of text or tradition to find emotional and moral bearings in the landscape. The topographies described in the poetry of exiled Chinese scholar-officials are no less familiar in structure for owing nothing to Homer or the Bible. So, for example, Han Yü after his banishment in A.D. 819 to Ch'ao-chou, far to the southern edge of the empire. Word of the sentence came through the palace, the sacred and civilized center, where a new day was beginning:

> In the morning a sealed memorial was presented
>   through the nine layers of Heaven . . .
> By evening, dismissed to Ch'ao-chou, an
>   eight-thousand mile road.

The route to exile led through darkness, miles of distance, and natural barriers ending only in death:

> Clouds stretch across the Ch'in Range—where
>   is my home?
> Snow snuffs Lan Barrier, my horse won't
>   go ahead.
> I know that when you come from afar, it
>   must be for this reason—
> Showing the kindness to gather my bones from
>   beside these pestilential rivers.[31]

Through countless variations of detail the underlying structure of exile territory in the modern imagination has hardly changed at all.[32] Bertolt Brecht was reverting to an archetype, if also drawing on his own experience, when he described his escape from Nazi Germany as a flight through a dark, Dantesque wood. The dark wood of Brecht's poem or the wastelands in Klaus Mann's novels about exiles are among the many ancient landmarks in modern exile literature. So are the sinister cities of asylum that exiles have viewed as something like facsimiles of hell, from Erich Maria Remarque's Paris of German refugees after 1933 to Solzhenitsyn's Karaganda on the Russian steppe, "the main capital and pearl of the exile world." Familiar too are the utopias, the perfect island and mountain retreats, or the idealized images of host countries in which modern exile writers have continued to mirror their hopes for, or liberation from, some world they have lost. Even Brecht allowed himself some joy over the gardens, fruit markets, and hillsides of southern California, and the desert of Kok-terek seemed a Beautiful Exile to Solzhenitsyn after his "release" from the Gulag Archipelago.[33] In "The View," the Polish émigré poet Czeslaw Milosz surveys a landscape which "lacked nothing except glorification." He asks: "And who here could manage to institute a phrase?" The answer is one that many writers in exile might have given:

> After forgotten disasters I was inheriting the earth
> Down to the shore of the sea, and above the earth, the sun.[34]

In medieval and Renaissance Italy the old and yet quite timeless contrasts between center and margin, fertility and barrenness, community and wilderness were repeated and renewed again and again. Dante's imagery of home and exile went deeper than even he could have realized. Florence he saw as a sheltering sheepfold, centered on the shrine of the city's patron saint; exile was a fallen valley, with stairs and bread that tasted of salt. Ser Pietro Faitinelli dreamed in a later generation of returning from exile to Lucca in time for ripe pears, ready to kiss its walls and embrace all his enemies within; in the territory of exile divine justice had disappeared and pagan gods returned. Later still, similar patterns returned in the observant playfulness as in the pathos of Niccolò Machiavelli's letters from a forced retirement. Business and, more important to the ex-secretary of the Florentine republic, politics went on in Florence without him. To those quintessential aspects of civic life his tumbledown farm at Sant'Andrea in Percussina was the classic antithesis—a *piccolo mondo* of bird-brakes, rustic gambling cronies at the rough inn across the road, and the fields that muddied the clothes Machiavelli exchanged at night for "curial robes" to write *The Prince*. Even the consolations of these Italian landscapes of exile were the tested ones. Under "the luminous spheres of the sun and the stars" Dante could spurn the Florentines within their walls, and it was "in a low position on the plain" that Machiavelli was better able to survey from exile the summits of worldly affairs.[35]

As premises and vestiges, then, physical and figurative features ran parallel in landscapes both presupposed and inherited through the experience of exile in medieval and Renaissance Italy. Geographical contrasts of territory "within" and "without" corresponded to contrasts in perception, function, and value. In this world of contrasts the paths of exiles are already well marked before they ever set foot on them.

A Framework for Facts and Rules

In the spaces provided for them, facts of exile are acted out and rules of procedure brought into play. The chronicles and histories of medieval and Renaissance Italy are rich in details of families, factions, companies, and whole communes of exiles—how they departed or were driven away, what they did abroad, who their allies were, whether they succeeded or failed at returning home. Judicial and administrative records and lawyers' commentaries dwell at length on legal requirements or institutional consequences. The sources are not at all identical, but they are altogether interdependent. Historical accounts show situations in action which it has always been the task of lawyers and magistrates to translate and, as nearly as possible, to regulate by law and protocol. "Conditions of fact," to use Emile Durkheim's distinction, must be transformed into "conditions of right" for an established order to legitimize "a common conscience against all enemies within and without."[36] In this process preconditions and past experience, premises and vestiges, are closely interwoven.

A striking analogy between the landscape and facts of exile in medieval and Renaissance Italy can hardly be missed—the shared pattern of division and contrast, that "particularism" which is one of the oldest and one of the most recent themes of Italian historiography. In the sixteenth century Francesco Guicciardini was already taking Machiavelli to task for supposing that the unity of Italy was either a possible or even a desirable goal. According to Guicciardini, "some destiny of Italy or the temperament of its people" had always withstood any encroachment on its particular liberties. Many calamities might well have been avoided if the Italians had been united. But, Guicciardini concluded, Italy "has had so many more flourishing cities than she could have had under a single republic, that I think unification would have been more unfortunate than fortunate for her."[37]

The cautious patrician, believer in *fortuna* that he was, would have been surprised by his modern followers. Against *Risorgimento* nationalism Catholic publicists and historians made much of the pluralism supposedly defended by the Church against the threat of a secular empire; to leveling tendencies they disliked in the modern world they offered the alternative of an old, corporative order, creatively diversified (as they chose to see it) and decentralized in networks of associations which protected particular interests and served particular needs. Antonio Gramsci had only to give the argument a critical Marxist twist. He asserted that the Italian bourgeoisie whose corporate order took shape in the Middle Ages and Renaissance was no more than "the solvent of any existing unity, without knowing how or being able to substitute a unity of its own"; as a result, Italian society was condemned to remain in a state of quasi-feudal, "economic-corporative weakness." Those judgments still run like a red thread through Italian historiography. "Lacerations and Contrasts" —the title of one chapter might be the motto of any volume in the recent Einaudi *Storia d'Italia*.[38]

Exile, as Guicciardini himself admitted, was one of the "calamities" which the political unification of Italy might have done much to prevent. Persistent rivalries among city-states meant that exiles from one town were likely to find support in other towns. The same civic independence the great historian admired was thus a source of *fuorusciti*, who were, he thought, "the worst thing a state can have."[39] Then too, political divisions invited foreign powers to pursue their claims on the peninsula, claims that exiles often used to their own advantage. German emperors had old inheritances and the French royal house and the rulers of Aragon newer interests to make good in Italy. The papacy had Italian territories and still greater pretensions to defend. The more fragmented the political situation, the more likely it was that, sooner or later, any particular regime would see agents of the pope or the emperor or the French or the Spanish at the head of a threatening army, spurred on by a contingent of exiles. Whether in the Guelph and Ghibelline alliances of the thirteenth century or behind the scenes of the French invasion at the end of the fifteenth, there were usually exiles to seek out foreign allies, inform (and misinform) them, and lend an aura of legitimacy to their expeditions in Italy.

But there were also forms of exclusiveness in the deepest levels of Italian social and political life of which exile was only an extreme expression. At one level the clannish solidarity of the family was not so easily dissolved as historians once supposed.[40] Much evidence suggests that the pattern of shared or contiguous residence among members of the same lineage, the family voting bloc in politics, and the family business firm were relatively late developments of the twelfth and thirteenth centuries in Italian towns. The pressures and complications of urban life may actually have strengthened, not weakened, the need for cooperation and loyalty within large-scale family units. In a major historiographical revision recent historians have begun to dispense with the conception of evolution from more to less "traditional" family structures, or even to turn the conventional view upside down. Carefully documented studies for Florence have shown how patrician families banded together and broke apart in various configurations, not to suit the theories of historians, but as generations and interests changed in the particular history of every lineage. As in Florence, so in Lucca, Genoa, Venice, and elsewhere in Italy it has become quite clear that family ties, however extended, remained binding or even grew more intense over the long term.[41] And this could only encourage the habit of drawing boundaries between one's own and others throughout the length and breadth of the social world.

So could those little communities centered on some gate, piazza, or church throughout the Italian cityscape. Initially these miniature towns-within-towns were responsible for maintaining their share of streets and walls. They manned the fire watch, policed the district, and distributed the tax burden; they mustered a militia and organized assemblies with elected officials. Townsmen are first collectively visible in the documents of such neighborhood groupings—for example, the *castrum, civitas*, and *burgus* which joined together to form the commune of Genoa in the eleventh century.[42] Long after much of the original autonomy had been lost to communal authorities, political offices continued to be filled, magistrates assigned, taxes assessed, and many types of record kept by neighborhood, district, or quarter. "When you can have the good company of your neighbors," Paolo da Certaldo admonished his sons in the fourteenth century, "don't leave it for the company of strangers."[43] In such a world to pass from one's home turf to some other part of town, inhabited by relative strangers, was already a kind of exile.

The sense of loyalty to the neighborhood was reinforced by the fact that the production of goods and services was rarely specialized by type and location as in the metropolis of the industrial age. While modern urbanites, their cherished self-sufficiency in many ways illusory, live in enclaves of income level, race, or age, it was common for every section, for every urban village, within the towns of medieval and Renaissance Italy to have its own main marketplace, wide-ranging economic activity, and social hierarchy, from great to humble and rich to poor. Renaissance Florentines, for all their collective dependence on the textile trade and their civic-mindedness, established networks of friendship, marriage, patronage, and business affiliation with their neighbors and, in the end, buried their dead among their ancestors in familiar ground close by. Newcomers gravitated from the same country districts to the same neighborhoods in town. In important respects, then, each part of the city duplicated, and stood distinct from, the rest. The rituals of civic and religious unity were all the more vivid because of the resistance they had to overcome as alternatives to the close horizons of everyday life.[44]

According to a familiar set of assumptions about the modernizing effects of wealth generated by urban economies, money should have worked to dissolve the supposedly traditional barriers of family lineage and neighborhood. The actual situation was by no means so simple. Around the turn of the thirteenth century the acerbic Sienese poet Cecco Angiolieri describes florins as "the best of kin" and the key to "all the world's vast possibilities."[45] Cecco's lines are underwritten by the experience of seeing money create new fortunes, breach social boundaries, and loosen old habits of loyalty and association. "New men" climbing their way to positions of authority on piles of florins are familiar figures in the chronicles by the early thirteenth century, and the grasping upstart is practically a literary obsession of poets' nostalgia for the imagined sobriety of the good old days. But the standard moral drawn by many writers was that money had become yet another divisive force in civic life. Businessmen were advised to hoard away their profits or, in the form of credits, to conceal them in secret account books. Both the chroniclers and the poets tell how new riches had produced new social distinctions and how new distinctions had elicited a fierce resistance from anxious men who had already arrived. It was usually conceded that there was little honor in being poor, and this cleared the way for a compromise view which legitimated the pursuit of wealth so long as it was put to the service of the common good. But the compromise could hardly prevent—for that matter, it probably encouraged—the kind of competition which set people against one another.[46]

Impulses to exclusion which were practically second nature in such a world were extended still further by voluntary forms of association. Links by blood and urban geography were institutionalized by agreement in "tower societies" uniting great families around a shared stronghold. The family consortium, or *consorteria*, provided for mutual support and collective defense among relatives, clients, and allies. Guilds regulated economic life, and confraternal societies performed works of charity and pious devotion. Written charters defined the obligations, administrative arrangements, and ceremonial protocol of these corporate interest groups. An oath—the *coniuratio*—bound members to maintain and defend their union. Matriculation lists drew lines of special allegiance, still other sets of boundaries, around many islands in the social sea.[47] In the language of the chroniclers—the annalists of Piacenza, for example—a party was not so much a political organization as a particular interest group or faction, and when the term became more exact late in the thirteenth century, it still betrayed its origins in legal disputes or armed clashes among more or less private associations.[48]

The communal governments of the Italian city-states were no exception. The word "commune" itself implied an ambiguous mixture of public and private authority. As a public entity, the commune was the collectivity of the inhabitants of a city, their common territory, assets, institutions, and interests, *ad comunem utilitatem* in a standard phrase. But Roman law also distinguished the "communal" sphere of private rights from the public arena, or *publicum*. When autonomous civic officials emerged around the turn of the eleventh century, full membership in the commune was restricted by oath to groups of property holders, episcopal or imperial functionaries, and important merchants or artisans.[49] The case of Genoa is revealing. In 1143 a "company" of the city offered membership over a fixed but renewable term of three or four years for the special benefit of those—and only those—who agreed to share its franchise, protection, and justice. Within twenty years a powerful competitor, one of several rival corporations, had sprung up to challenge the earlier commune.[50] This was a familiar turn of events in many other towns. As the lawyers put it, any *societas* with justice as its aim was as legitimate as any other.[51]

The debates of an earlier generation of historians over the origins of the communes sometimes turned on artificial and anachronistic ways of posing the question.[52] Where the historians drew sharp distinctions between democratic and elitist impulses or between public law and private interest, these apparent contradictions merged in the history of the communes. In practice, communal (and precommunal) exclusiveness was virtually inseparable from the exercise of public authority. Over the long term institutions originating with a corporate organization but claiming to stand for the common good gave way to institutions representing other organizations with similar claims. The apparatus of previous regimes—large assemblies, smaller councils, executive offices—was rarely dismantled; it was only pushed as much as possible from the effective center of political gravity by the latest group to organize, demand recognition, and insist on embodying, like the consuls of Tortona in 1122, "the honor and profit of all the people . . . of the city and its suburbs."[53] Public powers were not so much transferred as co-opted. The original commune of the twelfth century absorbed the civic prerogatives of bishops or imperial vicars; the guild-based *popolo* of the thirteenth century grafted its institutions onto the earlier commune headed first by consuls and then by the omnicompetent official usually known as the *podestà*; from the factions of the thirteenth and fourteenth centuries, in turn, the rule of a single lord and dynasty arose. Each shift in power was accompanied by (and sharpened) conflicts between the stalwarts of the old regime and the "new men" who sought to displace them.[54]

Machiavelli's conclusion in a particular case holds true for general practice: "those laws which were instituted were not for the common good but for the benefit of the victor."[55] That Florentine bastion of patrician privilege, the Guelph party, used its notorious veto power to bar the election of prospective officeholders whose Guelph orthodoxy could be questioned. On an unspectacular, everyday level provisions known as the *divieto, contumacia,* or *vacanza* according to place and context limited the access of designated individuals or families to the councils of the communes. Similar devices were scattered throughout communal legislation, and they were only the milder measures of a continual struggle for control.

A verse-making chronicler of Aquila lamented the most dramatic consequences for his and every other Italian town:

> Blessed Jesus Christ!
>> Every party learned about
> What wandering is
>> Once it got thrown out.

As it had been a corporate organization within the walls at home, so on the outside an "external commune" could maintain its own seal, officials, and fighting force until better days might bring it home again:

> Each one went out
> And each one found out
>> How to come back in a fury.[56]

In the sing-song lines of Messer Buccio di Ranallo the high drama of exile and return begins to seem only routine. The ability to exclude the rival side was, after all, a standard measure of political success as much by "normal" as by violent means. Already in the twelfth century the rectors of the Lombard League took a statutory oath to expel the partisans of the emperor from the cities they represented. The denial of political privileges to one faction in communes controlled by another was written into law during the interminable factional quarrels of the thirteenth century. The antimagnate legislation enacted in 1288 against the "rapacious magnate wolves" by the self-styled "gentle lambs" of the *popolo* of Bologna was a widely imitated model.[57] By the middle of the fourteenth century Bartolus of Sassoferrato could take it as a matter of good legal principle that those "who are so powerful that they might oppress others can be excluded by the regime." It was of course for the ruling regime to determine who its powerful enemies were, and, as the chroniclers make clear, "those who governed" meant to do so exclusively.[58]

In many dimensions of experience in medieval and Renaissance Italy, then, one finds sharp contrasts between insiders and outsiders, acceptance and rejection, those who belonged and those who did not. Visions of Italian unity have always been more grandiose and extreme for the formidable obstacles set against them. The real alternatives to divisiveness in the Middle Ages and the Renaissance were more limited in scale. The small size and great vulnerability of most Italian states promoted experiments with intensive forms of political organization and campaigns of territorial expansion in pursuit of larger resources, reputation, and power. The most faction-ridden communal institutions did claim to represent common interests and eventually challenged the separatist impulses of their own origins. As a result of one of those consolidating and centralizing phases which have come and gone in the history of Italy, the exiles of the fifteenth century were to have fewer options than their predecessors in the thirteenth. But whenever medieval or Renaissance exiles left some particular *patria* behind, they still remained within the broad and deep patterns of particularism in the Italian experience.

"Particular corps of interest can sanction a condition of fact; they cannot make it a condition of right."[59] To transform exile into a "condition of right," in Durkheim's phrase, professors of law, lawyers, notaries, and magistrates had their work cut out for them in medieval and Renaissance Italy. There was no shortage of rules possible in principle or received by tradition; the problem, as always in the law, was which rules to apply.[60] No consistent guidance could be expected from references spread across a vast sea of authorities—Roman law, barbarian codes, canon law, customary usage, or civic statutes. Terminology and procedure varied from one text to another. Rules for exile could be, and had been, formulated in terms of different conceptions of society and politics. Lines of historical development were unclear, as they still are on many points, despite the best efforts of legal historians.

The *Corpus Iuris Civilis* embodied these difficulties, and then some, on a massive scale. Emperor Justinian himself noted that his scholars had "plundered" two thousand sources for that great compilation of Roman law. The two chapters most instructive on exile among the notorious *libri terribiles* of Justinian's *Digest* included over sixty-one extracts from fourteen jurists of different epochs.[61] These chapters have little of that consistency and clarity for which it pleased the compilers, like most legislators, to congratulate themselves. Instead, ambiguities, contradictions, and anachronisms abounded in ways that only the most overawed medieval lawyers could have ignored. Even the clearest definitions were never quite clear or full enough. Marcian's formula of the third century A.D. was typical and very influential for the future:

> "Exile" may be threefold: either interdiction of certain places; or banishment whereby all places are forbidden but one; or the *insulae vinculum*, that is, relegation to an island.[62]

Different institutions and stages of development overlapped in this attempt at precise definition. The notion of interdiction recalled the ancient *interdictio aquae et ignis*, the denial to the wrongdoer of refreshment and warmth, and so of the basic physical necessities of life as well as the social ties symbolized by the well and the hearth. During the early history of the Roman republic the *interdictus* was subject to what amounted to a death sentence if he appeared in any place he had been forbidden to enter; his movements were not otherwise restricted, and he could become a citizen of some new community in which he took refuge.[63] A later development, relegation entailed "the limitation by the authorities of the free choice of a certain place of residence, whether by a command to leave a certain locality and never more to enter it—that is to say, by expulsion—or by a command to go to a certain locality and not to leave it—that is, by internment."[64] When Ovid admitted that, even at Pontus, his condition was preferable to that of an "exile," he was apparently distinguishing his "relegation" from the still more severe terms of "deportation" to exile under Roman law.[65] *Deportatio*—deportation or internment on an island or elsewhere—was always understood to be a capital sentence. While the *relegatus* retained his citizenship and his rights over his patrimony and his children, the *deportatus* lost his citizenship and all rights attached to it, except for the minimal concessions of the "laws" of nature. An individual could be relegated to exile in perpetuity or for a limited term; once deported, he was dead in the eyes of the law.

Although scholars have lavished much attention on these distinctions, the history of exile as a criminal penalty in Roman law remains problematic.[66] Only the main lines of what were actually piecemeal changes shifting with the course of politics seem fairly clear. Until the later republic interdiction was probably not so much a punishment as a confirmation of the right to evade it. In the face of some impending or actual sentence the Roman patrician could exercise an ancient privilege (and a quite untheoretical ability among the well placed and powerful) to fly for protection to his family or his allies. By laying on the *interdictio aquae et ignis* republican assemblies or magistrates were, in effect, recognizing a patrician privilege while warning the malefactor to keep his distance. Polybius, Cicero, and Sallust could still refer to exile in this sense. But anything like a "right of exile" had already begun to give way before the legislation of the dictator Sulla in the eighties B.C., and more and more restrictive conditions were grafted onto the old *interdictio* by Caesar, Augustus, and Tiberius. Under Tiberius deportation finally supplanted the older institution. All the while, relegation was being administered ever more strictly as a form of confinement.[67] Horace declared that even a respectable citizen would find flight from Rome as useless as a cloak in hot weather. The imperial peace, trumpets the complacent soldier-historian Velleius Paterculus, "has spread to the regions of the east and of the west and to the bounds of the north and of the south, [and] preserves every corner of the world safe and free from fear. . . ."[68]

By the time of the writers whose opinions were included in Justinian's *Digest*, and still more for Justinian's own lawyers, twists and turns of development were masked beneath conventional formulas and an overriding assertion of state power. Republican jury courts had lost much of their original jurisdiction to imperial prefects who were relatively professional, efficient, and unencumbered by the statutory requirements of "ordinary" justice. "Extraordinary" procedure under the emperors extended to any offense against public order and security, unlike the old republican system of courts, each limited to some specific category of crime.[69] Prosecution by official inquiry under imperial tribunals tended to replace prosecutions by private initiative, and many of the old enclaves of asylum disappeared with the spread of Roman citizenship and imperial power. Whatever the crime or the consequence, the right of exile belonged through proconsular *imperium* and the tribunes' *potestas* to the state. Justinian's own sixth-century legislation treated exile accordingly as a routine punishment which could be adapted to fit the type and gravity of any crime. The right of the individual, even in exile, was to submit, to obey the dictates of political obligation and practical necessity in a regulated world.[70]

For all the textual complications and inconsistencies, then, medieval and Renaissance lawyers received from Roman law a conception of exile in its various forms as a punitive measure sanctioned by an omnipotent state. At the same time, they also inherited very different rules of exile which had transformed or completely replaced the Roman model during the Middle Ages. As the centralized authority and institutions of Rome broke down, there was no effective tribunal to command obedience or hold the exile, as Cicero wrote to Marcellus, "still within the control of him [Caesar] whose power you were trying to flee."[71] What had been Roman territory teemed with particular peoples organized by tribe and clan, usually indifferent at best to visions of a unitary and all-powerful state. The elaborate constructions and procedural disciplines of Roman law were blurred, misunderstood, ignored, or lost. Controversies over the origins of medieval and, ultimately, of modern civilization still summon up the contrast between the written law, hierarchical political structures, and cosmopolitan rationalism of Rome and the customary law, communal institutions, and close-knit sociability of the invaders of the Roman empire.[72]

As historians of criminal justice have generally interpreted them, Germanic custom and tribal law regarded the malefactor as one at war with his community and his own better self.[73] As he had broken the sacred peace supposedly binding the community together in all things, so was he to be broken, utterly "without peace," *friedlos*. His chieftain or king could only consider him dead. His wife must be deemed a widow, his children orphans. His property must be destroyed or returned to common holdings. As prey, his body was left beyond the pale to the birds and beasts of real and figurative wildernesses; as predator, he haunted the forest in the symbolic guise of a wolf or werewolf fit to be pursued and killed on sight.[74]

It is a terrible picture—then again, perhaps not quite what it has usually been made out to be. In the first place, the "Germanic" conception of exile was surely not exclusively Germanic. Its menace and effect were similar to those of the *interdictio aquae et ignis* under the Roman republic. The Romans had once been barbarians themselves. Then too, the development of medieval institutions out of a general conception of *Friedlosigkeit* —literally, "the condition of being without peace"—proves difficult to trace in detail, in part because it *is* a conception, an ideal type or stereotype of the sort historians have used to represent (and misrepresent) the difference between Germanic and Latin institutions. In fact, every legal right was not always withdrawn from the exile under Germanic law; nor was the community always obligated rather than merely permitted to pursue and kill the outcast. The most serious misconception is to suppose that the wrongdoer was condemned for his misdeeds to be "without peace" in the same sense that the Roman malefactor had been sentenced to deportation on some Mediterranean island. On the contrary, the notion of *Friedlosigkeit* can be understood as confirming the inability of the community to maintain its peace or secure its satisfaction by bringing the lawbreaker to justice.[75] Against acts it could not control the community could only close gates and spirit, and rail at the enemy running free beyond the pale. By a familiar paradox in the history of the law the terrors of justice were inversely proportionate to the violence of its threats.[76]

The change in the rules of exile was profound in any case. Already in the Edict of Theodoric (507), with its uneasy conflation of imperial and tribal precedents, exile was becoming something other than a punishment for certain crimes. In specific instances and as a general rule Theodoric's lawyers anticipated exile for lawbreakers who failed to submit to prosecution.[77] Old terminology (*perpetui exilii relegatio; poena deportationis*) seems to have been adapted into an official recognition of contumacious behavior and an official threat meant to induce submission to duly constituted procedures. In language new to written law in the sixth century the term *bannum* referred both to the command of a ruler and to the consequences of disobeying it. To violate and so also to enter under the ban was to break bonds of fidelity to chieftain or king and the pact of concord embodied in society. The reward, or rather the fact, of persistent disobedience was expulsion from the collectivity. Thus, in the Frankish Edict of Chilperic (561), the malefactor who could not or would not compose his peace with those he had injured and "roamed through the forests" was placed (because he had already placed himself) beyond the "word" of the king, "so that whoever might come upon him might kill him without warning."[78]

Measures such as these disguised the impunity of the culprit by declaring him an outlaw. They prodded him to make his peace by exposing him to indiscriminate assault or the deliberate revenge of a vendetta.[79] The protection of the community from further attacks was still another consideration, if also a further recognition of the limits to official prosecution, in Carolingian capitularies. Exiling a homicide "as long as it pleases us" might prevent future crimes, force reconciliation in due course, discourage the escalation of violence which could be expected if the guilty party remained within reach of the friends and relations of the victim. *Exilium* was expressly prescribed "for the prevention of homicide" in a capitulary of 818–819.[80] Where the law could not hold the lawbreaker in, the best remedy was to keep him at a distance and await the outcome.

The most complete and influential elaboration of this remedy appears in canon law.[81] A summarizing canon of the *Decretum* cites the authority of Scripture, canonical precedent, and the Holy Spirit to authorize excommunication from "the lap of Holy Mother Church and the company of all Christianity."[82] There were other formulations—"to be taken as extraneous to the Church"; "to be expelled from the communion of the Church"; "relegation" from prayers, assemblies, and "all holy commerce"; "separation" from the Church; to be anathematized, or "made accursed."[83] Despite the variations in terminology, canon lawyers generally agreed that excommunication followed upon contumacy and regularly added measures for cancellation in case of repentance and return to the fold. In the thirteenth century Gregory IX brought this corrective or "medicinal" aspect into sharp relief by formalizing the distinction between major and minor degrees of excommunication. Under *excommunicatio minor* persons who flaunted their sins against every other discipline lost the benefits of the sacraments and the cult. Further sanctions might be threatened in an initial sentence, and in the event of continued resistance *excommunicatio maior* denied the guilty Christian aid, comfort, and community. Even contact with his family was forbidden although the Gregorian canons admitted a series of important exceptions.[84]

Supple but well defined, the system could be scaled up or down to induce repentance and submission. But here again the operative principles were not so much the exaction of punishment as the insulation of the community from the contaminating public sinner and the search for a remedy against disobedience. The rites of excommunication became all the more intimidating because of the unreliability of their practical effects.[85] In a repertory of words and ceremonies the spiritual exile was portrayed in the sufferings of a double death. Losing the sacraments, he lost the promise of spiritual life, and where the Gregorian exceptions did not apply, he was understood to be lost to Christian society as well. St. Augustine had already cast him to the devil, who waited as a gloating demon perched in a tree in thirteenth-century illustrations. (See Figure 2.) Malediction fell upon his city and his fields, on the fruits of his land, on his comings and goings, on his drinking and eating. Words were acted out by the ceremonial snuffing of candles, the symbolic breaking of a rod, the closing of church doors. The name of an excommunicate was cried aloud and posted so that all the faithful might know their enemy. But then, in the formula of the *Decretum*, the Church *non habet quid ultra*. In the homelier wisdom of the shepherd-heretics of the Pyrenees, "excommunication breaks no bones."[86] The ultimate recourse of calling upon the secular power was itself an admission of failure—and, for that matter, quite ineffective if the secular authorities were unwilling or unable to cooperate.

By the twelfth and thirteenth centuries civil and canon lawyers were acknowledging, and arguing from, analogies between secular and spiritual forms of exclusion. As the excommunicate was cut off from the communion of the faithful, so, the lawyers noted, persons under the imperial ban lost their standing in the secular community. In the twelfth-century formula of Hostiensis the excommunicate is like "one ejected from the city, as it were into desert and forest"; in the fourteenth century Alberico da Rosciate concludes that "the ban, and therefore to ban, denotes a kind of secular excommunication."[87] Developing the analogy further, a modern authority observes that, like excommunication, the imperial ban "is always a ban for disobedience and declared only against a contumacious party, either to lead him back to obedience or, if that is no longer reckoned possible, to substitute some other menace which contumacy made it impossible to carry out."[88] Again, like minor and major degrees of excommunication, the ban also had a milder form or initial phase and a more severe or subsequent stage at the end of deadlines variously set for the offender to submit. The major difference between the two institutions was that excommunication could be canceled as a result of repentance whereas the imperial ban, once definitively issued, was considered perpetual and carried with it the grim labels derived from Roman and barbarian law for the traitor and the enemy—*proditor et hostis, rebellis, reus maiestatis*. Disobedience to the emperor was thus equated with high treason, a capital offense which, even in the absence of the guilty party, entailed forfeiture of all rights, privileges, and possessions. It was in Italy, in the Sicilian constitutions of Frederick II (1220), that the institution of the imperial ban received its most exacting elaboration.[89]

Clearly, rules could be anything but lacking for facts of exile. And the extraordinary career of legal learning in medieval Italy insured that authoritative sources would appear, or reappear, as Italian lawyers and magistrates needed them. The recovery of Justinian's *Digest* early in the twelfth century triggered a quantum leap in the growth of legal studies in the university at Bologna. Principles of Germanic and early medieval law circulated in many guises—texts of barbarian codes, collections of customs, edicts and constitutions of the German emperors. To the *Decretum*, issued by Gratian around 1148, compilations and commentary were added from the time of Gregory IX until the so-called "closure" of the corpus of canon law in the fifteenth century. When the Magna Carta of communal liberties in Italy, the Treaty of Constance (1183), opened what has been called the Golden Age of codification in the Italian city-republics, the experts were only too well provided for. Confronted with the web of tradition and a welter of choices, they worked through gloss and commentary—to understand but, beyond the academic exercise, to accommodate and apply. They could often synthesize, but they were also obliged somehow to sort out the rival claims represented in different legal inheritances—and in their own history.[90]

Rules of exile were both a symbolic and a very real test. The Roman prototypes corresponded to impulses in communal experience toward disciplined public order, unquestioned political legitimacy, and efficient, professional civic administration. But there was also the alternative model, ready to concede the limits of public authority, the fragmentation of society, and the opportunity, even a grudging respect, for evasion. From the thirteenth century on, rules of exile were bound to change with the capacity of the Italian city-states to organize their territory, assert their authority, and enforce their demands against those who would resist.

Voices for Exiles

In language at least, exiles may return to their homes, revise the past to settle old scores, and plot a better future. Since antiquity there has been a literature of exile. Where the voices this literature contains register changing times and circumstances, they are no less historical than events, institutions, and laws. Even so, many themes and many tones have resurfaced and resounded from exile again and again over time. In one way or another all exiles must face the experience of repudiation, homelessness, and encounter with an alien world. They may take grief head on, refuse consolation, make all trouble their own, and cry out against real or imagined injustices. They can try to cut their losses by rationalizing, depersonalizing, or, what often amounts to the same thing, mocking them. If the mode is partly a matter of temperament, mood, and historical situation, it also depends on alternative literary conventions and contrasting views of the human condition.[91]

Understanding this long before the exiles of medieval and Renaissance Italy, the ancients wrote about exile as a historical experience and as a *topos* in which the vulnerability and the reactions of men to shifts in fortune could be explored. The elder Seneca remembered hearing Ovid as a schoolboy taking an imaginary exile's part. One line was prophetic:

I shall leave the city, shall flee, go into exile, endure my loss as best I can with miserable, cruel patience.[92]

Prophetic or not, Ovid's exercise at school compressed the conflicting voices of exile into a few words. Where the exile proposed to accept, even embrace, his lot with patience, he spoke with the philosophical forbearance of a tradition of consolations which went back to the Greek sophists. But he also contended with a rival voice of no less distant ancestry. Patience hardly sufficed if, like exile, it was miserable and cruel. Against the strategy of resignation, the exile might insist on his sorrow. In classical literature the most consistent and influential bearers of the consoling strategy and of the disconsolate insistence were the younger Seneca and Ovid himself. By listening to them, one hears distinctly what was to be borrowed or rediscovered in medieval and Renaissance Italy.

The particular person of Ovid at Tomis cannot be disengaged from the persona of the disconsolate exile. Biographers and historians have often complained that there is remarkably little detail of the kind they would like to know in all the nine books of *De Tristitia* and the *Epistulae ex Ponto*. Both works have also been faulted for lacking proper beginnings and endings, clear-cut progression through time or theme, and range of feeling. "Repetitiveness," "confusion," and "contradictions" are the standard charges. What passes for criticism might rather serve to describe the exile's mask that Ovid projected to the world.[93]

In his repetitions the exile-poet could dwell all the more obsessively on his grievances. The elegiac verse of his works in exile was itself a medium for mourning, the original *flebile carmen* of lovers' long laments according to some theories of classical poetry.[94] Elegiac meter, the "lame verse" of uneven couplets, suited a vocabulary of grief, of tears, trial, dejection, and death. Like the sounds and the words of lament, certain patterns of imagery return to intensify Ovid's sense of loss. Bright memories of Rome reappear in many lines, here laying out a remembered cityscape, there picturing a Roman springtime or an elaborate imperial procession. Family, friends, and sometimes enemies at home haunt the poet's imagination. But then, relentlessly and repeatedly, the spell of things longed for is broken by some counterimage—not Rome but Tomis, not friends or even enemies but uncomprehending barbarians, no spring, gardens, vines, and olive but empty sky, black water, and dull earth.[95]

Ovid's "confusion" is at least as willful and as fitting as his "repetitiveness" for his part. Rejecting consolation, he accepts the rise and fall of his feelings. His compounded hurt, protest, and hope he chooses, if anything, to magnify against any calming reason. Sometimes he grasps after straws;

in another mood he gives up "since some wounds only worsen with treatment."[96] With righteous anger, he can appeal for justice, brand his enemies unjust or his friends faithless, and dare to suggest resistance to the emperor himself. His mind and books, he cries, will transcend any imperial decree against his body. But then, this stubborn side dissolves in abject flattery and exhortation. The divinity of Augustus is hardly for poets to question; the merely mortal Ovid can only beg for pity and clemency. The responsibility for exile is the poet's alone—except (another shift) that the gods and the fates have ordained it.[97]

Ovid's poetry was itself the ultimate contradiction of his exile. Together with more obscure charges for having witnessed an imperial indiscretion he was not meant to see, his all too clever poem on the arts of seduction and intrigue had brought about his downfall. He ordered his epitaph to read: *Ingenio Perii Naso Poeta Meo*. But if Ovid "perished" by poetry, the poetic gift that was his undoing was also the source of all he could do in exile. He could only write, he said, as the laborer, shepherd, or slave-girl sang at hard labor. Having lost Rome, which was life itself to him, the poet represented himself as living still through his art.[98]

Like Ovid at Tomis, L. Annaeus Seneca remained an exile for eight years on the island of Corsica; like Ovid, Seneca had been convicted of an alleged moral offense against public decency and the imperial house, in his case adultery with the emperor's sister.[99] Other similarities between the two exiles were few because Seneca confronted his disgrace with prose and the reasoning patience that Ovid rejected. Seneca had reasons to spare. He claimed that it was his mother, not he, who wanted comforting, and his *Consolatio ad Helviam matrem* was a product of the carefully posed deliberation and detachment of a consolatory literature for exiles.[100]

Seneca played his chosen role as fully as Ovid played its counterpart. Rather than drawing on a lexicon of desperation, Seneca's watchwords were militant on the offensive or in defense. His was a language of victorious battles against fortune and besieged but triumphant virtues. The order of his arguments was strategically calculated from beginning to end.[101] His opening lines to Helvia make sure no one can believe that he, Seneca, may need consolation for himself. The first major argument is that the exile, of course, suffers no true ill. External things matter little to happiness; fortune is always untrustworthy—therefore, no necessary unhappiness or surprise can come from exile. Next, a parrying thrust: exile is no more than a simple change of place. The experience of the individual and history of the race are a record of movement; nature is in ceaseless motion—therefore, exile is no worse than the general rule of things. Then, a question designed to clear the field altogether: if the laws of nature are everywhere the same, if whatever virtues we can claim accompany us wherever we go, can there be such a thing as exile in this world? Seneca is, as always, ready with a response in which platitudes and rhetorical tactics are usually mistaken for high-minded conviction or true wisdom:

> This firmament, than which Nature has created nothing greater or more beautiful, and the most glorious part of it, the human mind that surveys and wonders at the firmament, are our own everlasting possessions. . . . Inside the world there can be found no place of exile; for nothing in the world is foreign to man.[102]

The remedy could not be complete until all the stock complaints of exile—servitude, poverty, dishonor—were swept into the net of the consoler's art, and silenced. The exile is free for virtue and contemplation—all that matters to the wise. Virtuous wisdom costs little or nothing. And then, was Marcellus not more respected as an exile than as consul? As poverty may be the way to spiritual riches, so may infamy bring forth true honor to challenge the illusions of the crowd. Seneca notes a possible objection: " 'Why do you artfully divide things which, if taken separately, can be endured, but, if combined, cannot be?' " But consolation must have the last word: "Reason lays low the vices not one by one, but all together—the victory is gained once and for all."[103] Resistance stilled and his mother remembered in a few final chapters, Seneca stands poised over the impulses Ovid could not or would not suppress, his mind disciplined and free (he says) for its own tasks.

In fact, long-standing traditions informed all his personal claims to self-mastery.[104] He tells Helvia that he has made use of the best among many works on consolation. "Remedies for the soul have been found by the ancients," he explains elsewhere, "how and when they are to be applied is for us to determine."[105] Perhaps he had already composed his consolatory letters to Marcia and Polybius or his *De remediis fortuitorum*, a manual of consolations for his friend Gallio. He certainly knew, with Cicero, who had himself written *de consolatione*, that the Greeks (as Greeks would do) had already collected and categorized solaces for poverty, dishonor, conquest, slavery, injury, death—and for exile. Stilpon and Bion of Borysthenes had written consolations on exile as early as the fifth century B.C., and Teles, another preacher who took popular philosophizing to the road two centuries later, had expanded on his predecessors in the earliest work of its kind to have survived.[106]

Seneca had only to imitate and to adapt the sort of versatile casuistry that the genre prescribed. *Consolatoria* had always been eclectic and pragmatic. The most systematic attempt to classify them according to particular philosophical schools has only succeeded in tracing a mixture of influences from the Sophists, Pythagoreans, Cynics, Stoics, and Epicureans.[107] This is hardly surprising. The consoler was not so much concerned with what was strictly true or philosophically correct as with what worked. Leaving the philosopher to reason out the truth of things by dialectic, he favored the quick pace of the diatribe to establish rapport with an audience, soothe it, exhort it, and, not least important, keep it alert through the sententious remedies. Where the treatise taught *ex cathedra*, and so to the general run of men not at all, the conversational ploys of the consoler dissolved uninterrupted and weighty discourse and made the lessons palatable with leading questions, protests, jokes, little paradoxes, and anecdotes. The patent medicine and instant therapy of the consoler's art had little use for slow methods or deep subtleties.[108]

Over the long term, and at short range, the consoling and disconsolate voices of Seneca and Ovid were related in the way that one set of convictions depends for definition on the existence of another. Ovid let himself be tossed by the rush of wayward sentiment, by conflicting perceptions, recollections, and ideals. His feelings were too pressing for detachment, if not too personal for reenactment in poetry. Sorrow should not, could not perhaps, be rationalized away or held to proprieties and prose. Seneca granted the diagnosis only to apply the cure of persuasion, half-reasons rather than strict reasoning, and a disarming readiness to flatter, enchant, or scold. The consoler would argue with anguish, keep it at a distance, break its power. It was for the sufferer to endure, to adjust and not to protest or rage or, for that matter, reason deeply to overturn the order of things. The release of high and vivid feeling was closed; helplessness was itself a *topos*, part of the game. And yet the very human susceptibility, not to say gullibility, which made consolation possible meant that the effects were not likely to last. The conventions of complaint might still surface within the consolatory machine, as in Ovid's exercise at school, or strong emotions might burst out again on their own, vehement and grieving as ever.

So, the old lines were spoken by a succession of new actors. From the first to third centuries complaints and consolations on exile were passed on in Greek by Plutarch, Musonius Rufus, Dio Chrysostomos, Favorinus, and Cassius Dio. Favorinus's consolatory essay was actually written in exile. Plutarch paces an anonymous victim through four familiar lessons—the evil of exile lies in opinion only; the whole world is our native land;

exile does not deprive us of many external goods; life on earth is an exile from heaven in any case.[109] In his *Roman History* Dio represents Cicero weeping in exile, for once wanting rather than giving advice. "It is not at all the same thing," Cicero admits, "to speak for others as to advise oneself . . . ; where some affliction overwhelms the spirit, it becomes turbid and darkened and cannot reason out anything that is opportune." The philosopher Philiscus stands by to administer arguments that none knew better than Cicero himself, and even then the unhappy exile is only "somewhat" comforted.[110]

The fathers of the early Church carried out the characteristic conversion.[111] Exile served them as a metaphor for the distance of the earthly life of men, like Jews in Babylon, from the heavenly Jerusalem. Expanding on a Pauline distinction (but meaning to call a backsliding bishop to account), St. Jerome exclaims that the world should be a place of exile for monks. St. Augustine lists exile in the catalogue of ills that infect the human condition. In Isidore of Seville's *Lamentation of the Sinner's Soul* the sorrows of the exile rise once again: "I suffer the pain of exile; under the damnation of exile I groan . . . in heat, in snow, in cold, in glowering storms, in every labor exposed to every danger."[112] The consoling voice had already made its response in Christian guise. Christians, the fathers insisted, could hardly be exiled by human means because virtue and faith were their defenses and heaven was their true fatherland. The "maimed muses" and "gloomy songs" of Boethius and his medieval followers were perfect foils for the quasi-Christian figure of Lady Philosophy. The "few small questions" of that severe and long-winded mistress of consolation, consoler turned at last divine, drown out her own creator's sad refrains in a litany of old lessons on transcending the miseries of his worldly "exile."[113]

Except that the refrains and the lessons would be repeated, even when the classical literature of exile was lost, dispersed, or only half-understood. In strange settings and crippled Latin, Carolingian bishops resume an old encounter.[114] Only echoes of an original fullness remain, sounds heard faint or distorted across a great distance and resonant with biblical overtones. But the lamentations of Bishop Theodolf of Orléans, exiled by Louis the Pious around 816, are familiar enough in his correspondence in verse *de suo exilio*. To Bishop Modoin he bids the muse carry sad tidings of his condition:

An exile is he, poor, a pauper, most miserable,
    anxious, in need,
Spurned and abject, everywhere in sorrow.

Should Modoin ask how the exile passes his time, the answer is to come in lines borrowed from Ovid but tinged by readings in the Old Testament:

> And perhaps he will ask what I do: I live, say
>   to him,
> A life than which death would be the better good.[115]

The exile can scarcely read, teach, or say the sacred office. His world is smoke-filled, a place of fever and festering wounds. While even the slave or the servant girl have their little pleasures, the exile has none.

Bishop Modoin's reply came back with what reads like caricature of the old consolations. Against "hard iron," he admits, his "soft wax" promises little protection. He is, he says (truly), no poet. Still, his friend's prudence can accomplish much; his wisdom will bear any burden. Let Theodolf remember the great men who have gone before him into exile —Ovid, Boethius, Virgil (Modoin supposes), Seneca, and many good Christians. Let him cast off his hurt in serene peace, free from the encumbrances of worldly existence. But if he will appeal, the emperor will surely yet provide for him.[116]

For centuries the dialogue was not so clearly or directly resumed. It merged into the more general fortunes of the texts of Ovid, Seneca, and Boethius. Here and there images and metaphors of exile still surfaced.[117] But when the facts and rules of exile became again, in Italy, very real and widespread, medieval and Renaissance exiles would fully possess—and be possessed by—the ancient voices of their condition.

2

Facts of Exclusion
and Exile in Medieval Italy

On 19 September 1305 the bishop of Mende and Abbot Pilifort of Toulouse disembarked at Pisa as papal legates on a mission of peace. For two months the legates held court in Tuscany. They published the pope's true at Lucca, Pistoia, and Siena, met with representatives of warring towns or factions, and issued ecclesiastical censures against those who refused to submit. Then, criss-crossing the Apennines, they carried their mission to the Marches and Romagna where they were at first deceptively well received, and on to Umbria, where they were hardly received at all.

The legates' reports to the pope have survived and, like all documents, contain facts which fit different histories.[1] Some of the details belong to the long story of foreign attempts to dominate the Italian peninsula, and there is much evidence of the stubborn independence of city-states and territorial lords in a landscape checkered with towns and the uncertain spaces between them. The facts of exclusion in the legatine reports belong to a less familiar history, though they confronted the legates at every turn. From the beginning to the end of their journey the papal emissaries found exiles everywhere. Pisa and Lucca harbored whole communities of émigrés. Pistoia, the seat of a recent schism between the factions of Black and White Guelphs, was under siege from its Black Guelph outcasts in alliance with the Florentines and the Lucchese. Ghibelline and White Guelph *fuorusciti* were menacing Florence, and exiles in Umbria were operating outside Todi, Nocera, Foligno, and (perhaps) Spoleto. In the

Marches the towns of Iesi, Fano, Pesaro, Senigallia, Castroserra (Serra-valle), Castrosingoli (?), Ascoli, and Urbino all had parties in exile. So did many places in the Romagna, where the pope's representatives were "hardly obeyed in anything."[2]

Similar reports were made at other times during the preceding 150 years and continued to be made for many years to come. Facts of exclusion were never lacking in medieval Italy. Exile was a particular manifestation of a general state of affairs, and the particular phenomenon needs to be seen in terms of both the complexities of Italian history in the Middle Ages and the larger patterns which give the Italian experience shape and significance.

The External Dimension:
International Accomplices from the Outside

One may begin, as the legates of 1305 did, from the outside. It is striking that they, heavy with finery and matters of state, concerned themselves with bands of exiles scattered beyond the walls of even the smaller Italian towns. They had no local pride to mislead them about the importance of Todi or Fano or petty towns in Tuscany. Whether they had been present or not, quick changes in obscurely local political alignments would have sufficed to bring about the expulsion of individuals, families, and factions or to allow them to return home again. But the legates were interested, and their interest connected internal facts of exclusion with external influences acting upon them and linked local histories to a larger historical context. Although the Italian communes were quite capable of making or unmaking exiles on their own, they did so regularly with international accomplices and far-reaching consequences until the mid-fourteenth century. Sometimes external agents intervened directly. Even at a distance they could push or pull rival parties to and from their places over a shifting field of forces.

In the long view and over the long term those external forces can be described as geopolitical *avant la lettre*. The legates of 1305 came to Italy as barbarian invaders, German emperors, and French or Spanish princes had come—from beyond the Alps or across the seas sheltering the peninsula only enough to enhance its attractions to outsiders.[3] International interests funneled into the Mediterranean center of the medieval world in search of power, wealth, and the real or symbolic sun of a dynamic civilization. A divided center, physically stretched and fragmented from north to south, Italy was virtually impossible to unify and, for that rea-

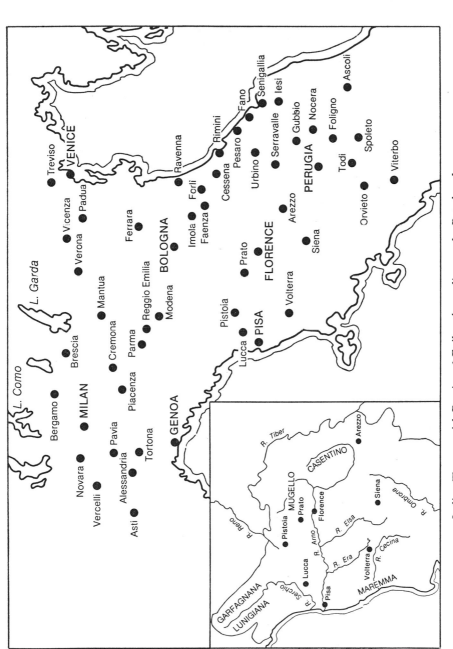

Italian Towns with Parties of Exiles According to the Papal and Imperial Missions of 1305 and 1313. Insert: Tuscany.

son, quite possible for foreigners to penetrate and hold in some particular part. By playing competing interests off against one another Norman adventurers established themselves in southern Italy during the eleventh century. German emperors intervened from the north, effectively in the case of Conrad II (1024–1039) or with mixed results as in the case of Frederick Barbarossa, whose fifth expedition on the peninsula saw the defeat of the imperialists by the Lombard towns at Legnano (1176). At the end of the twelfth century the imperial dynasty of the Hohenstaufen inherited the Norman kingdom in the south through diplomacy and marriage. But the Hohenstaufen were crushed by the Angevin invasion from France (1265–1268), which was eventually challenged in turn by the house of Aragon from Sicily. In all their campaigns on the Italian peninsula foreign invaders angled on the borders of regional divisions and behind the lines of political differences for factions, towns, and territories, and for exiles, to use against some outside rival.

The history of the papacy as a territorial power in Italy is the classic study in the geopolitics of external intervention. If the popes could somehow have united the peninsula, their fear that Rome and the lands of St. Peter might be isolated and encircled by a foreign power might have given way to other anxieties. But the resources of the papacy, however great, were always too few; the resistance of local autonomies and of the land itself was too strong. Since the best alternative to collective security was to divide and weaken the opposition, the popes cultivated regional coalitions against a long series of foreign invaders and their own expendable foreign allies. Threatened by one ultramontane contender in Italy, they could always call in another. Both Machiavelli and Guicciardini thought that the traditional aim, or actual outcome, of papal policy was to keep Italy disunited.[4] This is surely to take a cause of papal strategy for its effect. What is clear is that foreign powers and their supporters in exile tended to return or recede in proportion to the degree of political fragmentation on the peninsula.

Theoretical claims of emperors and popes introduced conflicts over matters of principle into an environment suited to invaders and to exiles. From the Hohenstaufen campaigns in Italy in the twelfth century to Henry VII's Italian mission a century and a half later, imperial constitutions, diplomas, charters, and epistles asserted the emperor's authority over and often against his Italian subjects. The assertion ran from claims to imperial prerogatives under Roman law to Otto of Freising's practical disappointment that so fine a prize as Italy should be divided among rebellious city-states. It soared highest in Dante's contempt for rebels "against the glory of the Roman prince, king of the world and minister of God." The papal case "for the correction of sin" in secular affairs found its way into the arguments of the theologians, and filled papal letters, bulls, and documents of ordinary routine.[5] It has become fashionable for historians to discount the force of abstract principles or ideas in favor of "realistic" explanations. Much of the evidence does suggest that imperial and papal interests were superimposed on local circumstances, that their effects came relatively late and were often temporary, that theoretical consistency and steadfast allegiances were conspicuously lacking at the local level. But there is still a place in any account of the conflicts between the empire and the papacy for the deceptively simple proposition that powers claiming universal authority will attempt to exercise it if they can.[6] Emperors and popes did attempt to exercise their ideal claims in Italy. Factions within the towns or regions of the peninsula chose sides, and while one side rode high, the other was excluded, forced into opposition, and frequently driven into exile.

The Guelph and Ghibelline "exits" of the mid-thirteenth century are a good test of external facts of exclusion at closer range. Only in Dante's *Inferno* could Farinata degli Uberti have boasted that he and his Ghibellines alone had driven the Guelphs out of Florence in 1248 and 1260; only to outdo the insult could Dante reply as if his Guelph ancestors, when their time came, had cast out the Ghibellines unaided in 1258 and 1267 (*Inferno*, X, 46–51). Both Farinata's Ghibellines and Dante's Guelphs had been losers in the internal disputes between Florentine factions, but they were also victims of realignments of forces on the Italian peninsula at large. Behind the Guelph exodus of Candlemas Day 1248 lay a papal deposition of Frederick II (1245) and the compensating push of imperial power from its southern base over the borders of Tuscany. (See Figure 3.) The emperor had countered his loss to the pope's allies at Parma in 1247 by ordering his son Frederick of Antioch to increase the pressure he could bring to bear on Florence as its resident vicar. The pressure was intense, the vicar's alliance with the Uberti and other Ghibelline magnates was openly threatening, and the Florentine Guelphs abandoned the city. In 1260 it was outside pressure again, this time applied by Frederick's heir Manfred, which forced the Guelphs from Florence once more after their blood had stained the river Arbia at Montaperti. A similar process in reverse order pulled the Ghibellines out of Florence when Hohenstaufen power receded upon the death of Frederick II and his sons. After disastrous losses by the Ghibellines at the battles of Benevento (1266) and Tagliacozzo (1268), a new papal-Angevin settlement held the Guelphs in power just as Hohenstaufen supremacy had once sustained their Ghibelline rivals. All over Italy the pattern of Guelph and Ghibelline return or retreat was very much the same.[7]

But the more sharply the pattern comes into focus, the less impersonal and abstract it seems. Party labels pointed to particular places, ties of family, and events in history or legend. Scathing epithets were spoken in winding streets or shouted in the piazza to sound out purely local circumstances—*raspanti* ("scratchers") and *bergolini* ("dupes") in Pisa; *malcorani* ("evil hearts") and *befatti* ("the mocked") at Orvieto; *montecuccoli* ("cuckoos") and *montegarulli* ("chatterers") near Modena. A richly detailed lore grew around the best-known political labels. "Ghibellino" was probably an Italian stab at the German name of the Hohenstaufen castle of Waiblingen; "Guelfo" was the Italian version of the Welf family name of Frederick II's Bavarian rival for the imperial crown. But mythical origins were invented to explain that "Ghibellinus" and "Guelphus" had been Tuscan brothers who had quarreled and taken different paths or that "Gibel" and "Gualef" were demons with scourging swords. According to a famous story recounted by the Florentine chronicler Giovanni Villani, it was in 1216, when a Buondelmonti-Donati betrothal at Florence had broken up in bloodshed, that "for the first time new names were heard—Guelph party and Ghibelline party."[8] Guelph and Ghibelline organizations actually seem to have been formed as such at a much later date. They were first recorded around 1242 in Florence. They appeared at Arezzo, Siena, Pistoia, Prato, and San Gimignano only during the next decade, and it was not until Charles of Anjou came to lead the anti-Hohenstaufen alliance of the 1260s that the great party names spread throughout the rest of Italy. Even so, communal chroniclers projected "Guelphs" and "Ghibellines" back much earlier in time and turned them local so as to root the origins of contemporary history in the past.[9]

In that history the outsider assumed several different guises. He might appear alternately as a warlord, a party chieftain, a feudal suzerain, a meddling administrator, the descendant of a great dynasty, an impresario of pageantry, or a partisan peacemaker. Often he was a leader of an army reinforced by exiles, like the Hohenstaufen and Angevin forces of German or French knights with their supporting contingents of Italian émigrés. The expeditions of foreign champions were welcomed or resisted by cities which broadcast their allegiances in the shape of their battlements, rectangular for the papal or swallow-tailed for the imperial side. Coats-of-arms, banners, and the color or cut of cloaks, ribbons, armbands, and liveries displayed partisan connections and traditions. After the foreigner had passed, storytellers, poets, and chroniclers went on to tell of how he had been favored or despised, of battles he had won or lost, of "the fury of the Teuton" or the arrogance of "the French, Provençals, and Picards."[10] However they might be justified by appeals to high ideals or universal principles, international interests in Italy were acted out in specific events and settings.

When a combination of city-states, internal factions, or parties in exile grouped together in the foreigner's behalf or against him, their alliances and leagues were understandably loose and usually unstable constructions. It was only natural for Farinata's Ghibellines to be received, with Manfred of Hohenstaufen's Germans, in Ghibelline Siena after their retreat from Florence in 1258; so too for the Guelphs who survived Montaperti to take refuge, hoping for papal aid, in Guelph Lucca.[11] The twelfth-century prototype of formally chartered leagues on a regional scale was a response to Hohenstaufen intervention in Italy. In 1164 the most exposed towns in Lombardy formed a "concord" fronting the Alps against Emperor Frederick Barbarossa. They were joined in 1167 by another coalition of parties and towns, from Milan to Bologna. At its height, the Lombard League was a *societas* with its own rectors, assemblies, and rules for coordinating diplomatic and military operations. The association was renewed in 1185 and 1195, and by the time that it was revived against Frederick II in 1226 an antiimperial Tuscan League of 1197 had already introduced the first of several experiments in regional alliances to central Italy. But these experiments could not supply a viable federal solution to the still unresolved challenge of Italy's political diversity. The Lombard League held together just long enough to drive Frederick Barbarossa, still uncomprehending, from the peninsula; a Guelph alliance stood behind the final defeat of the Hohenstaufen and the conquest of southern Italy by Charles of Anjou between 1265 and 1268 and then fell apart in disputes over the spoils. Binding ties remained weak and were dissolved as opportunity and advantage beckoned. One of the most certain consequences of regional alliances was a steady stream of exiles, victims of the standard clauses providing for the expulsion of the opposing side.[12]

It was characteristic of the tangibly particular interests at stake that ties of business, finance, and property were knotted into these agreements, especially in the Guelph system of alliances. In 1262 Pope Urban IV placed merchants of Ghibelline towns under interdict, voiding their contracts and liberating their debtors. The fortunes of Siena and Genoa were hard hit at the fairs of Champagne. To redeem their credits, and perhaps even their souls, the bankers of Siena went into voluntary exile. In March 1263, during its second Ghibelline interlude, Florence was struck by similar measures, and precise terms of submission were demanded of Florentine bankers. The Angevin adventure in Italy was partly financed in this way; Charles of Anjou's expedition was a political and an economic speculation, a business deal for a Guelph syndicate. The house of Anjou and its papal sponsors needed the financial resources, political support, and military contributions of Guelph towns. Guelph businessmen recouped their investments many times over in the grain and rich offices of the Italian south and in the accounts of papal finance, and to profits from abroad they added the spoils from confiscated Ghibelline property at home.[13]

Indemnities guaranteed by the political authority and military presence of a great foreign ally were not altogether unwarranted. When one party left or was driven from town, confiscation or destruction of their property was the usual result. In Florence more than seven hundred structures belonging to Guelphs in exile were reportedly dismantled or razed between 1260 and 1266. Returning victorious in 1267, the Guelphs charged damages against Ghibelline possessions amounting to something like the annual revenue of the commune. This figure was surely greater than real losses incurred; the proceeds must have lined private purses and actually served to establish the Guelph party as a substantial financial institution. Fragmentary records suggest a similar story after the Lambertazzi were forced into exile from Bologna by the rival Geremei in 1274, and examples could be multiplied.[14] However necessary in politics, ties to outside support which could drive the opposition into exile were, for the winners at least, good business and standing surety for a profitable series of economic arrangements. In the features of Arnolfo di Cambio's statue of Charles of Anjou, at once remote and shrewd, it is tempting to see the king as chairman of the board.

There is no more revealingly intricate illustration of the connection between external interests and exile than an episode in the chronicle of Fra Salimbene of Parma.[15] On 15 June 1247—the day explodes into detail as Salimbene describes it—a few Guelph knights in exile from Parma, bitter over injuries the emperor and his party had done them, leave their place of refuge at Piacenza. Longing for the sight of home, they take counsel on the field at Noceto in speeches reminiscent of the Old Testament books of Proverbs, Maccabees, and Judges. The *podestà* of Parma (who had been, Salimbene admits, a good friend of his brother Franciscans) rides out against them but falls in battle with many of his followers.

As the *fuorusciti* approach the walls of the city, Salimbene admires the signs of the cross they make to sounds of peace and good will. He overhears the German garrison talking betrayal and notes the indifference of artisans too busy at their trades to enter into the quarrels of their betters. He knows, as the defenders do not, that the gates are open, with broken locks and missing bolts. The day and the town soon belong to the party of the Church, exiles no longer.

Most details in Salimbene's account have some outside point of reference. He begins the narrative of the exiles' return after relating how Frederick II, like a bear caught in chains, had been deposed by Pope Innocent IV. The exiles had left Parma in the first place because they feared the power of the emperor there. They had gone to Piacenza because it was safe in the hands of the papal party. After the *fuorusciti* overwhelm the *podestà* of Parma and his men, the emperor's German garrison stands aside and the Germans say, "Come to Parma and take the city securely because we will not resist you!" The small episode merges into the great history of "the most valid and intricate war between the Church and the *respublica*, between the pope and the emperor," and Salimbene caps the story off with a little sermon on the ingratitude of emperors.

Tallying up a list of reasons for what had occurred, Salimbene is sure that the exiles' success depended on what was happening outside the city. The emperor's son Enzio had left his post as castellan of Parma to besiege the castle of Quinzana near Brescia; Frederick II himself had been far away at Turin, scheming to capture the pope and his cardinals at Lyon. While the chief actors on the imperial side had been absent or remiss, the exiles had expected aid from sources spread far and wide but linked and led in the interest of the Church. Innocent IV had relations and friends in Parma where "against the emperor, his enemy, he wished to fight and now let loose his blow." The papal legate of Lombardy, Gregory of Montelengo, had made preparations to come from the north with the pope's brother-in-law Bernardo de' Rossi of Parma and a Milanese striking force. The men of Piacenza, Bologna, and Ferrara, Count San Bonifazio from Verona, and the whole party of the Church had sealed Parma in a ring of external power against the party of the emperor. When the imperialists' turn in exile came, they made their way to Reggio, Cremona, and Modena where "the party of the Church was outside the city, the party of the emperor within." There they waited, as their rivals had done, for some great change to bring them home again.

Ghibellines all over Italy waited decades after the Anjou conquest and final Hohenstaufen defeat of 1265–1268. No emperor intervened effectively until Henry VII in 1311. In the emperor's absence compromises between factions such as Pope Nicholas III's attempts at peacemaking in 1279–1280 were possible, though they were usually short-lived.[16] It is all the more telling, then, that the dynamics of external influence continued to affect the making and movements of exiles. Parties gravitated to the French or against them. Around the turn of the thirteenth century the Guelphs of Tuscany divided into Black and White factions, partly in response to the "Ghibelline" tactics, as chroniclers called them, of Boniface VIII in his contest with the king of France and his enemies in Rome.[17] A few years later Corazza of Signa reminded the Guelph councils of Florence (they must have nodded agreement) how many men were still Ghibellines, or wanted to be, especially if they were exiles.[18] Like fish eggs in a dry stream bed, says the chronicler of Piacenza, Ghibellines could still come to life whenever "the flow of imperial excellence" reappeared.[19]

The dubious zoology makes an accurate historical point. Long after the international conflicts of the thirteenth century in Italy, exiles were still searching for foreign champions to serve as their great accomplices.

Internal Organization: Companies of Exiles

The exiles of Tuscany, Umbria, the Marches, and Romagna who appealed to the papal legates of 1305 did so generally in groups or for groups. Had Dante appeared before the legates, what might have struck them most about him was not that he was a poet but that he had come alone, that he had chosen to separate himself from the company of White Guelph and Ghibelline exiles he came to call "wicked and senseless"— *la compagnia malvagia e scempia* (*Paradiso*, XVII, 62; see Figure 9). Like most political exiles, Dante had been condemned together with other members of his party; if the Black Guelphs in Florence had not kept a collective register of their enemies, the sentences against him and the White Guelph faction would be lost. The earliest surviving document of his life in exile shows him signing the pact between the White Guelph *universitas* and its Ghibelline warrior-allies who met at San Godenzo in the Apennines early in June 1302. In the spring of 1304 Dante wrote (if the letter is genuine) to the cardinal of Prato in the name of his party. Some years later he addressed Henry VII on behalf of "all Tuscans who desire peace." Searingly personal as his encounter with Farinata degli Uberti is in the *Inferno*, it is also presented as a confrontation between rival factions.[20]

Since the solitary figure was the exception inside a city or outside the walls, the legates of 1305 had no difficulty in granting the corporate recognition and identity exiles expected for themselves. Proctors of "the party of the Whites in exile" from Florence, Lucca, Volterra, and Prato met the legates on the same footing as representatives of the White Guelphs who still held on under siege inside Pistoia. The syndic of the "expelled Blacks of the party of the Church and of the Guelphs of Pistoia" also had his hearing.[21] Black Pistoia in exile, like White Pistoia on the inside, had its *podestà*, captains, and councils, its seal, army, and emissaries for diplomatic negotiations. The difference between parties at home or in exile was one of location not of legitimacy. Lopped off communal organisms to grow on their own, parties in exile reproduced in miniature the political structures they had left behind. They could grow wherever they happened to be because the institutions of communes and parties were practically indistinguishable.

Chroniclers recorded deeds done by both the *intrinseci* and the *extrinseci*, the *pars intrinseca* and the *pars extrinseca*. Chancellery officials made no special distinctions in script, formulas, and seals they sent to "internal" and "external" communes alike.[22] As equal partners in military and political negotiations, the exiled *podestà*, knights, and men of Modena "favoring the party of the Church" had contracted with the commune of Bologna between 1247 and 1249 to garrison Bologna's boundaries with the Modenese. The Sienese Guelphs in exile were at least as well organized. In 1265 the "captains of the party and corporation of the Guelphs of the city and *contado* of Siena" met at Città della Pieve where they named delegates to the Guelph League, read dispatches from the pope, and chose "a captain and rector of the said Guelph party."[23] Ghibelline Tuscany had its corporate structures too. It was at a congress of Ghibelline parties, some of them still in exile, that Farinata degli Uberti had spoken, *a viso aperto*, to save Florence from destruction after the Guelph defeat at Montaperti (*Inferno*, X, 91–93).

The corporate units of communal and party politics were modules which could be assembled in various combinations. The Ghibelline regimes of Pisa and Arezzo, the White Guelphs inside Pistoia, and the White exiles from Florence, Lucca, Volterra, and Prato sent letters in common to the papal legates in 1305. The White party in exile from Florence included Florentine citizens and men from the countryside. The legatine acts listed sixty members of a branch convoked in Arezzo by Guidino of Forlì, judge and vicar of its Ghibelline captain-general, Ciappetino degli Ubertini. A committee of four and a council of twelve members elected Ser Lapo Recuperi syndic for peace negotiations, and a group of at least 112 Florentines in Pisa notified the legates that Ser Lapo represented them as well. Whether Florentine refugees maintained a separate organization in Pistoia is unclear. It is certain that they did so in Bologna where Buccino of Barga had borrowed 150 *lire bolognesi* by June 1303 "for the stipends of said party in payment of horsemen and foot soldiers." Scarpeto Ordelaffi (a former captain of the White Guelph militia), twelve councillors, and 120 members of "the *universitas* of said party" had guaranteed the loan, which, to Bolognese displeasure, was still outstanding in June 1305.[24]

Men of high standing predominated in these exile companies and coalitions as they had in the councils at home. Between 1267 and 1268 the Ghibellines of Florence and Prato were persecuted by degrees. Some were ordered to leave communal territory, some were to remain within it, and others were held only to good behavior. The important personage was the one likely to be dealt with most harshly.[25] When, to take another example, Padua agreed to repatriate its exiles in May 1323, the more prominent of them were obliged to wait as long as a year while the lesser fry were restored unconditionally to their rights and possessions.[26] It is true that there were woolworkers, tanners, butchers, shoemakers, and stonemasons as well as the ragpicker and the juggler who were either suspect as Ghibellines or actually in exile from Florence by 1269.[27] Notaries were a special case because the expertise which made them indispensable in communal affairs also made them vulnerable when a particular regime was overthrown. Exile was a kind of occupational hazard for the more important civil servants.[28] Still, Salimbene's picture of artisans, tradesmen, and money changers too busy to care about the *fuorusciti* returning to Parma in 1247 is probably a fair reflection of the passive political role played by many minor and middling sorts of people at home or in exile. In the official business of the Florentine *fuorusciti* with the legates of 1305, Gerino the tailor was the only identifiable member of the lower orders to be recorded.[29] In short, those with the most at stake were those to suffer most—if also to have the best resources for survival.

Nobles and magnates, notorious for their family feuds and their factional quarrels, were especially marked for exclusion and usually first in rank among exiles. The regimes of guildsmen which came to power in the thirteenth century had set them apart as a distinct group subject to political disabilities and legal restrictions. Measures confining or banishing the overmighty, as in the model antimagnate legislation of Bologna or the outright expulsion of the nobles of Viterbo in 1283, were the logical extension of a common policy.[30] But this extension was often ineffectual and sometimes self-defeating because nobles and magnates were in many ways beyond communal control. Their far-reaching political alliances, territorial strongholds, extended kinships, large rural and urban clienteles, and readiness for warfare made them independent and dangerous enemies in any location. In 1248 the Guelphs who were expelled from Florence harassed the city from their fortresses in the countryside; in 1259 Piacenza was blockaded by its nobles.[31] More than a century after returning to Prato in 1267 as "glorious victors over their perpetual banishment by the imperial party," Count Guido Guerra and his family were remembered for their feats of arms and French connections during their absence. A far stronger commune than Prato would have been hard-pressed to resist them.[32] Lucca was prey to its *fuorusciti*-turned-soldiers on two occasions early in the fourteenth century, and the great city of Milan was very nearly seized in 1339 by an army of powerful exiles and unemployed mercenaries who had formed one of the earliest of those freebooting military companies which terrorized Italian city-states for more than two generations.[33]

Genuine nobles from feudal families were more or less indistinguishable at home or in exile from the merchant-bankers whose overweening manner and capacity for trouble caused them to be designated magnates by communal regimes. Rich merchants and bankers put an aristocratic veneer on their business skills and their international interests in trade and finance. The merchant everywhere tended to maintain ancestral ties in some rural area or reacquired a landed base, and the great territorial lineages had their business dealings and their towers or whole districts in town. The marriage market was, as always, a mediator between the claims of money and those of blood. Modern models of class conflict or stereotyped conceptions of an inevitable opposition between feudalism and capitalism are, at best, deceptive guides to the social world of this Italian elite.[34]

The legates of 1305 met a number of émigré White Guelph bankers in Tuscany whose situation illustrates both the urban and the territorial bases of their power in exile. Messer Vieri de' Cerchi was said to have taken the vast sum of 60,000 florins from Florence into exile at Arezzo. Cerchi consorts and clients in Pisa—the Scali, Tedaldi, Macci, and Malespini—opened their houses and purses to exiles from Florence, Prato, and Volterra. White Guelph credit was good in Bologna. By moving money from place to place, by collecting and cutting off credits (or by hiding them in secret registers), the townwise Cerchi and allied banking houses kept their fortunes intact to buy time and tactics. Only a year after the expulsion of the Whites from Florence, Boniface VIII restored his protection to the Cerchi bank, with its thirteen Cerchi partners and associates from other families. Profitable Cerchi business continued with Edward II in England and even with Black Guelph bankers in Florence. It is true that all the banks which sided with the Whites were not so fortunate. Assets left behind could be destroyed or confiscated; through Black Guelph influence in Rome and Naples, ecclesiastical censures and embargoes on trade with southern Italy were imposed on White Guelph businessmen. But in at least four of seven cases which are well documented, the Ammanati company of Pistoia, the firm of Berto Frescobaldi, and two Mozzi companies survived and flourished after 1302.[35]

With the barons of feudal Tuscany, too, the contacts of the exiled White Guelph bankers were close and elaborate. Banking ties linked the Cerchi with the magnate houses of the Mozzi and the Bardi, who were related in turn by marriage to the Ubaldini family of the Mugello and bound by political traditions to the Ubertini of the Casentino. Through their Adimari relatives and banking partners the Cerchi could claim kinship with the great Ghibelline clan of the Conti Guidi, whose Guido Novello had also been a client of the Cerchi-Portinari bank and, again, with the Ubaldini. Through the Cavalcanti the Cerchi were also connected with the descendants of Farinata degli Uberti. This network of overlapping associations ran to deep roots. Conflicts between Florentine families and factions at the beginning of the Trecento still followed the alignments of the Buondelmonti-Uberti feud one hundred years earlier.[36] Ghibelline grievances from the mid-thirteenth century still rankled fresh among backland clans. "For more than forty years," wrote Dino Compagni, the Uberti "had been rebels of their homeland, nor had they ever found mercy or pity there, remaining exiles in great estate; and they never lowered their honor but stayed always with kings and lords and set themselves to great deeds."[37] The alliance between Tuscan feudatories and the White Guelph exiles of the early fourteenth century was obviously not an isolated affair. Behind their union lay bonds of blood and politics and a shared social experience in which nobles and merchant-bankers were as often associates as adversaries at home or abroad.

Formidable in their organization and their leadership, companies of exiles moved in and out of local lines of vision. The legates of 1305 found White Guelphs and Ghibellines in urban bases—Arezzo, Pisa, Pistoia, Bologna—ringed around Black Guelph Florence; friendly Umbrian and Romagnol towns constituted a second line of defense, a source of reinforcement, and a route of easy retreat. Along the edges and within these

1. The Figure of the Exile. According to Cesare Ripa's *Iconologia* (Rome, 1603), the exile should be represented with the costume and the staff of a pilgrim; the falcon's hood and tethered feet signify that its master has been condemned to exile by a prince or a republic. The inscription on this mid-sixteenth century engraving by Enea Vico reads: *Extorris patriam dulcesque relinquo penates* ("Driven into exile, I leave sweet hearth and home behind").

2. *A Medieval View of Secular and Spiritual Bans.*   On the left a victim of the secular ban is beheaded on orders from a judge. On the right a priest proclaims a sentence of excommunication by extinguishing a candle (?) and breaking a rod; the soul flees the body of the excommunicate and is grasped by the devil perched in a tree. Miniature from the Heidelberg *Sachsenspiegel*, early thirteenth century. Universitätsbibliothek, Heidelberg, Ms. Pal. Germ. 164., fol. 37r.

3. *Foreign Intervention and Exile in Medieval Italy.* On the left the army of Emperor Frederick II enters Florence in 1248; on the right the Ghibellines, with shields bearing Florentine insignia, drive their Guelph enemies into exile. Miniature from the *Cronica* of Giovanni Villani, mid-fourteenth century. Vatican Library, Chigi Ms. L. VIII, 296, fol. 80r.

4. The Company of Exiles in the Thirteenth Century.

a. An army of Milanese exiles in the 1270s listens to a harangue by Ottone
Visconti, archbishop of Milan. Fresco, Castle of Angera, early fourteenth century.

b. Ottone Visconti enters Milan with his entourage in 1277 after fifteen years in
exile. Fresco, Castle of Angera, early fourteenth century.

5. *The "Art of Returning Home" Fails in Florence.*

a. Cardinal Niccolò of Prato abandons Florence in 1304 after unsuccessful negotiations for the return of the White Guelphs and the Ghibellines. Miniature from the *Cronica* of Giovanni Villani, mid-fourteenth century. Vatican Library, Chigi Ms. L. VIII, 296, fol. 178v.

b. The White Guelph and Ghibelline exiles are defeated at the gates of Florence on 20 July 1304. Miniature from the *Cronica* of Giovanni Villani, mid-fourteenth century. Ibid., fol. 180r.

6. A Success in Milan for the "Art of Returning Home." After the
pitched battle shown at the top, Guido della Torre and his faction
are sentenced at the bottom by Emperor Henry VII in 1311. As a
result of this sentence, the Della Torre left Milan and their rivals
the Visconti returned to power after nearly ten years in exile.
Miniature from the *Codex Balduinus*, fol. 10r, early fourteenth
century. Staatsarchiv, Coblenz.

7. Rules of Exclusion. A copy of the death sentence issued against Dante and fourteen others by Cante Gabrieli of Gubbio, *podestà* of Florence, on 10 March 1302. Archivio di Stato, Florence, *Libro del Chiodo*, p. 14.

8. An Archetype of the Disconsolate Exile. "As Hippolytus departed from Athens . . . so from Florence must you depart" (*Paradiso*, XVII, 46-48). Dante is shown the banishment, death, and resurrection of Hippolytus, unjustly exiled from Athens. Illumination by Giovanni di Paolo for the *Divine Comedy*, mid-fifteenth century. British Library, London, Yates Thompson Ms. 36, fol. 158r.

9. Dante as the Disconsolate Exile. Dante is driven from Florence and, weeping, works on a manuscript in Verona. Illumination by Giovanni di Paolo for the *Divine Comedy*, mid-fifteenth century. Ibid., fol. 159r.

circles, on key passes, fords, and roads, lay the Apennine fortresses of the Ghibelline clans which were either in exile themselves or allies of the *fuorusciti*.[38] Similar patterns of resettlement and resistance were common in other times and places. A generation earlier the Lambertazzi of Bologna had relocated in Faenza and Imola after their defeat by the Geremi in 1274. A generation before that, the exiles who left Ferrara after Azzo d'Este took control of the city in 1240 had gone to Ravenna, Mantua, Bologna, and Verona. In the twelfth century refugees from Frederick Barbarossa's razing of Milan (1162) had been welcome in the Milanese quarter of Sant' Ambrogio at Genoa and in all the cities which eventually formed the Lombard League against the emperor.[39] On the land some strongholds opened their gates to exiles from one generation to the next— so, for example, the Tuscan castles of Montaguto and Montagutolo. In the mid-thirteenth century these backcountry outposts rebelled against Florence in support of Count Guido Novello, leader and then archexile of Ghibelline Tuscany, just as they were to do again for the exiled White Guelph Adimari in 1305.[40] Geography gave exiles shelter and staging ground which long histories of conflict between rival towns or between towns and neighboring lords filled with a choice of willing allies.

But the company of exiles was often a sizable force in its own right. In 1301–1302 the White Guelphs of Pistoia banished 380 men and two women, many of whom must have been among the Pistoiese exiles who sent their representatives to the legates of 1305. During the same period the victorious Florentine Blacks sentenced 689 members of the White opposition, and four years later most of them were still at large. Dino Compagni was reminded of the *fuorusciti* of the mid-thirteenth century, when more than 3,000 Florentines, as the chronicler said of their White Guelph successors in exile, went "wandering sorely pressed through the world."[41] Still more dramatic figures are on record. According to one chronicler, 1,500 families abandoned Ferrara after the Estensi takeover in 1240; as many as 12,000 partisans of the Lambertazzi may have fled from Bologna in 1274.[42] If these figures can be trusted, they mean that anywhere from a third to a half of the population of Ferrara and Bologna was in exile at one time. In 1323 there were 4,000 exiles to respond to an amnesty declared by a Florentine government threatened with invasion from Lucca, and in 1334 at least 1,500 persons were in exile from Bologna, some of them in places as far distant as Naples.[43] Matteo Bandello must have had circumstances such as these in mind when he imagined a kind of anti-Florence filled with the exiles of the Florentine past.[44]

There was no need to imagine whole communities of exiles in their colonies abroad. Although Dante's wife—one wonders, was Madonna Gemma rejecting or rejected?—never joined her husband in exile, his sons and heirs did. Petrarch was born in 1305 when his father was an exile at Arezzo, and he grew up among the Florentine expatriates residing with their families at Pisa and in the south of France. In the next generation Petrarch's disciple Coluccio Salutati was taken by his mother to Bologna to live out his father's exile as a Ghibelline from the little Tuscan commune of Stignano.[45] Giovanni Villani reports that Ghibelline ladies gave birth to their children while in exile with their husbands on Monte San Pellegrino between Lucca and Modena, and in the 1320s the chronicler heard that *fuorusciti* from Genoa were "living with their households, practicing their occupations and trades just as they had done in town."[46] One of the most terrible visions in the lament that Fazio degli Uberti wrote for an allegorical Lady Florence in the 1340s pictures bloodlines broken by exile, "widows and orphans of her best blood" begging their bread in strange lands. Without family connections they wandered in "great shame" and "mortal dread." Where honor and shame were involved, as they always were when the family and the household were threatened, the complaints of exiles reached their most moving tone. In a sense, the severity of communal statutes which sometimes forced sons or kin to accompany exiled fathers or relations was a kind of concession.[47]

Like family ties, protective ties of patronage and friendship were reconstituted in exile. The case of Messer Duccio di Tignoso's horse offers a revealing glimpse of favors exchanged and services rendered. On Tuesday, 22 April 1270, Guccio di Buonaccorso told the *podestà* of Guelph Prato that Count Alessandro of Mangona had summoned him to fetch a sick horse from the count's country seat. Guccio testified that he had been ordered to take the animal to Prato so that it might be treated and equipped with a saddle if it could be cured. The horse allegedly belonged to Messer Duccio di Tignoso, a leading Ghibelline rebel of Prato; the Alberti counts of Mangona were famous for their old Ghibelline sympathies, and Guccio di Buonaccorso was known to be Count Alessandro's man. When the *podestà* asked whether Guccio had known whose horse it was or whether he had parleyed with its rebel owner in the Alberti castle, he pleaded ignorance.[48]

No community at home or in exile would have been complete without its underworld. Vanni Fucci, the "beast of Pistoia," was surely not the only cutthroat exile in the eighth circle of Dante's *Inferno* (XXV, 1–2). Witnesses to his escapades and commentators on the *Divine Comedy* re-

port that Vanni was only the most savage of the brigands who ran with
him in the mountains above Pistoia for nearly two decades at the end
of the thirteenth century.[49] There were thieves among exiles and exiles
among thieves because the line between principled and unprincipled
violence was a very thin one. Uprooted, armed, and in a virtual state of
war against their hometowns, exiles turned readily enough to brigandage
and piracy. One reason for the legatine mission of 1305 was a series of
appeals from the Florentines, whose food supplies had been cut off by
a White Guelph blockade. In the 1320s exiles privateering in more than
a dozen galleys came close to starving out the Genoese.[50]

The honor of exile-thieves did not necessarily include loyalty. Bounty
hunters often lurked on the fringes of exile companies. These shady
characters lay in wait for some likely prey to hand over to communal
officials who were authorized to pay rewards or commute the sentences
of bandits ready to turn in their own kind. According to the experienced
lawyer and magistrate Alberto da Gandino, some turncoats were only
too ready to betray their fellow exiles. Many of these traitors seem to
have got their blood money or their pardons. Others only succeeded in
compounding their trouble with the law. In 1269 or early in 1270, for example, two *fuorusciti*, Buriano and Guiscardo da Vinci, assaulted a Pratese
rebel in hiding at Carmignano and delivered him to the authorities, but
instead of being rewarded, they were detained together with their captive
in Prato.[51]

In some cases, then, companies of exiles were quite as "wicked" as
Dante declared his own *compagnia malvagia e scempia* to be. That they
were also "foolish" or "senseless" is a proposition on which one can dis-
agree with Dante, and still more with those who suppose that establish-
ments inside real or symbolic walls are the only sensible ones. Dante had
his reasons and the excuse of his resentment. The fact remains that the
internal organization of companies in exile made no less (or more) historical sense than the structure of politics and society in the communal
age.

Tactics of Resistance: The Art of Returning Home

Dante taunted Farinata degli Uberti because the Ghibellines had failed
to learn the art of returning home from exile after 1266. The mocking
retort was deserved: Dante too would discover "how much that art
weighs" (*Inferno*, X, 22–51). Returning home was no light or easy matter,

except in the poet's verse and his dreams. But Dante and Farinata were acknowledging that there were certain regular maneuvers, an "art," in the strategies by which exiles could return.

Partisan peacemaking was one of those maneuvers. It was only after Frederick II imposed himself as arbiter between warring factions in Florence that Frederick of Antioch, the emperor's son and vicar, presided over the mass exodus of the Florentine Guelphs in 1248. The pacification policies of Clement IV had a similar outcome for the other side in 1266. The first step was a papal proclamation of peace between the "internal" and "external" communes, the *intrinseci* and the *extrinseci*, of Italy. Next, the pope sent his legates to Piacenza and Cremona. The reason seemed plain to the Ghibelline annalist of Piacenza: the party of the Church was in exile from those two towns. In places from which the *imperialists* had been exiled—Parma, Milan, Mantua, Ferrara, Lodi, Vercelli, Novara, Como, and many other towns—the annalist did not expect any papal intervention. On 3 December 1266 negotiations opened in Piacenza. Discussions were still in progress when the alarm was raised: "The exiles are entering the city!" After two days of fighting, the representatives of the pope proclaimed their peace by turning Piacenza over to a Guelph stalwart. It was rumored that they had arranged the surprise attack themselves.[52] Cremona was soon pacified in the same fashion, and the ruler of the city for sixteen years, Uberto Pallavicino, was expelled, thanks to what Salimbene called the "mild words of priests."[53] The papal mission of 1305 followed a long tradition when it came to Italy in the name of peace but actually supported the White Guelphs under siege at Pistoia and at large in exile.

Partisanship was suspected as a matter of course in professionals at pacification.[54] The full title of the peacemaking Order of Knights of the Glorious and Blessed Virgin was soon displaced by a nickname hinting at peace made for high bidders and at good tables—*frati gaudenti*. Founded at Bologna in 1260 by a group of Emilian knights, the order mediated among factions at the behest of a *podestà* or judge. Missions were sent to draw up conciliating statutes and celebrate the kiss of peace in many towns of Emilia, Romagna, and Tuscany. Sharing the zeal for spiritual renewal and social justice that had spread with special intensity during the first half of the thirteenth century, Fra Guittone of Arezzo insisted that his brother *gaudenti* were content to favor the cause of God alone. Nevertheless, in one of their first missions (1263), they joined the *podestà* of Bologna in a partisan decision to send the Ghibelline Lambertazzi into exile while allowing the rival Guelph faction of the Brizzi to return to their homes in Imola. Three years later Fra Catalano and Fra Loderingo brought about the pacification of Florence which landed them among the hypocrites in Dante's hell (*Inferno*, XXIII, 103–108).[55] In the opinion of many people in Florence and elsewhere the two *frati* were hypocrites at best. Giovanni Villani was relatively mild: "under the cover of false hypocrisy they were in accord more for their own advantage than the common good."[56] Commentators on Dante generally agreed with Jacopo della Lana that Fra Catalano and Fra Loderingo "were corrupted by the Guelphs and took bribes in coin so that the Ghibellines were driven into exile."[57]

It was not petty tyranny, then, but realism which led the Visconti of Milan and the Scaligeri of Verona to ban the call of "peace" in their territories.[58] The events made famous by Dante's part in them show in detail how the peacemaker's mission could become a Trojan Horse for exiles. In the fall of 1301 Black Guelph exiles preceded Dante's last-ditch embassy to Rome on behalf of the White Guelph regime in Florence. Boniface VIII had already named Charles of Valois papal *paciarius*—in the interests of the Black Guelph exiles and their allies. The pope's terrible tongue gave him away in Dino Compagni's report of his interview with the Florentine ambassadors: "Humble yourselves to me, and I will tell you the truth that I have no other intention than peace for you." Contemptuous, then protesting too much, these are words Pope Boniface might well have said. It was hardly necessary for Dino to add that "the appearance was very good, but the resolution contrary, because he [the pope] wanted to crush the Whites and raise up the Blacks and make the Whites enemies of the house of France and of the Church."[59] Even Giovanni Villani, no friend of the Whites, chose to see through the camouflage of Boniface's brand of arbitration.[60]

When Charles of Valois actually entered Florence on 1 November 1301, Black Guelph exiles rode showily on parade with his French knights or followed close behind.[61] The armor of the peacemaking force glistened, and mules carried supplies for an army of twelve hundred men. The White Guelph government, too late, talked peace. Exiles were already slipping into the city. Where Corso Donati and his men had gathered beneath the east wall, the Porta di Pinti was breached and San Pier Maggiore taken. To the west the French were opening the Porta della Cucilla to Gherarduccio Buondelmonti and other exiles. During six days of violence Charles of Valois took hostages from both sides (but released Black Guelphs) and saw only huts burning (where palaces were in flames). The official version of events blamed the helpless Whites for what Villani admitted was actually the work of "tyrants, malefactors, and bandits" who had made their way into the city.[62] The new signory—by the grace of God, the patron saints of Florence, Pope Boniface and the Church, and the son of the king of France—was Black Guelph. Those who had been condemned and exiled under the White regime were absolved, and on 7 November 1301 the news went out that the true Guelph party had triumphed over "certain sons of iniquity, rebels in spirit and by their works. . . ."[63]

That the new pope, Benedict XI, was saintly only meant that the White Guelph exiles would tread more lightly with similar tactics. In 1304, under the blue skies of a Florentine spring, Nicholas Cardinal Alberti of Prato preached the peace of Pope Benedict. The cardinal was a papal favorite and a firm supporter of the Whites. Dino Compagni imagined the Blacks reconciled among themselves and "humbled by sweet words" to a more universal concord.[64] Bonfires were lighted. Church bells rang as proctors of the White Guelphs and the Ghibellines, with Ser Petracco, Petrarch's father, as their notary, entered the city on 26 April 1304. Before agreeing to a settlement, the Blacks insisted on certain terms. There must first be peace in Prato, in the White stronghold of Pistoia, and in the districts of the countryside held by the Whites. As the Blacks surely knew, these conditions could not be met without delay—and probably could not be met at all. The cardinal of Prato shuttled from one town or party to another until it became clear that he must abandon his mission or change his tactics.

At the end of May, playing on pity but also showing his strength, the cardinal summoned the leaders of the *fuorusciti* to Florence. Men and women poured into the streets to watch the spectacle. The descendants of Ghibelline families that had not been seen in Florence for forty years rode in procession, and ancient Ghibellines kissed the arms of the Uberti as they passed by. After their arrival, the exiles fortified the houses and towers of the Mozzi on the Oltrarno, hard choices in the art of returning home lying before them. The cardinal (and Dino Compagni) would have had them deal, and win, from strength, but they "proposed to be led by the Blacks . . . so that [the Blacks] would not have any excuse to evade the peace."[65] Negotiations, wearing to the breaking point, wore out the exiles' determination. When their supposed allies the Cavalcanti refused to mobilize their houses and friends for an attempted coup, the exiles and their cardinal, leaving his malediction behind him, were forced to withdraw. (See Figure 5a.)

With the failure of such attempts at pacification, guerrilla warfare was likely to resume. Poised on the borders or in their enclaves, allied with rival powers, ready to raid or subvert the regime within the walls, companies of exiles tested the "foreign policy," the military preparedness, and the internal security of the communes at home. The countryside was particularly vulnerable because it was open to forays from neighboring towns, always of uncertain allegiance, and accustomed to outbursts of violence. Beginning in the 1220s, Ezzelino da Romano had enlisted the support of the country-based warrior nobility, many of them under communal ban, to build a proto-principate on the northern edges of the Lombard plain. Nearly one hundred years later Matteo Visconti, like his uncle Bishop Ottone before him, gained time and followers in the foothills and towns of Lombardy for his return from exile to Milan in 1311.[66] From their castles Guelph nobles exiled from Pisa—the Uppezinghi, the Visconti, a Casalberti—terrorized the Pisan countryside up to the suburb of San Marco in 1288–1289. In Romagna and the Marches conflicts between local lords and papal representatives early in the fourteenth century were very often contests to determine whether exiles could be drawn in from some territorial refuge to tip the balance of forces within the towns.[67]

Here again a Florentine case is especially revealing.[68] Within two months of their defeat and expulsion in 1302 the Florentine White Guelphs and their Ghibelline allies had raised rebellion to the south and east of Florence. To old war cries, the Ubertini and the Pazzi took Figline with 130 horsemen and 600 foot soldiers and lost Pian-tra-Vigne farther up the Arno only after they were betrayed. While Florentine troops hurried from the siege of Pistoia for a counterattack, the Gherardini entered the Chianti castle of Montagliari and the fortress of Brolio so as to control the roads in the valleys of the Greve and the Pesa. From skirmishes in the south the Florentines veered to the Mugello, where Ubaldini men, reinforced by Florentine and Pistoiese Whites, were bullying and burning villages around the Ubaldini stronghold near Firenzuola. The Mugello was devastated in retaliation, but not before the market towns of San Piero a Sieve and Gagliano on the pass to Bologna were razed by the rebels and castles down the length of the river Sieve were incited to revolt. The *intrinseci* were harassed and beaten piecemeal in this first war of the Mugello. A year later, in the summer of 1304, they lost a pitched battle to the exiles at the castle of Montaccianico.

Although the walls at home were usually strong enough to withstand guerrilla raids, the same fortifications which kept exiles out could hold captive the cities within when lifelines to communications, provisioning, and trade were cut. Throughout the winter of 1302 Black Guelphs in

Florence had good reason to fear that their exiles meant to finish what the preceding year's drought had begun. Grain prices were already twice normal before exile attacks closed the roads from the granaries of the Chianti and the Mugello. *Fuorusciti* were intriguing at Pisa and as far as Genoa for policy or pirates to intercept the flow of supplies from abroad. An assembly of representatives from the whole guild community of Florence met on the emergency. Formal protests were sent to Pisa. Shipments of grain that the merchant houses did succeed in importing from the south were diverted to smaller and less conspicuous ports. But the Florentine winter and spring of 1302 were leaner than they might have been. Thanks to exile blockades there were also hungry times at Piacenza, Modena, Genoa, Orvieto, and other towns.[69]

Even within their walls towns were not secure from conspiracies hatched between insiders and exiles. The fifth column was another favorite tactic in the art of returning home. Wives and sons and branches of families left behind by exiles were a dangerous pool of potential spies and supporters. Stumps of factions, like the old Ghibellines greeting the cardinal of Prato's procession of *fuorusciti* in 1304, might come to life again. At least 650 of the 1,050 Ghibellines listed by the Florentine Guelphs in 1268 were not exiled outside communal territory. This proportion was probably representative. In 1276, nearly ten years after the leading Ghibellines of Prato were expelled, the Ghibelline remnant was large enough to select sixteen representatives, two for every city gate, and to pay a special tax assessment of 2,000 *lire*. With an exile bridgehead in its midst, it is not surprising that even in alliance with the Guelph League of Tuscany the commune of Prato was reluctant to campaign against its own rebels.[70]

In 1311, forty-six years after the subjection of Vicenza by Padua, the Vicentine exile Sighelfredo Gonzara entered his city unnoticed disguised in a Greek beard.[71] Helped by his son-in-law and perhaps by tricks learned in the service of the king of Cyprus and the pope at Avignon, Gonzara laid his plans with a group of conspirators and then withdrew to Verona to watch the results. On 15 April 1311 the gates of Vicenza were betrayed on schedule to soldiers sent from Verona and Mantua. The Paduan garrison was taken by surprise, and the castle of Isola was plundered and burned. Communal statutes should have prevented Gonzara's adventure and others like it.[72] Although exceptions were sometimes made for family, to receive or aid rebels or exiles from one's town was to risk a fine, a sentence equal to their own, or the destruction of the house where the fugitives had been sheltered. The frequency and severity of provisions such as these suggest that the fear of exile intrigues ran deep—and that the success of the communes in defending against them was limited.[73]

Direct assault was the ultimate weapon. During nearly fifteen years of exile, Archbishop Ottone Visconti had tried every other maneuver in the art of returning home to Milan. Late in 1276 he launched a fleet on the river Po and assembled an army of more than eleven thousand knights and foot soldiers. His own following of exiles marched with men recruited from Monferrato and at least six friendly Lombard towns. The Della Torre inside Milan prepared for a siege. The city was called to arms, and trenches were dug around the fortified suburb of Desio. On the night of 20 January 1277, after a day of bombardment from catapults and crossbowmen, the gates of Desio were thrown open while the Torriani defenders slept. Trying resistance, Francesco della Torre was thrown from his horse and, with a cousin, killed and beheaded. At least six hundred surprised defenders were taken captive. On the Feast of St. Agnes the cry of "Peace!" was sounded in Milan, and the next day Ottone Visconti made his entrance at the head of his troops—not conqueror, he announced, but peacemaker. By then, the houses of the Della Torre had already been sacked and destroyed "without any order from the commune."[74] (See Figures 4a and 4b.)

Like Salimbene's account of the attack on Parma in 1247, Dino Compagni's description of the exiles' assault on Florence in July 1304 is a great moment in his chronicle.[75] (See Figure 5b.) The cardinal of Prato's arbitration in the spring of 1304 had failed, but his efforts did draw away a large number of would-be Black Guelph defenders to proclaim their innocence before the papal court at Perugia. Seizing the occasion, Ghibellines and White Guelph exiles gathered in their enclave at Lastra, two miles down the Arno from Florence. Guerrilla bands and soldiers were called in from outposts in Florentine territory. With reinforcements summoned from Bologna, Arezzo, and the Romagna, the exiles commanded at least 1,200 cavalry and as many as 10,000 infantry. By night, friends from the city crept into the camp at Lastra to urge a show of force.

On 20 July 1304 a mounted vanguard led by Baschiera della Tosa appeared before the walls of Florence. Like some apocalyptic vision Compagni might have dreamed, the warriors were dressed all in white. They held olive branches and swords. All were calling for peace. As the sun bore down and burned over the scene, the Porta degli Spadai near San Marco opened miraculously and not (Compagni was sure) to treachery or tools for a siege. Many attackers entered, but Baschiera and most of his men stayed fused to their places, hearing sounds of thundering catapults and watching flames and smoke rising from the city. Only after the raiding party inside the walls had been trapped did Baschiera and his men move at last—in retreat. "Their hope and joy [turned] to tears because the adversaries they had defeated were defeating them and had taken heart like lions and streaming forth pursued them. . . ." Many exiles were killed in their headlong flight, and many of them and their allies were captured and hanged. Whether or not their plans for a siege had been "wise and bold," as Dino Compagni wanted at first to believe, only the high drama of his account made their tactics seem altogether exceptional.

Partisan peacemaking, guerrilla campaigns, blockades, subversion, and siege—these were standard tactics in that art of returning home from exile which was sometimes but, as Dante and Farinata degli Uberti and Dino Compagni knew very well, not always successful.

Facing the Facts: Henry VII and Exiles

As emperor-elect, Henry of Luxemburg expected his mission in Italy to transcend the facts of exclusion in communal politics and society. His coming in the spring of 1310 had the blessing of Pope Clement V. His embassies had been received in Lombardy and Tuscany, where he assured suspicious cities that he would show no undue favor. Imperial justice and clemency were to be the only art for bringing exiles home. The dead ends of the imperial expedition, the irreducibility of the facts it exposed and confirmed, have always seemed more certain for the sense of new beginnings with which it opened.[76]

The initial Italian reaction followed stubbornly predictable patterns.[77] Anticipating the usual imperial ambitions and hostile alliances between the emperor-elect and their own exiles, communes turned to their external allies. Close to the route of Henry's descent from Mont Cenis, Asti negotiated for the protection of King Robert of Naples against a forced return of its *fuorusciti*. Next in line, rulers in Lombardy raised the prospect of a Lombard League with the old papal-Angevin connection. From Tuscany came a report of the Lucchese saying "several times" that "they would obey, if [Henry] conceded letters stating that they could keep lands they held of the empire and that he would not restore the exiles."[78] The Florentines urged traditional forms of resistance openly, complaining to King Robert that Henry's policy was to replace Ghibellines in Guelph lands.

It is true, as the Florentines alleged, that Henry followed the counsels of Ghibelline and White Guelph exiles "for the most part."[79] Although

Henry considered himself above faction, exiles saw in him the long-awaited successor of the Hohenstaufen emperors, the new hope of an old cause. There could be no genuine settlement in Italy so long as there were exiles to disturb it; they were symptoms of a disorder intolerable to an emperor and a standing challenge to set the world right. But the prospects for peace were no better if the exiles were restored because to bring one party home was to create the conditions for forcing its rival into exile. Exiles had everything and *intrinseci* nothing but enemies to gain by imperial arbitration. There was a double bind in the intervention of the outsider, just as there was a double edge in Giovanni da Cermenate's remark that Henry's plans for peace were a true expression of his "simple soul." [80]

Members of exile companies, a decade's cross-section of leading *fuorusciti*, surrounded the emperor-elect in key positions.[81] Among the White Guelph exiles from Florence, Ugolino of Vico was a papal knight, an imperial emissary to Lombardy, and the first of Henry's vicars appointed in Italy. Palmiro Altoviti had been condemned along with Dante by the Florentine courts which he condemned in turn as a member of the imperial tribunal, and Vermiglio degli Alfani was so far from ruined by exile from Florence that he was able to loan money to the house of Luxemburg. Black Guelph Pistoia expelled Cione de' Bellasti; Henry VII appointed him judge for sentences to banishment and confiscation in Milan. Messer Cione's fellow fugitive from Pistoia, Simone de' Reali, had lost his property at home but served as treasurer of the imperial expedition. Niccolò di Bonifazio Buonsignori was a great exile from Siena—and imperial vicar at Asti and later at Milan, where he came to be hated as much as he had been at home. As many as three Ghibelline exiles—Matteo Visconti, Manfred Beccaria of Pavia, and (perhaps) the Florentine banker Guido di Filippo dell'Antella—sat on Henry's council for Italy. Nearly half of the twelve imperial vicars who can be identified in an official list of February 1311 were exiles from Tuscany.[82] The staying power of companies of exiles is understandable.

So is their strategy. The talents and ties of town and countryside were, as usual, combined in their leaders—nobles, bankers, magistrates, and would-be *signori*. Sure of support, exiles regrouped once again in strategic places on the land or in receptive towns. Riccardo Tizzone, the persistent chieftain of the Ghibellines in exile from Vercelli, offered the emperor-elect his band of one hundred knights, who had occupied the territory around Feltre; Vercelli itself, Riccardo promised, would be forever loyal once his party returned. Giovanni de' Cerchi and the Florentine Whites who had held out in Pisa prepared their case and their presents for Henry.

Some one hundred White Guelph expatriates from Lucca picked proctors to pledge him their devotion and, more impressively, their property.[83]

The exiles were not disappointed. Chieri was the first commune to receive the imperial expedition, and in November 1311 it became the first commune forced to reinstate its *fuorusciti*. A few weeks later the exiles returned to a grudging Asti because "the plenitude of imperial majesty" was much nearer than distant promises of protection from Robert of Naples. At Vercelli and Novara the virtue of clemency was quickly learned when the exiles approached in the name of the king of peace with five thousand imperial troops. Similar patterns unfolded all over Lombardy. Wherever beneficiaries of the emperor-elect's intervention were restored to their homes, their rivals were likely to take their places in exile.[84]

Matteo Visconti proved himself a master of the art of returning home. For eight years he had been an exile from Milan. Moving with his family and followers between country strongholds and friendly towns, he had played a waiting game with the Della Torre who held Milan against him. Petrarch tells how a messenger from Guido della Torre once found Matteo fishing on the shore of Lake Garda. For the time being, Matteo said serenely, he was tending his nets; when Guido's crimes outweighed his own, he would return by the same road that had taken him away.[85]

In 1311, "now in a pilgrim's habit, now as a shield-bearing squire, often under cover of night," Matteo made a supposedly secret way to meet the emperor-elect.[86] Finding the court at Asti, he posed as a nameless wanderer, too filled with important news and longing devotion to wait for a regular audience. By day the Ghibellines, who had expected Matteo all along, broadcast his identity, sent him an armed escort, and staged showy demonstrations for the "Ghibelline *Italicus*." Guelph lords knew the treacherous apostle of the kiss of peace that Matteo forced upon them in a formal reception staged for the benefit of the emperor-elect. Mistaking their tone and misunderstanding the language of their protests, Henry smiled and said, "Good, you are almost reconciled already."[87]

Matteo's next step was to subvert Milan on the inside. An elaborate pact was made between the Visconti and defecting Della Torre cousins.[88] The Visconti agreed to terms of mutual coexistence and promised to submit to the archbishop of Milan, Cassone della Torre. The fact that Messer Guido della Torre, not Cassone and his brothers, managed Milan was conveniently ignored. Matteo made concessions which hint at the resources underlying the survival and resistance of a great exile. His agreement not to molest the country holdings—castles, fields, water rights—of the archbishop and his brothers or even to acquire land near their own shows him still a threatening force in Milanese territory. Matteo's urban connections were at least as dangerous. The Della Torre demanded that he renounce his claims to encircling towns, from Como and Tortona in the north and south to Bergamo and Pavia in the east and west. Chroniclers understood the consequences even if the archbishop and the emperor-elect did not. The leader, Henry of Luxemburg, was about to be led into becoming a partisan peacemaker in spite of himself. Dino Compagni delighted in his understanding of Matteo's appeal to Henry: "*Signore*, my hand can give or take Milan; come to Milan where there are friends of mine so that no one can take it away from us."[89]

The time for Guido della Torre, in Dino Compagni's play on words, "to take" (*torre*) Milan had passed. On 23 December 1310, his anger obvious to everyone but the emperor-elect, Guido escorted Henry and the Milanese exiles into the city. Even his name, as if it no longer really mattered, was forgotten in the lists of luminaries who marched in the procession. Within hours Guido agreed to peace, swore fidelity to Henry as the "true and natural" lord of Milan, and surrendered his office as captain of the Milanese to Henry's vicar. On the Feast of the Epiphany, 6 January 1311, Henry was crowned in an epiphany of his own with the iron crown of Lombardy. One of his first acts as king was to knight faithful followers, who included, of course, Matteo Visconti.[90]

The expulsion of the Della Torre completed a familiar scenario.[91] Tensions already ran high in Milan when Henry proclaimed a general amnesty on 23 January 1311. Anticipating his rivals' response, Matteo seems to have lured the Torriani into arming against the king by encouraging the restless younger Visconti to appear to make common cause with them. When German troops investigated rumors of an uprising, they found Matteo in quiet conversation with a few friends; the Della Torre were armed to the teeth. Fighting broke out on 12 February. "With superb wisdom and quick thinking," Matteo commanded his men to lie low and hurried to present himself, unarmed, before the king. Too hasty in the attack, Guido della Torre was more fortunate in his quick retreat over garden walls to the edge of the city and escape. After two months' confinement outside Milan, Matteo returned at Easter. The Della Torre, refusing humiliating terms of reconciliation, were left to contemplate for themselves the art of returning home.[92] (See Figure 8.)

Early in April 1313 two imperial ambassadors set out from Pisa on a mission in Italy as the papal legates of 1305 had done.[93] Eight years had brought about many changes, but some things had hardly changed at all. Despite the emperor's expedition, the unruly independence and vitality of the towns and territorial lords of Italy were very much what they had been. So were the facts of exclusion in the Italian experience. Like the bishop of Mende and Abbot Pilifort before them, Giovanni Rosso de' Gualandi and Vermiglio degli Alfani found exiles nearly everywhere from the outset of their journey, and the records they kept for the emperor reconfirm what should seem by now a routine state of affairs. (See Map 1, p. 33 above.)

Of the two parts of the ambassadors' assignment—winning support for another imperial campaign and collecting information on rebels who were operating in Lombardy and elsewhere in the north—only the second was successful. Men and money for the emperor were scarce; rebels and exiles were not. In February 1313 Henry had already condemned a long list of rebellious subjects in Tuscany. Robert of Naples was declared guilty of lese majesty on 26 April 1313, and a number of towns allied with him were charged with rebellion in terms defined by the "Pisan constitutions" and incorporated by Henry's lawyers into imperial law.[94] When the ambassadors arrived at Brescia, the imperial vicar there pleaded desperate circumstances and produced the names of 333 rebels—those who had broken terms of confinement; those known to be in hostile territory; and those of a marauding gang of "assassins, homicides, robbers, arsonists, and other perpetrators of nefarious crimes." These three groups formed the hard core of the nearly ten thousand men who had held Brescia under siege for weeks on end. At Verona, Cangrande della Scala supplied thirty-three rebel names; since the sons, brothers, and nephews of the individuals mentioned were known to be outside the walls with them, the force harassing Veronese territory from exile must have been very much larger, perhaps as large as the group of 356 rebels listed by Cangrande's agent in Vicenza. Although the names requested from Passarino Buonaccolsi in Mantua do not appear in the ambassadors' records, Buonaccolsi's lieutenant at Modena counted 225 exiles and 36 rebel castles in his district. It could not have been much consolation that the ambassadors also came across many Tuscan *fuorusciti* on the imperial side—7 in Brescia; 35 in Verona; 12 in Vicenza; 27 in Mantua.[95]

The situation at Modena was like that in many parts of Emilia, Lombardy, the Romagna, and Tuscany:

> the *extrinseci* of Modena hold many castles in the district of Modena and are waging war against the town; and the Bolognese and the men of Parma and Reggio, sometimes openly, sometimes in secret, are giving aid to the

extrinseci. . . . No one is living or working [in the Modenese countryside], except in the direction of Mantua; there are no merchants or routes [for transporting] merchandise and other necessities, except on the Mantuan road. . . .[96]

Many reports of this kind must have been made during the communal age. Modena was divided into factions, each hoping for outside aid. The losing party of the moment was in exile but still a power to be reckoned with. The company of exiles was well organized, entrenched in the countryside, and allied with neighboring cities. Flying their own flag, *fuorusciti* were blockading Modena and threatening to mount a full-scale assault. Sympathizers inside the walls had already attempted to betray the gates.[97]

Henry VII may not have received the full text of the ambassadors' gloomy report before his death at Buonconvento near Siena on 23 April 1313. It was perhaps the only way that he could have transcended the facts of exclusion in Italy. Some exiles were repatriated after the emperor's death, but others filled their places to await some change in circumstances that might bring them home.

3

Dante and His Judges:

Rules of Exclusion in
the Early Fourteenth Century

And so if Justice is left out, what are kingdoms except great robber bands? For what are robber bands except little kingdoms?

St. Augustine, *City of God*, IV, 4–6

By the fourteenth century Italian lawyers and magistrates had many names and many rules for exile at their disposal. The *Corpus Iuris Civilis* read by the scholars at Bologna referred in scattered rubrics to the *relegati* and *deportati* of ancient times or to the *banniti* ("outlaws") and *hostes et rebelles* ("enemies and rebels") of medieval emperors. The theory and practice of ecclesiastical censure and excommunication paralleled or crossed over into the concerns of civil lawyers. Communal statute books contained a vast quantity of legislation on the *banniti, exbanniti et ribelli*, and *confinati* ("internees") whom papal legates and imperial ambassadors found beyond the walls of most Italian towns. The names and the rules were fairly certain; the rationalizing task of the professionals was to decide which names and rules to apply.

The case of the most illustrious of Italian exiles is an especially revealing test of how far the judges, officials, and doctors of law had come with this task by the early Trecento. For official justice dwelt on Dante at length, if not blindly, during his nearly twenty years in exile.[1] Although the original records are lost, copies do survive. Dante's name appears three times in the *Libro del Chiodo*, the oversized and bristling register in which the Guelph party of Florence transcribed lists and sentences of political outcasts after its own return from exile in the middle of the thirteenth century.[2] The *Chiodo* copy of a condemnation dated 27 January 1302 nails down the initial moments and modes of Dante's case. According to this document, he was charged with various offenses, including barratry, extortion, and resistance to Pope Boniface VIII and his Black Guelph allies, who had just returned triumphant to Florence; after being tried and convicted in absentia, he had been sentenced to two years of exile, fined, and permanently excluded from public office. A second condemnation of the poet is recorded for 10 March 1302: as a result of his persistent refusal to appear and accept the first sentence, he was condemned along with fourteen other former White Guelph officials to be burned to death should he ever fall into the hands of the commune. (See Figure 7.) Under 2 September 1311 the *Libro del Chiodo* includes the text of an amnesty which, far from pardoning Dante, explicitly reaffirmed the conditions of his exile and extended them to his two sons. These documents, together with outside copies of yet another death sentence proclaimed against Dante and his sons in November 1315, have none of the poetry they elicited from him. But they do have an eloquence of their own on the possibilities and the limitations of a legal profession and a political establishment straining after order, legitimacy, and mastery.[3]

The issue at stake was whether the court and the magistrate could exact obedience to their rules and routines. The outcome was still in the balance because the rules of exclusion in medieval Italy were as many-sided and as intractable as the facts underlying them. While Dante's judges laid claim to preeminent authority, like Roman magistrates or modern "servants of the state," their jurisdiction and their means of enforcing it were still very limited. In the face of defiant evasion the courts and their executive agents were left to assert wide-ranging powers, develop elaborate procedures, and formulate exhaustive definitions in order to exclude those whom they could not otherwise include and punish under the sway of the law. The powers, procedures, and personae of exclusion were expressed in the tortuous language of highly technical distinctions. The documents are difficult, but, closely read, they bring to life the terms of an unresolved contest between established authority and a still-powerful and unrepentant opposition.

Powers of Exclusion

In the winter of 1302 Messer Cante Gabrieli of Gubbio, *podestà* of Black Guelph Florence, acted against Dante and the White Guelphs "as well, by every legal mode and right, as we are able." This was a formality of course—but then, not a finished convention, altogether predictable and opaque. The affirmation also betrayed the need to search ("as well . . . as we are able") among different sources and styles of authority.

The sentences of 27 January and 10 March 1302 conferred, in their opening lines, a kind of charismatic authority on the representatives of the law. Before specifically identifying his office, the notaries of Messer Cante Gabrieli dignified his person with attributes of command. "Noble" and "potent," the knight and lord in Messer Cante, the power in his title as *podestà*, preceded the judge and obscured the bureaucrat in his identity. More than officials, his entourage were a "family," surrounded by "the sound of bells and the voice of the herald" and not to be seen as mere functionaries at their desks. The amnesty-by-legislation of 1311, which deliberately omitted Dante and others like him, opened in something of the same aura. No routine or impersonal act, it was known by the name of its most influential supporter, Messer Baldo d'Aguglione, formidable even as Dante's *villan d'Aguglion* or as the "Great Dog" in the epithet of Benvenuto of Imola.[4] Bypassing the regular authority of the commune, Messer Baldo's peace was enacted after the co-option of twelve "wise and upright men" to form a *balìa*, an emergency commission given special powers in times of crisis. There were no references at all to the regular courts of the commune in the formulas of 1315. What mattered first to the notary was that the condemnations flowed from the "nobility" and "potency" of Messer Ranieri di Zaccaria of Orvieto, vicar of King Robert of Naples during the first Florentine experiment with despotism.

Trappings of charisma were granted by statute and glossed by a whole literature of advice for the model magistrate.[5] The anonymous author of *The Pastoral Eye* (ca. 1222), the earliest known example of this genre, wished to see in the ideal *podestà* the image of Justice, Honor, and Love on which legitimate power rested. His actions were supposed to mirror tags of wisdom from Scripture, good Greeks and Romans, and the books of law. He would fear failings of immoderate laughter and self-praise, shun eavesdroppers, spies, flatterers, gifts, and invitations to easy familiarity. His comings and goings would make fine processions, where people might marvel, as Orfino of Lodi did, at the beauty of his weapons, his horses, hounds, monkeys, falcons, and songbirds singing. "It is not enough [for the magistrate] to abstain from evil," declared Giovanni of Viterbo, "without also doing good."[6]

As Messer Giovanni would have known very well after serving as a judge in Florence during the 1240s, the actual situation of the magistrate was nuanced and complex. The real *podestà*, Captain of the People, or Executor of Justice normally paid a bond for good behavior on assuming office and was subject to formal review at the end of terms kept short by statute in order to forestall long-range ambitions. Ordinarily a foreigner, he was quartered in a fortified palace of the commune where he could be closely watched. Communal commissions, like Baldo d'Aguglione's, could overrule him. By the later fourteenth century the foreign official, hedged in by rules and shut up in his palace, was a butt of insiders' jokes and a subject for satire as a *podestà* without *potestas*, a power without power.[7] On the other hand, regulations and irreverence are unnecessary where they do not matter. The rituals and the personifications of politics are never entirely unreal, though they are often intentionally deceptive. In any case, the awesomeness of a Messer Cante Gabrieli, lord in Umbria, familiar of popes and French royalty, author of 209 condemnations in 1302, was not illusory.[8]

Both the aura and the fact of power had distinct functions. The majesty of the law always depends in part on awe-inspiring paraphernalia calculated to produce effects of reverence, loyalty, and submission. Starting from the premise that secular institutions often draw upon or mimic sacred imagery and ritual, recent historians have rediscovered the importance of just such spiritual sanctions where historians used to see little more than pragmatic operations of political power.[9] The powers of Messer Cante Gabrieli can be understood accordingly as much more than matters of worldly routine. The regime he served claimed the blessing, however hollow, of Pope Boniface VIII. He bore titles setting him apart from ordinary men; he took vows of fidelity on entering office and caused bells to ring for rites of condemnation or absolution. Like members of real religious orders, this "lay monk" discharged an important ministry in the world while remaining detached from it, cloistered behind high walls, surrounded by an all-male company, regulated (in principle) by strict discipline, and pledged to conduct an unimpeachable life. Neither sacred nor altogether profane, his intermediate or double identity gave him leverage to enforce the supposed commands of the spirit against the demands of the flesh and to translate Providence to the world of circumstances.[10]

Messer Cante Gabrieli was also a "soldier of the law." His titles were knightly, signs of physical prowess and emblems of the military commander. As *podestà*, he rode mounted in procession as a captain-at-arms to the beat of drums, armor ready and weapons ranged around him. Soldiers outnumbered the judges and notaries in his entourage.[11] These attributes were not simply for show in a society where the competition and conflict among corporate groups could burst openly into battle over some tower, piazza, or fortified street. Insofar as legitimate rule was the rule of the strongest, the *podestà* and captain of Italian communes or factions entered the lists as a warrior-champion and leader. Since personal presence and physical possession were symbolic and actual forms of political domination in a society of corporate bodies, the body and "family" of the magistrate were bound to clash for control against the bodies and family ties that rallied in resistance. The spectacle of trial by ordeal and of justice by combat were still incarnate, at once concealed and exposed, in the person of Messer Cante Gabrieli, *nobilis et potens*.[12]

Yet none of these charismatic sanctions was sufficient authority for legal powers of exclusion. Saints or soldiers of the law are not easily called to account. Their position is at the same time archaic and revolutionary because it is grounded in the primitive violence and mystery which both precede and to some extent persist outside the rules and routines of ordinary politics. They enforce the law only to the extent that pretensions to majesty and the practice of command do not interfere with the regularity and even banality on which the authority of the magistrate also depends. Dante's judges and their notaries stopped short of endorsing such interference. Their opening accolades were brief.

The formulas of 1302 passed abruptly from Messer Cante Gabrieli, "noble" and "potent," to his collateral judge Messer Paolo of Gubbio, "wise" and "discreet." It was Messer Paolo who took the case, delegated not to the person of the *podestà* but to an office of his administration, "the office on extortion and illicit gain." Messer Paolo was a specialist among specialists, certificated and sanctioned in committee "by the will and with the counsel of the other judges of the said *podestà*." His actions were not those of show and sound and combat but of official procedures duly notarized by Ser Bonora da Pregio. The amnesty and exceptions of 1311 covered Baldo d'Aguglione's personal influence beneath layers of legal expertise, which, as a lawyer and judge, he must have contributed to them. In words and phrases at least, the lines of authority were delegated, disembodied, and depersonalized. Even Messer Ranieri di Zaccaria of Orvieto, though the personal representative of King Robert of Naples in Florence, spoke in 1315 through his notary's formulas in an abstracting first-person plural and "with the consent of his judges."

Through such appeals to established precedent or written law, magistrates become (or seem) all the more orderly and objective. In 1302 Dante's judges claimed to be proceeding "according to the form of the law, the statutes of the commune and of the people of the city of Florence, the Ordinances of Justice, the reformations thereof, and by virtue of our will."[13] Arbitrary action came last in this formulation, necessarily acknowledged, but deliberately scaled below less makeshift and personal sanctions. First in rank came the common law—the consensus of doctors, doctrine, and judges in gloss, commentary, treatise, and case law. The formula set Florentine statutes and legislation between arbitrary decision making and universal prescription, as if to describe their standing midway between the most contingent and the most general sources of legal authority. This hierarchical arrangement made Florentine laws appear to be, in effect, species of the genus *ius comune*. Historical priority belonged to the communal statutes because the commune had taken on a formal organization in the twelfth century and, after absorbing or excluding its major corporate rivals, had eventually lodged executive and judicial powers in the office of *podestà*. The Ordinances of Justice (1293) were cited next in recognition of the fact that they had been an instrument of constitutional consolidation after the guild community of the thirteenth century had fought its battles and framed its statutes under a Captain of the People. Additions or changes to these political and legal charters were left to the legislative councils and those "reformations" which figured only a notch above magisterial will in the formula of 1302.

Thus, in a few routine phrases, Dante's judges and their notaries produced a schematic cross-section of Florentine history, charted the levels of their authority, and traced its flow. All the dimensions of Max Weber's classic typology of legitimacy figured in their formula—the charismatic, the traditional, and the rational-legal or bureaucratic. The synthesis was impressive, as it was surely meant to be. But so was the potential for conflict and challenge it served to formalize. By acknowledging three sources of authority—common law, statute, and *arbitrium*—the formula also acknowledged that one source might be appealed against another. More than a century of legal learning and practical experience had cut the worst risks. The romanizing rigidity of twelfth-century glossators had dissolved in thirteenth-century commentary. Concessions forced from German emperors or from popes in the drive of the communes to rule themselves (since higher powers could hardly rule them) had reduced the application of common law to matters that were not covered by communal statutes. By the fourteenth century, statutes were silent about very few things, certainly not about magistrates given ample power, only to be sharply restricted in exercising it. But the problem of consistency and of limits remained. Florentine law, like communal law everywhere in Italy, was multiform, a patchwork of irregular parts. Lacking certainty and simplicity, it did not close openings for interpretation and argument. Nor could Dante's judges claim a monopoly either on magisterial will or on common law when Emperor Henry VII and Dante could turn these same claims against them.[14]

Counterclaims were the more damaging because the bias of faction showed so clearly beneath (and through) the ritual invocation of duly constituted powers. If the solemn preambles of 1302 introduced Messer Cante Gabrieli and his court as agents of the law, the text exposed them as political instruments acting for "the good state of the city of Florence *and of the Guelph party*." Messer Baldo d'Aguglione stood, more bluntly, "for the exaltation of the Guelph party." Again, in 1315, the "regime [*status*] of the Guelph party" was at stake in the condemnations by Messer Ranieri di Zaccaria of Orvieto. Even the dating of sentences "in the reign of the lord Pope Boniface VIII" or "under the royal vicar" insinuated partisan dependence on the papacy and the Angevin alliance. Leonardo Bruni, in his fifteenth-century *Life of Dante*, did not doubt that the Black Guelphs had passed "a perverse and iniquitous law" in 1302 to prosecute the White opposition after the usual statute of limitations had expired.[15] It is unlikely that constitutional guarantees were so explicit or the powers of the court so restricted as Bruni supposed. Dante's judges let their political color be seen quite independent of some special law. The Black Guelph cause surfaced in their own formulas, where the spell of legal legitimacy that they had begun to cast broke on the reality of a Guelph regime even more partisan than the Guelph party because it was limited to one victorious faction alone.

Between 1311 and 1313 the high imperial tribunal of Emperor Henry VII called the Florentine bluff. The city and faction condemning Dante were themselves condemned. The credentials and language of the sentence were weighted down with righteousness and recollections of imperial authority. To resist, declared the emperor's judges, was to contravene the holy power of imperial majesty, ever vigilant for peace and rightfully supreme in Christendom. Roman *imperium*, apostolic mandate, and divine decree stood offended. For the emperor's grace, his dependents, like vermin in ripe pears or serpents at the breast, had returned contumely; to his benevolence they had responded with contempt. Before the throne of the just judge, let the offenders of his majesty, rebels against the empire, suffer devastation of their cities, death by hanging, revocation of all imperial privileges, fines and confiscations, release of their vassals and debtors, and eternal infamy on their names.[16]

The powers of Dante's judges paled by comparison. Their authority could only seem perversely provincial to an emperor. Their bench was overshadowed by his throne. The *Libro del Chiodo* counted for little against an imperial constitution condemning more than five hundred Florentines and nearly one hundred other men from Florentine territory, including Baldo d'Aguglione, "who is called a judge." Dante's judges held to their cramped legal formulas. But the emperor's case lumbered through his decrees and finally took flight in Dante's treatise calling for a world monarchy and in Dante's poetry, where three allegorical ladies, symbols of perfect justice, were battered exiles but at home in the poet's heart.[17]

If this was fantasy, then judges, lawyers, and seasoned politicians were remarkably fanciful. The legal profession took the emperor seriously enough to comment and respond at length in a war of legal briefs. In one of the most radical responses Oldrado of Lodi argued on commission from King Robert of Naples against the emperor's right to condemn such a ruler, but in another opinion the same writer granted his client only a technical case on grounds of procedural oversights. Forty years later communes and lords in Italy were still buying their way clear of sentences that they had armed against and had pretended to ignore. The Florentine descendants of the Black Guelph regime of 1302 paid Emperor Charles IV 100,000 florins to cancel the edicts his grandfather Henry VII had proclaimed against them.[18]

Dante's judges, then, had not yet insulated the regime they served from rival tribunals. Higher authority still loomed on the outside, and their own powers were still mixed, makeshift, peremptory, and, in the end, unable to exact obedience. The opposition could still resist in the name of some better cause and join with allies to claim true justice beyond the span of a city's walls.

The Procedures of January 1302

Despite the ambiguity of their authority, and to some extent because of it, Dante's judges went through all the laboriously recorded protocol of contemporary courts of law. If the great aim of an impulse to order and objectivity is to appear dully routine, in this, very often, they were only too successful. Like the legitimacy of the court, however, its efficiency was incomplete and open to question.

The sentence issued against Dante on 27 January 1302 was at once an artifact of particular Florentine procedures and a fragment of a larger legal culture.[19] The formula announcing the condemnation was standard in Florence and elsewhere: "These are condemnations or sentences of condemnations made, decreed, and promulgated by the noble and potent knight, lord Cante Gabrieli of Gubbio." Behind the conventional phrases lay the checkpoints of an elaborate judicial process. The kangaroo court so much imagined in Dante's case would hardly have cared about such niceties; the less connected proceedings of an earlier period would have deposited quite different records in single parchments or references scattered through notarial protocols.

By Dante's time, the official preliminaries were written down piecemeal by a notary on slips or scraps of paper or in a journal for engrossing, case by case. Citations variously announced, posted, and recorded summoned the defendant before the court. Such specialized documents were transcribed or cited in larger registers—the sentence of 27 June 1302 was presumably copied from one of these into the *Libro del Chiodo*. These larger volumes had evolved as instruments of navigation through the judicial sea, like the contemporary portolan charts that guided sailors from port to port. Sometimes separate and sometimes comprehensive books were kept for proceedings by official inquisition and by private accusation, respectively; much of the material in these volumes was transferred again into books of official sentences and condemnations. On the other hand, there was no altogether consistent organizing principle of registration beyond a rough-and-ready sense of chronology. Formal registers must still have sat among trunks and sacks of documents. Dante's case had no alphabetical listing, number on the docket, or manila dossier. There were technical reasons for this—paper made in odd sizes for instance. But the inconsistencies also point to deep-seated habits of improvisation in a world not yet delivered over to standardization and system.

Even so, Dante's judges managed aggressively in the guise of the secular inquisitors they adopted in his case. Historians of the law have traced the origins of the inquisition process in the thirteenth century.[20] Sharply contrasting old accusatorial with new inquisitorial procedures, a traditional interpretation held that "the injured party pursues his rights" in the former while in the latter "the state prosecutes crime."[21] Doctrinaire assumptions about the supposedly necessary (and necessarily desirable) evolution from primitive to progressive institutions have been advanced under the cover of such theories. In any case, classifying the procedures of the courts by their technical starting points is misleading. Both accusation and inquisition could coexist, as they did in Messer Cante Gabrieli's court, without the court being for that any the less inquisitorial. The important point is the claim in Florence as elsewhere that it was the duty of government to conduct judicial proceedings *ex officio* and to investigate the facts as the arbiter of objective truth.[22]

Exceptional early but increasingly common later in the thirteenth century, official inquisition was partly a response to specific technical changes, such as the abolition of trial by ordeal in the twelfth century. But these changes were themselves propelled by (and also reflected) the great campaign of the High Middle Ages, from the universities to the workshop and the village, to harness and shape explosive new energies. The Church and the Italian communes were fundamentally at odds in many respects because they were among the most nearly universal and the most narrowly circumscribed of medieval institutions. They were alike, however, in generating a steady stream of experiments defining and giving concrete expression to new conceptions of order. Arguments for strict priorities in the development of the inquisition process—canonists over civil lawyers, civilians over canonists, practice over theory—are probably wasted for what might rather be seen in terms of complicated parallels and interactions.[23] Most revolutionary discoveries stem from mixed and lengthy pedigrees.

Whatever its intellectual sources, judicial inquisition had become a powerful weapon by the early fourteenth century. It put professional tribunals at the service of Church and State alike. It gave the ruling powers a claim to a monopoly on truth, access to the thoughts of their subjects, and a rationalization of the pursuit and persecution of internal enemies. Dante's judges were up-to-date inquisitors in full command of the procedural steps and formulas available to the model medieval magistrate.

Step One: Messer Paolo of Gubbio, *sapiens* and *discretus*, was delegated special judge on crimes of public officials by Messer Cante Gabrieli's court.

According to nearly contemporary Florentine statutes, three judges on criminal cases were attached to the court of the *podestà*. Ordinary criminal jurisdiction, four notaries, and a number of bailiffs were assigned to each judge for two of the six districts of Florence during a three-month term. When the term had elapsed, the judges rotated to different districts for the remaining three months of the *podestà's* tenure. But the statutes provided as well for extraordinary assignments. In this special capacity Messer Paolo was ready for the inquiries which Ser Bonora da Pregio duly recorded, "by the will and with the counsel of the other judges of said *podestà*."[24]

Step Two: Messer Paolo's tribunal initiated proceedings, investigated specific charges, and brought indictments against individuals or
groups of individuals.

The court might begin inquiry on receiving written notice of accusation from a third party, as in the case of Gherardino Deodati, "denounced and accused" by Bartolo Banchi of San Lorenzo on charges Ser
Bonora must have summarized from documents of accusation. More
often, cases were opened and continued "by inquisition conducted by
virtue of our office and by our court"—the procedure employed against
Dante and three other former priors cited together with him. Although
the two formulas of the notary preserved the traditional contrast between
private redress and public prosecution, what may have been a slip of Ser
Bonora's pen undercut the old distinction. Gherardino Deodati had apparently been "accused" by a private citizen, Bartolo Banchi; he would
not normally have been "denounced," as Ser Bonora also wrote, unless
the charges against him had been lodged by a magistrate acting in his official capacity. This suggests the overriding role official inquisition played
in court.

When that role could be expressly admitted, there was no lapse in the
formula. It was "by inquisition ex officio . . . upon and about that which
has come to our ears and to the notice of our court by common public
knowledge" that the court prosecuted the case of Dante and his three codefendants.[25] The full powers of inquiry and investigation granted to the
podestà in the Ordinances of Justice thus became operational. These prerogatives were all the more effective thanks to the breaches contemporary
lawyers had made—when a crime was very serious, for example, or when
indictable offenses were uncovered in the course of ordinary investiga-
tions—in the old-fashioned prohibition of the glossators against regular
ex officio inquiry.[26]

What the court discovered, or chose to see and hear, was set down in
a list of seven counts which Ser Bonora evidently drew from detailed
records of inquisition. While they had held their office of prior and before
or after their respective terms of office and together or singly—so begins
the cumbersome review of the charges—Dante, Messer Palmiro Altoviti,
Lippo Becchi, and Orlanduccio Orlandi had:

1. Committed extortion for their own or others' gain in money or
goods or by tacit promises or by tampering with public documents.

2. Received money or goods for corrupting the selection of new
priors.

3. Intervened in the appointment of officials for the administration

of the city of Florence or its territories in return for credits in money or property on the books of certain merchants.

4. Appropriated monies from the fisc or the palace of the priors in greater amounts or otherwise than allowed by legislation.

5. Perpetrated fraud and extortion to suborn resistance to the pope and Charles of Valois and the "pacific state of the city of Florence and of the Guelph party."

6. Accepted bribes of money or other payment in negotiations concerning public works.

7. Plotted to divide the town of Pistoia, to expel its Black Guelphs, "faithful and devoted to the Holy Roman Church," and to incite Pistoia to rebel from union with Florence and subjection to the Holy See and Charles of Valois.[27]

Was Dante guilty on all, or any, of these counts? The surviving evidence is slight and circumstantial.[28] There are a few terse references to Dante's joining his colleagues in advisory or legislative councils to approve, among other things, proposals for keeping the exiles of Pistoia at bay, measures for electoral reform, and an amnesty for the son of Gherardino Deodati. There is the fact that Dante was a member of the signory which reaffirmed a sentence against three Black Guelph bankers intriguing in Rome; the same priors had sent leading Black and White Guelphs into exile after an imbroglio on the Feast of San Giovanni in June 1300. Then there is Dante's nomination, in April 1301, to superintend public works on the new street of San Procolo, along which property owners collected indemnities for the right-of-way. Above all there is a notorious report of his words in council on 19 June 1301: "Let nothing be done in the matter of a subsidy for the pope."[29] All this would have been enough to incriminate Dante in a partisan court guided by "common public knowledge" on sharp Florentine tongues in the tense winter of 1302.

It is no defense to imagine that Dante's politics were polite and disinterested. They were not, and many well-meaning admirers who have pleaded his innocence have only diminished the passion of his political convictions and trivialized the hard choices that faced the White Guelphs as their enemies closed in on every side. But even without falling back on the odd illusion that poets are blameless, it is quite possible to suppose that there was no way to be innocent *and* White Guelph during the Black purge of 1302. The fleeting references to Dante in council are inconclusive at best. The sentences against the Black Guelph bankers in Rome had been passed before his term as prior, and members of both factions, including Dante's "first friend," Guido Cavalcanti, had been exiled after the affair of San Giovanni's Day in 1300. The San Procolo project had been under way since 1298. Dante's *nihil fiat* spoke against spending public funds, not for misspending them, and during the crucial period immediately before the entry of Charles of Valois on 1 November 1301 Dante was not in Florence but on a mission as Florentine ambassador to Rome. Although there may be better means—ballots or bullets or the ass Philip of Macedon loaded with sacks of gold—to eliminate the political opposition, the courts can generally be relied upon to find evidence against the losing side in any political crisis.[30]

Step Three: The court cited Dante and his three codefendants to appear in their own defense before a certain deadline.

The citations had gone out, Ser Bonora was careful to note, "legitimately, by the messengers of the commune" and so along a network of legal requirements. Communal *nuntii* were obliged by statute to be citizens of Florence and ten-year residents of the city. They took an oath, posted a bond for good service, and wore peaked caps of wool—those precious symbols were explicitly protected by law—emblazoned with four lilies of Florence. The summons, the title of the summoning magistrate, and the name of the messenger were to be written down on a citation slip. Whenever possible, this notice was to be delivered and read aloud to the person cited. (One imagines chases, cat-and-mouse.) In the absence of the party summoned, the citation was to be affixed on his front door or, in the case of vagabonds and foreigners, posted on the palace of the commune after being proclaimed in the main public squares. All the details of delivery, usually with repeat performances, were to be recorded. In Florence and elsewhere statutes and legal commentators insisted on strict observance of form.[31]

Step Four: The communal ban closed around Dante, Palmiro Altoviti, Lippo Becchi, and Orlanduccio Orlandi in distinctly differentiated but tightly meshed judicial moments.[32]

In the most general sense, "to ban" meant "to bring information to the notice of the public in an official manner on the direction of an appropriate authority." The information and the directives might command or prohibit certain kinds of behavior, with a penalty for disobedience. Consequently, "to ban" could also mean "to prohibit or to command an action under penalty." Since the penalty was often a fine, the terms for ban, penalty, and fine—*bannum*, *poena*, and *multa*—are practically indistinguishable in some of the standard notarial formulas.[33]

When Dante and his codefendants failed to respond to the citation, as the messengers would have informed the notaries of the court, they were subject to being "called under ban" in a quite specific way. The *cridatio in bannum* was the work of still more imposing officials than their colleagues the messengers. Duccio di Francesco, the communal herald (*banditore*) assigned to Dante's case, must have been one of those six "true Guelphs" elected to office annually by the signory. Resplendent in costumes of different colors each year, mounted on horseback, and preceded by banners and trumpet blasts, Duccio and his fellow heralds were the major medium of official communication for a watchful government in an increasingly complex society. They announced fairs and festivals, meetings of councils, levies of taxes, militia parades, bankruptcies, and public auctions. To spread the word of criminal or civil sentences issued by the courts was one of their routine assignments. Amidst pressing public business and on a set itinerary—the church of Or San Michele, the palace of the *podestà*, two places in each district of Florence—Duccio di Francesco must have cried out the ban at least once against Dante in January of 1302.[34]

The "you must come," or "comminatory," declaration of the herald took note, under instruction from the court, of failure to appear as cited. At the same time, the herald proclaimed that Dante and the others, because of their contumacy, "had allowed themselves to be placed under the ban of the commune of Florence in the amount of 5,000 florins each."[35] Whether the court set the additional terms usual in such matters—in Florence one ordinarily had three days to respond and fifteen days before further action was taken—is unclear. It is clear, however, that Florentine procedures had been adapted to the quick pace and the counting-house mentality of urban life; the standard grace period was briefer and the fiscal penalty more specific than in Roman law or in that closer model of despotism, the Sicilian constitutions of Frederick II. Dante's absence in Rome would not have counted as an excuse. Nor would the fines imposed have been revoked even if the defendants had appeared in time or, still more unlikely, had been found innocent. From the moment of the herald's "you must come" warning the suspects became *banniti*.[36]

Step Five: Any question of innocence was thrust aside by the definitive sentence.

On 27 January 1302 the court equated the contumacy of Dante and the others with confession and sentenced them to specific penalties for their guilt as charged. The equation rested on the legal fiction of a simulated trial, the *ficta litis contestatio* of the legal commentators.[37] Since they had not contested the charges, Dante and his codefendants were, "because of their contumacy, held to be confessed criminals" and subject to sentencing. All four were condemned to pay the 5,000 florins' fine within three days and to restore illicit gains to any legitimate claimant. Anyone who did not meet the deadline was to have what property remained to him after restitution confiscated and destroyed. Even if payment were made, he would be confined beyond the borders of Tuscany for two years. His name was to be inscribed in the public statutes as a forger and embezzler of public funds, and he was to be barred in perpetuity from public office. Thus, "the fruit may be harvested according to the quality of the seed and misdeeds committed . . . met by the retribution they deserve." [38] Due process honed the self-indulgent imagery of retribution to this single line.

Step Six: The sentence was formalized and officially registered by the court notary.

In formulas that must have come by rote to Ser Bonora da Pregio, "the said condemnations were decreed, pronounced, and promulgated . . . by the lord *podestà* aforesaid for the tribunal of the commune of Florence in general council assembled." Ser Bonora had read the sentences "in said council by the mandate of said lord *podestà*, on the XXVIIth day of January, in the one thousand three hundred second year from the birth of the Lord, *indictione* IV, in the time of the lord Pope Boniface VIII." Ser Agnolo, Ser Pace Tomè of Gubbio, the heralds Duccio di Francesco, and many others present in council had witnessed the act. [39]

Inquisition, citation, contumacy, condemnation, registration—the trajectory of the process had been unremitting. Even the aggressive court of Messer Cante Gabrieli could pause at this point, if only because it had set other official machinery in motion.

In June 1302 the Black Guelph signory named Ser Puccino di Tommaso of Gubbio to administer the confiscations ordered by the court. Fresh legislation defined what was expected of him, and he had his own staff of bailiffs, messengers, and scribes. Ser Puccino's office as Notary on Rebel Property may have come to him through some combination of election and delegation by the *podestà*. (The "of Gubbio" in his name suggests plainly enough whose man he was.) In the future the post was held by a judge working with a citizens' panel, such as the six officials whose rubric appeared in the statutes of 1322–1325. [40] These variations may reflect the difficulty of the assignment for whoever was in charge.

Searching out houses, shops, farms, credits, and scattered belongings for confiscation was both subtle and strong-arm work. To inventory and dispose of property and personal effects called for the notary's expertise and the less fastidious methods of the bailiff. Despite the orgies of destruction imagined by historians or actually reported in the chronicles, many confiscated holdings were sold; more often, income-producing property in town and country was assessed and rented or, in the absence of willing tenants, forced upon subject communes or corporate groups. Creditors had to be heard in any event, among them the wives of *banniti* and rebels, who were allowed a closely regulated annual return from their dowry portions. Whatever was left over was assigned to the fisc for purposes ranging from soldiers' wages to buying grain for the communal storehouses. No exceptions to the standard routines were apparently made for Dante. Ser Puccino and his successors seem to have kept his property on their books and rented for more than twenty years. Gemma Alighieri was still collecting payments on her dowry in 1329.[41]

Here again the procedures of 1302 are not easy to fault for flaws of form. Generations of critics have done them the unintended honor of picking at details or of conscientiously criticizing them in light of later and supposedly more enlightened norms. As a result, their real shortcomings have often been missed. Correct form and effective form are not necessarily the same. Closely examined, some slight line of the formal protocol in Dante's case turns suddenly dense with the self-defenses of a society of family ties, local allegiances, and corporative interconnections in the face of bureaucratic meddling.

"A certain sale was made of said house located in said parish of San Martino."[42] This cryptic notarial reference means that Dante's house was probably not destroyed as the court had directed—perhaps because the house also belonged to Dante's brother Francesco. In a carefully notarized testimony of 1337 Goccia di Lippo dei Lupicini claimed possession of the farm of Sant'Ambrogio that had once belonged to Dante. The Alighieri were cousins of the Lupicini, who returned the Sant'Ambrogio property to them as a dowry gift to Francesco's daughter in 1352.[43] Did the Portinari, whose Beatrice led Dante through paradise, deliberately hold his bit of earth at San Marco in Camerata for his sons? It is impossible to know, though not unlikely judging from a few opaque official references of the 1330s.[44]

What is certain through all the practiced legal formalities of 1302 is the fact that Dante was never present, never entirely in the power of his judges. If anything, the formal routines held *them* captive to rounds of repetition. On 10 March 1302 Dante and fourteen others under communal ban and condemnation were sentenced to death by fire—if captured (which they were not). The formulas of inquisition, citation, ban, and attestation were much the same as they had been in January. Again, in 1311, the law of Messer Baldo d'Aguglione could only reaffirm the commune's ban against the likes of Dante, and in 1315 Messer Ranieri di Zaccaria of Orvieto could only ban and kill him one more time in words. Dante's judges could not command obedience. The elaborate procedural cage had been empty all along.

Personae of Exclusion

Each step taken by Dante's judges transformed his status in the eyes of the law. In the beginning he was a Florentine citizen under citation; by the end, in the sentence of 1315, he had become an outlaw and rebel of the court and commune. From beginning to end, and in the stages between, the court drew on a repertory of increasingly menacing legal identities for which there were rubrics in the statutes, glosses, commentaries, treatises, or consultative opinions in the lawyers' literature. Moving through a hierarchy of personae at law, Dante's judges flexed and extended the labeling and defining power of their own judicial competence and of contemporary law. But here too they exposed their limitations.

Dante entered the legal limbo of a *citatus* when the communal messenger posted notice of citation on his door in San Martino del Vescovo.[45] Rumor and the early inquiries of the court had been formulated in the seven charges against him and his three companions in citation. The burden of appearing within a certain term "for the purpose of defending and excusing themselves" rested with them. Under the circumstances any appearance would have been risky. Inquisition and citation were undertaken on the presumption of guilt; ordinarily the citation slip did not indicate the charges which those cited were supposed to defend themselves against. It is true that the statutes did specify fines for notarial mistakes; officials were also required to deposit bonds against good conduct, and there were penalties for bearing false witness. But the most likely result of such slight guarantees for the defendant was that anyone under citation would steer as clear of the court as he could. Dante was no gambler, saint, or fool. He could not have been expected to appear, even if he had been nearer Florence than Rome; the court, not expecting him, fished for him with a citation, the threatening terms of which made his disobedience virtually a foregone conclusion.

When Dante did remain disobedient in fact, the herald Duccio di

Francesco proclaimed him a *bannitus* of the court and the commune. Few legal identities were more common in the criminal statutes and the papers of the courts; fewer still were so vexing to contemporary commentators. Although the degrees, refinements, and implications of *bannitus* status remain problematic for legal historians, this much seems probable in Dante's case. From the first moment of the ban, in its anticipating or "comminatory" phase, Dante would have been a *bannitus* in the sense of one who had not obeyed the directive of a magistrate and had been fined as a result. Still failing to appear ("having persisted in contumacy," as his absence was interpreted), he became what the statutes and the lawyers knew as the *bannitus* or *exbannitus pro maleficio*. Under Florentine rules this new status ordinarily took effect eighteen days after the "you must come" warning of the herald and became final after another fifteen days. From that time forward Dante would have been considered a confessed criminal. He had no right of appeal and lost the privileges of citizenship. His name inscribed in communal registers of those banned and condemned, he would have been open to assault and even assassination with impunity by anyone within Florentine territory. There was of course a punitive element (and certainly a punitive purpose) in measures such as these. But the real point of *bannitus pro maleficio* status was that the court had been unable to exact full punishment. Dante could not be punished in person if he refused to submit; he could only be banned under a series of legal fictions and indirect reprisals. Its "you must come" warning rebuffed, the court was reduced to saying "you must go."[46]

A long labyrinth of legal reasoning had wound around these subtle distinctions since the twelfth century.[47] More, as usual, than merely glossing Roman law, Accursius had supposed that the *exbannitus* was like the Roman *deportatus* or *relegatus*.[48] This was a first false start. The Roman categories referred to penalties for crimes, not to contumacy—to exile and the loss of all but the minimal rights of natural law in the case of the *deportatus*, to exile with civic rights and property preserved for the *relegatus*. There could be no trial and sentencing in a defendant's absence under Roman law; nor did Roman law permit what amounted to a capital sentence for contumacy, among other reasons because the penalties for crimes involved might well be less extreme. Roman imperial magistrates expected to get their man.

For Alberto da Gandino and Jacopo d'Arena at the end of the thirteenth century the Accursian analogy was difficult to relinquish, or to retain. A legitimating link between contemporary practice and ancient precept still passing for *the* law could not be given up lightly. Alberto repeated Accursius faithfully, then glossed the glossator with insistent, practical questions from his magistrate's experience "in Lombardy, the Marches, Tuscany and elsewhere all over Italy."[49] Roman law had no clear-cut answers. In what may have been the first treatise *De bannitis*, Jacopo d'Arena appreciated the distance between ancient Rome and the communes of his day. While his contemporaries hoped to keep their outlaws beyond the gates, the Romans, Jacopo remembered, had deported and relegated their malefactors throughout the world.[50]

The commentators, though continuing to tinker with Accursius's comparison, were driven to try other analogies. According to Nicola Matarelli, the *ban* proceeded from public authority as the armies of emperors proceeded against lawlessness under the imperial *banner*. The *bannitus* was so called for his resistance to legitimate authority represented by and gathered around the imperial insignia.[51] Jacopo d'Arena pointed to an analogy Hostiensis, following the latest formulations by Innocent IV and Gregory IX, had already seen between the *bannitus* and the excommunicate in canon law. As the excommunicate was cut off from the sacraments and the community of the faithful, so was the *bannitus* deprived of civic rights and the benefits of the secular community.[52] By the next generation, in his synthesizing *Questions on Statutes*, Alberico da Rosciate reported the canon law parallel as a matter of course, despite awkward difficulties.[53] The fact remained that the communal *bannitus* was a marked man only in the territory where he had been condemned whereas the excommunicate bore his identity, "as the leper his leprosy," throughout the Christian world. Besides, excommunication was not in itself corporal punishment and could, after repentance and satisfaction, be rescinded.

It was like Bartolus of Sassoferrato to object and to simplify. Neither the *deportatus* nor the *relegatus* nor the *excommunicatus* seemed apt analogies to him. He chose rather to argue for a comparison between *banniti* and *hostes et transfugae*, the traitors and deserters of Roman law. This was a convenient way of branding the *bannitus* a public enemy who had, in effect, declared war on his homeland (and vice versa); it also brought into play the formidable sanctions of Roman law against treason. The opinion was an influential one. Yet by insisting on the comparison, Bartolus gave further impetus to the old practice and all the problems of finding some single inherited master key to a complex communal institution.[54]

A major problem with analogies, as Alberico da Rosciate realized, was that the ban and the *bannitus* could be traced only "in the newest laws."[55] Novelty is rarely welcome to lawyers, and when "the newest laws" must have included, for example, the Sicilian constitutions of Emperor Frederick II, it could be positively threatening. Imperial authority was still a standing challenge to the integrity of communal statutes.[56] If the emperor's outlaws were similar to communal *banniti*, imperial procedures were sufficiently different to call communal practices into question as rather shabby imitations. The *bannitus* under Emperor Frederick's legislation had two months after citation to appear in court. A third of his movable property was declared forfeit, the rest sequestered for one year, as in Roman law. After two months had elapsed, he became a *forbannitus* and could be freely assaulted or killed, unless, under safe conduct, he chose belatedly to appear for trial. Dante's judges, by contrast, counted deadlines in days, not months, and imposed fiscal penalties after, not before, clear evidence of contumacy; once established, Dante's contumacy had stood for confession and convicted him of crime. By imperial legislation this ultimate condition under ban was reached after a year and a day. Only then did the *forbannitus* become a *foriudicatus*, a confessed criminal by reason of contumacy, with no right to trial or appeal.[57]

The more the lawyers pored over precedent, the more tangled the question of the *banniti* became. A rubric *De bannitis pro maleficio* in a treatise by Alberto da Gandino can be read as confirmation of a crisis of coherence and as early evidence of a kind of provisional solution. Where authoritative precedent, analogy, and deductive reasoning seemed useful or necessary, Alberto drew on them in scholastic style. The results—his failure to give up the Accursian analogy, for instance—were often inconsistent and misleading. But if interpreting statute was the source of the difficulties, statute also forced a way around them. Whether justified and precise in theory or not, the *bannitus* was there in statute to be contended with.

"But suppose," Alberto asks in a characteristic question, "it is contained in the city's statute that *banniti pro maleficio* can be offended with impunity and in particular that they can be killed?" The statute may be deemed illegal because the divine commandment says "Thou shalt not kill," and divine law cannot be abrogated by the weaker ordinance or law of a city; for if equal cannot command equal, much less, according to Justinian's *Digest*, can the minor command the major power. The statute also seems contrary to *ius gentium* and natural law, which enjoin man not to assault his fellow man; the positive law of a particular community, which is mutable, cannot change immutable principles. *Sed contra*, it seems that the statute is valid because the *Digest* concedes absolutely and without distinction to every city the right to establish laws among its citizens. What more is there to say? The Roman emperor himself granted that certain malefactors could be killed, among them the fugitive, the assassin, and the adulterer. "I say," Alberto concludes, "that the statute is valid; for although it is quite correct that by divine and natural law it is not permitted to kill, it is nevertheless true that, general and particular positive law permitting, this may legitimately be done."[58]

This was one of many questions-and-solutions too particularly practical and too urgent to wait for some more perfect or, for that matter, more convincing statement. Could a *bannitus* be killed without penalty when not under an explicit capital sentence? This had happened at Lucca in 1281 during Alberto's tenure there as appellate judge. Were two Piccolomini brothers rightly condemned because they had wounded a priest under ban? They had been condemned in fact while Alberto was judge and editing his writings in Siena. Could a *bannitus* be killed while in the custody of the *podestà*'s men or if he had paid the fine imposed by banning?[59] Alberto's answers would have been too cautious for Dante's judges in some respects, particularly where he was disinclined to conflate contumacy with confession or fiscal with capital penalties. But Alberto had made statute and everyday experience a proper object and end of judicial interpretation. He could be pragmatically blunt and agnostic toward supposedly authoritative analogies outside statute. It is easy enough to imagine Messer Alberto on the bench with Messer Paolo of Gubbio "for the tribunal of the commune of Florence in general council assembled."

If Dante's judges had been able to confine him to certain conditions of exile, as they proposed to do at one point in the sentences of 1302 and 1315, his legal identity would have been relatively simple. The *confinatus* was already a familiar figure in communal legislation. Parma's statutes of 1255 allowed the *podestà* "to confine" in exile those who took private quarrels to the streets, even if they had made peace with their enemies. After the tumult of San Giovanni in 1300, the signory to which Dante had belonged had ordered White and Black Guelph chieftains to reside for set terms in certain locations outside Florence. In such cases confinement could be punitive, preventative, or both.[60] Since the great breakers of public peace were the magnates, the antimagnate laws of the second half of the thirteenth century had commonly granted magistrates full power "for sending magnates . . . to confinement whenever and as long as it may be necessary in the event of crimes, disturbances, or rioting which have been or may be committed or, God granting warning, may be expected to occur. . . ."[61] Bartolus put his seal of approval on such legislation in the fourteenth century, and by his time the pretense of limiting confinement to magnates alone had long since fallen away.[62] The *Libro del Chiodo* began with lists of some 1,600 suspected or outright Ghibellines subject or actually sent to confinement in exile in 1267. Little Prato measured political time between 1260 and 1266 as that period "in which the Guelphs lived *ad confines.*"[63]

Dino Compagni protested when the Black Guelphs of Florence executed two *confinati* in 1303.[64] Broadly humane or narrowly partisan as the outrage of a White Guelph chronicler may have been, it also had the sanction of common law and statute. It should have been enough that the unfortunate victims had apparently kept beyond or within prescribed boundaries on oath and under bond and had observed deadlines laid down by the sentencing magistrate. If that was, of course, a great deal, confinement did not in itself jeopardize life or limb or possessions. The Black Guelph executioners in Compagni's account were blind to the law; but so, more surprisingly, were the lawyers, who had strained to force the *bannitus* into some Roman prototype only to neglect the clear analogies between the *confinatus* in communal statutes and the *relegatus* in Roman law. Relegation was more strictly punishment for crime than communal confinement; the destination of the Roman *relegatus*—from Mediterranean islands to Ovid's Tomis—was sure to be closely defined. Like the *confinatus*, however, the *relegatus* retained the rights of citizenship and his property under law. Perhaps the lawyers paid little attention to these similarities because confinement, if effective, was a temporary condition quite limited and quite straightforward in its consequences; when ineffectual, confinement was quickly passed over for sterner measures.[65]

The severest measures were reserved for those who had been declared rebels. In September or early October 1315 Messer Ranieri di Zaccaria of Orvieto cited Dante together with the Ghibellines who were suspected of conspiracy or had actually fought against Black Guelph Florence in the army of Uguccione della Faggiola, lord of Pisa. When they failed to pledge guarantees and accept terms of confinement, Messer Ranieri moved from a comminatory ban to the definitive sentence of 6 November 1315. "As Ghibellines and rebels," Dante and his sons were condemned in absentia to be decapitated "at the place of execution . . . so that they may die utterly and completely."[66]

There were precedents for the terms of this condemnation. No clear distinctions had been drawn among Ghibellines, rebels, and *banniti* in many of the sentences recorded for 1268 in the *Libro del Chiodo*. Dante's property had been administered by those "Officials on the Property of Rebels" whose jurisdiction the statutes of 1325 would extend to the property of "rebels, *exbanniti, condempnati,* and delinquent taxpayers of the commune of Florence."[67] This suggests a pattern of analogies—that the rebel was like the Ghibelline, outlaw, or tax defaulter—and of causality— that he was a rebel *because* of those identities. Certainly the condition of the *bannitus pro maleficio* and that of the rebel were overlapping and interconnected. Both lost all civic rights and property, and both could be offended in their persons and their possessions within the borders of the commune that had sentenced them.[68] The executioner's fire for Dante the *exbannitus* and the headsman's sword for Dante the rebel may have been different in dignity; the intended effect was not. The similarities are understandable because the circumstances were so much the same. "Rebel" only pointed openly to what *bannitus* more nearly obscured in protocol and procedure—that Dante still defied his judges.

Even so, the status of rebels was at once more general and more specific than that of *banniti.* On the one hand, the statutes associated the rebel with broadly related legal personae—*inimicus, hostis,* and *bannitus in perpetuo.* Bartolus supplied an academic translation. The rebel was "unfaithful by that infidelity which leads to rebellion"; and rebellion was "to resist something" by commission or omission, in spirit or in deed.[69] This was simple, comprehensive, and unencumbered by procedural detours. On the other hand, not every criminal who disobeyed a magistrate was necessarily considered a rebel. Although Messer Ranieri sentenced Dante and the others in 1315 "lest they glory in their disobedience," he also charged them with specific crimes "against the good state of the commune of Florence and the Guelph party."[70] The verb "to rebel" had transitive meanings in contemporary speech, meanings as concrete as the possession of power in contemporary politics. Messer Ranieri must have meant that those condemned had "rebelled" territories, communes, strongholds, and fortresses, raised banners and armed against Florence. In this sense rebellion was different from a common delict against some private person. Bartolus became authoritative on this distinction too.[71] In his opinion rebel acts were properly so called because committed against prince or republic by their subjects. The punishment prescribed was correspondingly severe —death, confiscation, and perpetual infamy. Although Messer Ranieri actually followed ordinary procedure, the gravity and notoriety of the crime of rebellion would have warranted summary justice. And if the legitimacy of broadening the criminal ban to include descendants and relatives remained controversial, there was no question that Messer Ranieri could legitimately condemn Dante's sons for the rebellion of their father.[72]

Tanquam rebelles—the sentence seems deceptively easy, a virtuoso performance, when in theory and in fact it was deeply problematic. *Rebellio* was originally a Germanic and medieval term for hostilities against one's superior. Since personal bonds held medieval people together (when they could be held together at all), to violate such personal ties was to commit the most serious of crimes, a felony. *Fellonia* carried sinister connotations—wickedness, baseness, cruelty—long before the great seventeenth-century lawyer Sir Edward Coke decided that term had come from the Latin word for "gall." In the twelfth century Hostiensis defined a felony precisely as "a fault or injury for which a vassal loses his fief."[73] Bartolus preserved the notion of infidelity in his definition of a rebel. So, perhaps, did Messer Ranieri of Orvieto in his sentences of 1315. For Dante had broken faith in the eyes of the court by violating the command of a superior. His rebellion was obviously not the broken faith of a vassal, but it could be interpreted as violating the allegiance—"rebellion" in Bartolus's more specific sense—subjects owed to their rulers and magistrates.[74]

But who ruled Dante? Certainly not the Black Guelphs of Florence. Their "good state" was partisan, factional, without altogether secure standing in public law.[75] Even in the best of times the Florentine commune did not have the unquestioned legal sanction Messer Ranieri assumed for it. Bartolus did not mean to grant any prince or any republic the right to declare hostile subjects rebels; he was referring to the *Roman* prince and the *Roman* people, and his definition appeared in the course of commentary on the imperial constitution *Qui Sint Rebelles* ("Those Who May Be Rebels") issued by Emperor Henry VII in 1311.[76]

Messer Ranieri, then, was mimicking the emperor in 1315. It may have come easily to him as vicar of the Angevin king of Naples, whose French cousins and their lawyers had learned to imitate imperial officials in the twelfth and thirteenth centuries. To the question of whether one owed aid to the king in preference to one's feudal lord, French civil lawyers had responded that the monarch was the major tribunal, administrator of the entire kingdom, and defender of the common good. They had also taken for their king the formulas the canonists had developed to defend the Church by inciting royal particularism against the universal claims of the empire. By the middle of the thirteenth century northern lawyers were used to applying Roman public law and the attributes of Roman emperors to their kingdoms and their kings. According to Jean de Blanot, the king of France had *imperium* to reign and to rule over all his subjects by virtue of those passages in Roman law designating the emperor supreme ruler of the world. Bracton's English king had "all law in his hands," with dignity and power to judge, enforce, and even, breaking through the prevailing conception of law as something "found" and not "made," to legislate.[77]

If kings could pose as emperors, so could Italian cities pretend to be the "Roman people." In the famous formula of Bartolus, they could claim to be *civitates superiorem non recognoscentes*, "cities recognizing no superior."[78] The claim was made over and over again, though the actual degree of civic independence varied from one city or lawyer's opinion or occasion to another. In 1315 Messer Ranieri di Zaccaria of Orvieto needed every possible independence. While he, a blustering little emperor, was declaring Dante a rebel, his Florentine and his Angevin clients were themselves rebels of the empire. For, of course, the imperial constitution *Qui Sint Rebelles* had been directed against them.

By 1315 the rules of exclusion had run out. Their surest effect had been to insure that Dante would remain beyond reach. De jure, his loss of civic rights in Florence had gained him another, higher citizenship as *civis Romanus*, whose rights, the lawyers admitted, no purely provincial ordinance could ever take away.[79] And as "Roman citizen," a citizen of the world, Dante could refuse the only recourse left to his judges.

It was no contradiction for the regime to offer him amnesty. When procedural rigor does not correspond to effective controls, the clement magistrate may try to terrorize the opposition and then command gratitude. This play at Providence with apparently unconditional pardoning power can also serve expedient purposes which the ruling power may be at a loss to achieve by ordinary means. If the letter "to a Florentine friend" is authentic, Dante must have been offered one of those ritual amnesties meant, among other things, to put a good face on the limitations of communal authority. Had he accepted, he might have paid fines at a discount to join some procession of penitents dressed in sackcloth, mitred to show shame and carrying candles as signs of satisfaction to a mass in the baptistry of San Giovanni.[80] Dante's refusal was both true to the man and timeless. It put unanswerable questions before the oracles of the law:

> What now? May I not look upon the luminous spheres of the sun and stars wherever I may be? Shall I not contemplate wheresoever under the sky the sweetest truths without first rendering myself inglorious, nay, abject to the people and city of Florence? I shall not lack my bread.[81]

Dante's judges had no better reply than the sentence of 1315. The case closed, they adjourned and withdrew. One wonders whether they could see far enough beyond the rules of exclusion to appreciate the reversal of roles. They withdrew; Dante's presence filled the larger world beyond and minds inside Florence. They had condemned Dante, whose works remained to condemn them there and thereafter. They reached the limits of what was possible while Dante's power grew beyond possibility as the pilgrim of whom strange stories were told. The gossiping ladies of Ravenna were sure that his complexion had been burned dark in hell. As the sorcerer—*magister Dantis*—he was supposedly called to Milan to cast spells on a silver image of the pope. It was rumored that his restless ghost showed his son where his manuscripts might be found. Eight years after his death he was still the unexorcized enemy whose book *De monarchia* a cardinal legate would burn for heresy.[82]

Dante's judges were finally silent; their original sentences were lost. But Dante still spoke, the commanding voice in a chorus of exiles who would have filled some circle and canto of his *Divine Comedy*.

4

Facts and Rules of Inclusion:

Exiles in the World
of Renaissance States

No great bands of exiles met the ambassadors who made their way from northern Italy to Naples in 1454 to complete negotiations for an Italic League. Florence, Milan, and Venice had agreed in August to fifteen articles for mutual defense. The agreement excluded foreigners and included the minor Italian states only as satellites of the major powers. Arriving at Florence in October, the ambassadors set aside the scruples of the Florentines over their traditional ties to France. Pope Nicholas V adhered in November and blessed "the most holy peace" as a first step toward a crusade against the Turks. Facing a *fait accompli*, Alfonso of Naples, who did not care for principles or peace, ratified the league to scenes of jubilation on 26 January 1455.[1]

There was more than coincidence to the failure of companies of exiles to appear along the ambassadors' itinerary, for the Italic League confirmed the loss of conditions for their existence over the preceding century. The league did not unite Italy, bring a stable peace, fight the Turk, or, in the end, keep out the foreign invader. But it did represent an altered scheme of political relations which had transformed the terms and increased the costs of dissent and opposition. The easy openings to international intervention on which exiles once depended had narrowed since the middle of the fourteenth century. The empire and the papacy were shadows of what they had been under Henry VII and Boniface VIII. The king of France was distracted by the Hundred Years' War and then by the problems of reconstruction; Spain was still divided and still at war with its Moors. The Florentine ambassadors belittled Milanese worries over the emperor's claims in Italy as "windy and of no importance."[2] Other international interests were dismissed as bluntly by the five major Italian powers which had expanded over the course of three generations to the edges of regional boundaries and, occasionally, beyond them.

There were still outlaws, bandits, and *fuorusciti* of course. But with the parceling out of Italy among something like territorial states the land-based and urban strategies of exiles during an earlier age could be more closely controlled. Internal consolidation extending watchful institutions and intensifying pressures for ideological conformity within each political unit left still less room for the brash maneuvers and clear consciences of exiles in the thirteenth and early fourteenth centuries. After the middle of the fourteenth century the facts and rules of exile registered profound changes within an emerging order of Renaissance states.

Enclosure on the Outside

Political maps of thirteenth-century Italy show both the cellular particularism of the medieval communes and connecting shades or arrows of international influence emanating from Rome, Germany, France, and Spain. In a fragmented political landscape parties and whole companies of exiles had found staging grounds and had taken on the shading and moved with the arrows of outside influence. By the fifteenth century connections on a map of Italy are more and more likely to appear as internal connections, and in many places the outlines of Italian states on a regional scale encompass many fragments of the older order. The artifices of power and the power of artifice intruded on nature in Renaissance politics as in Renaissance art. The same culture that admired the forced symmetries and controlled spaces of Quattrocento painting and architecture suppressed and enclosed the old external shelters of exile.[3]

This was in the beginning (and always in part) enclosure by default. In 1355 Petrarch imagined that Emperor Charles IV must have been condemned on his compromising and mercenary way to Italy by the ghost of his grandfather Henry VII. Fazio degli Uberti cursed "those gluttonous modern Germans" with a Ghibelline's bitterness over the loss of a traditional ally, and Antonio da Ferrara branded Emperor Charles as "miserly, servile . . . the most servile of serfs."[4] Gaudy imperial processions staged in an International Gothic style could not conceal the opportunism or the weakness of the three emperors who followed Charles

**THE MAJOR STATES OF
ITALY IN THE MID-FIFTEENTH CENTURY**

DUCHY OF MILAN

REPUBLIC OF VENICE

REPUBLIC
OF FLORENCE

STATES
OF
THE
CHURCH

KINGDOM
OF
NAPLES

KINGDOM   OF
SICILY

IV over the Alps during the next one hundred years. Unpleasant realities would break in. Alliances among Italian city-states in the fourteenth century had already included clauses against the emperor as an undesirable foreigner. In 1401 Milanese mercenaries routed Rupert of Bavaria at Brescia, and Emperor Sigismund of Luxemburg was forced to hole up in Siena for nine months in 1432. After the middle of the fifteenth century Frederick III came to Italy as an attractively ineffectual guest.[5]

If never so completely as the labels "Babylonian Captivity" and "Great Schism" may suggest, the popes had also lost much power and influence in Italian affairs.[6] Clement V left Rome in 1305 for Avignon; Eugenius IV was driven away from Rome again in 1434. In the interim there were three effective papal campaigns in Italy, and as many retreats. The Bolognese expelled a papal legate in 1333 to undo the designs of Pope John XXII on Emilia, Romagna, and Lombardy. The ablest fourteenth-century tactician of force and favor in the papal states died with Cardinal Albornoz in 1323, and despite the end of the schism and the partial restoration of papal authority after 1417 under Martin V, Eugenius IV spent nine years in exile while another warrior-cardinal fought another campaign against the unruly subjects of the pope. According to Machiavelli, the popes were able to stand above the rules of normal politics. "These ecclesiastical princes alone," he wrote, "have states without defending them, have subjects without governing them. . . ." But Machiavelli also thought that until the end of the fifteenth century "the Italian powers, and not only those which were called powers, but every baron and little tyrant, even the least of them, held the Church in slight esteem so far as its temporal power was concerned. . . ."[7]

Even the French were not the exile allies they had been in the thirteenth century.[8] There was much to foreshadow the invasion of 1494 in the continuity of French ambitions in Italy. But this is hindsight. In the 1260s Charles of Anjou had been backed by a broad Guelph alliance on his anti-imperial crusade. After the middle of the fourteenth century, expeditions from France were skirmishes on the margins of the Hundred Years' War; they were interrupted by military defeats, dynastic divisions, and an Italian resistance Italians themselves found surprising. The death of King Robert of Naples in 1343 threw the old French establishment of Angevins with Italian names and titles into an anarchy of internal conflicts and family quarrels with new Angevin, Armagnac, or Orléanist pretenders. By the early fifteenth century, when the history of the Italian south turned outward and briefly coherent again, Ladislaus of Naples was an Italian prince in a new style. Like his ancestors, Ladislaus imagined himself at the head of an Italian kingdom, but only distorted echoes of the old Guelph cause remained in the street rhymes of Naples addressed in his name to the rest of Italy.[9] The exiles who campaigned for the French after the middle of the Trecento could not have supposed for long that their unreliable allies were good champions or good Guelphs. Although the Florentine chancellery of the 1390s trumpeted the restoration of the Guelph system in its new classical style, there is no evidence that anyone believed it.[10]

Deprived of traditional sources of outside support by the retreat or recycling of ultramontane interests, exiles were also hemmed in by Italian states aggrandizing themselves in the relative absence of effective foreign opposition. Early in the fifteenth century the territories of the house of Savoy in the northwest were rejoined under one branch of the dynasty and tilted farther into Italy, from Monferrato and Saluzzo to the Ligurian coast. To the northeast Venice, threatened by the Turks and uncertain of the sea, had turned to the mainland after 1423 to reach from Treviso and Ravenna to the river Adige by mid-century. Giangaleazzo Visconti had set Milanese front lines as far south as Florence and Perugia; after his death in 1402 and the dismembering of his empire, the later Visconti and their Sforza heirs could still fall back on most of Lombardy and the ducal title that Giangaleazzo's ducats had bought in 1395. In central Italy the Florentines had drawn much of Tuscany together—Arezzo (1384), Montepulciano (1390), Pisa (1406), Cortona (1411), Livorno (1421). Even the papal states, Italy's Balkans, had begun to show the effects of the long process of territorial unification that sixteenth-century popes would complete. The kingdom of Naples was the largest of the Italian states, and despite its geographical diversity, its overmighty barons, the failures of its Angevin rulers, and the troubled accession of Alfonso of Aragon (1435–1458) on the mainland and in Sicily, the kingdom was probably the most powerful of the territorial states that had come to dominate the peninsula by the time of the Italic League.[11] As Pope Nicholas V told Emperor Frederick III in 1452, "there are at present in Italy no Scala, Carrara, and other *signorotti* . . . who were once so desirous of change." *Potentie grosse*—"great powers"—had prevailed. They would not tolerate the foreigner, except perhaps for sport, and "even then they will band together to undo him in the end."[12]

It was like Pope Nicholas to be cheerfully unrealistic in politics as in most things. The politics of tension continued. Foreign intervention was bound to come sooner or (as it happened in 1494) later, and Italian states still angled for change at one another's expense, whether piecemeal or in the aggression mounted on a grander scale by Milan and Naples early and by the papacy and Venice late in the fifteenth century. Rather than impersonal institutions or a continuous set of orderly political relationships, *lo stato* still designated a regime of particular persons who might possess and lose power in discontinuous and unpredictable ways.[13] The "state" of Milan, for example, was divided and distributed like private property when Archbishop Giovanni Visconti died in 1354; it disintegrated on the death of Giangaleazzo Visconti in 1402, and it sprouted the anachronism of the Ambrosian republic in 1447, despite the preceding century and a half of Visconti rule. Even the apparent mastery of Venice over its mainland possessions has been exposed as a "fragmentary and inharmonious structure," "a heterogeneous conglomeration" of compromises leaving many municipal liberties to supposedly subject cities.[14] If this was the case in the republic of St. Mark, sudden reversals and quick territorial changes among the petty lords of the Romagna were so numerous as to tax the patience and understanding of the most persistent historians.[15] The academic scenarios and abstract policy considerations of modern political science are even less relevant than usual in describing much Renaissance state building. Italian Renaissance politics were notoriously a theater of feint, finesse, exception, and expediency, in which contemporaries detected the disruptive hand of the goddess Fortuna.

But there was more than complacency or bluff to Pope Nicholas's remarks in 1452. He had understood quite well the ultimately conservative implications of Italy's relative independence. The consolidation, however tentative, of territorial states on the peninsula did have the stabilizing effect of reducing the prospects for great gains in the wake of a foreigner's intervention. With or without foreign support, the possibilities for territorial expansion were increasingly limited because the larger states that had swallowed up their lesser neighbors encountered rival states or spheres of influence like their own over the borders. The costs of imperialism mounted at the same time that the tactical refinements of mercenary captains, who often consumed half or more of the budget of the Renaissance state, were decreasing the chances for decisive victories. This was not the distracted political space in which the *fuorusciti* of the thirteenth and early fourteenth centuries had been practically invulnerable.

An outstanding exception tends to prove the rule.[16] Braccio da Montone was a mercenary captain unsurpassed at the daring gesture and the quick maneuver early in the Quattrocento. He was also an exile from Perugia for more than twenty-five years after the early 1390s. Beginning with a small corps of fellow exiles, he built up his own fighting force, sold "protection" to small towns, and amassed clients, reputation, and capital for the victorious homecoming that remained his overriding goal. The model condottiere found, or made, operating room for himself. On the other hand, he did not succeed in forcing his way home as lord of Perugia until 1416, and even Braccio da Montone could not hold out against the major Italian powers. He recognized the need to expand and consolidate a much larger territorial base than Perugia could afford; some contemporaries were sure that he would not settle for less than the crown of Naples. The response of Naples, Milan, and the pope was a league against him. In 1424 he was defeated by an allied army and mortally wounded while besieging Aquila. Perugia submitted to the pope and was formally reincorporated into the papal states.

While Braccio da Montone could be his own general in exile, most Renaissance exiles were thrown upon the calculating mercies of the greater Italian states, and aid from those sources was likely to be sporadic and stinting, a quite dispensable ploy of strategies largely beyond the control of even the most important *fuorusciti*. The battle of Anghiari in June 1440, when a combined Florentine-papal army routed a Milanese force with its contingent of anti-Medicean exiles, would never have been fought if Filippo Maria Visconti of Milan could have prevented it.[17] (See Figure 12.) The duke had encouraged the exiles openly, but the threat from Venice in alliance with the Medici regime in Florence worried him into summoning his troops back to Lombardy. The interests of the exiles were no longer useful to him. That a battle was fought at Anghiari was due to the commander in the field and the outdated optimism of the exiles that there would be an uprising of their supporters behind the lines at home. After the defeat, the *fuorusciti* recognized that their cause was hopeless. Their leader, Rinaldo degli Albizzi, consoled himself on a pilgrimage to the Holy Land, and two of his sons became citizens of Ancona. Milanese promises were no more rewarding in the 1450s when Francesco Sforza sacrificed his Sienese allies in exile because coming to terms with Venice and Naples required it.[18]

Nor could exiles count on the smaller territories that had once been a ready source of shelter and support. Unmanageable areas did remain, like the Maremma and the Lunigiana in Tuscany or the redoubts of pocket barons in the Alps, in much of the kingdom of Naples, and in fractious Romagna. But even Ferrara, Mantua, and Urbino kept their own rulers and Lucca its republic largely because it suited the convenience of one or another of the larger Italian states. The Della Scala of Verona and the Carrara of Padua whom Nicholas V cited as the old type of *signorotti*, "desirous of change," were displaced first by Milan and, after 1405, by Venice. The sons of the last descendant of Cangrande della Scala to rule the court that had welcomed Dante in exile died as refugees beyond the Alps. Francesco da Carrara died a prisoner of the duke of Milan; his son was executed with two of *his* sons in Venice.[19]

Even under the best of circumstances exiles were closely monitored by governments at home. States greater in means, boundaries, and enemies, but less able to maneuver than medieval communes had been, needed surer diplomatic instruments than the informal networks of travelers, merchants, and clerics or the cumbersome formal missions by heralds, special emissaries, and procurators of thirteenth-century diplomacy. Resident embassies developed in step with the Renaissance transformation of the political environment.[20] By the middle of the fourteenth century there were Mantuan agents residing at the court of the emperor because the empire mattered a great deal in Italian affairs. Around the turn of the century city-states in Italy were engaging in transitionally indefinite and interrupted exchanges of "ambassadors" among themselves. By the 1450s both the emperor and small states such as Mantua mattered less than they once had, and so it was among the major states of the Italic League that the first permanent embassies were established. What seems to have been the earliest manual on the duties of a resident ambassador has a dignified Latin title. But *De offitio legati*, the little treatise Ermolao Barbaro composed in Venice around 1490, substituted unadulterated power politics for much traditional moralizing on the Christian and chivalric principles of the ideal diplomat. "The first duty of the ambassador," Barbaro writes, "is exactly the same as that of any other servant of a government, that is, to do, say, advise, and think of whatever may best serve the preservation and aggrandizement of his own state."[21]

Philippe de Commines had only to cross the border from France to learn that an Italian ambassador's duties included close surveillance of *fuorusciti*. In May 1478 Commines was on his way to take up his post as French representative in Milan. Stopping at Turin, he granted an interview to Roberto da San Severino, an important Milanese exile who promised loyal service in return for French intervention. Commines refused to go beyond the letter of his instructions—wisely, as it turned out, since the court of Milan had the details of the interview from its ambassador at Monferrato long before Commines arrived to present his credentials.[22] Such information was to Renaissance diplomacy as money was to Renaissance warfare. Barbaro was quite explicit. His model ambassador was to keep his government informed of the comings and goings of the great and near-great, of the affairs and intentions of his hosts, and of the activities of its own citizens *in partibus*.[23]

Fuorusciti were fortunate if they were only watched. A thirteenth-century chancellery might well have written, as the Florentine chancellery did to an ally in 1360, "the continual damaging of the enemy, our rebels, pleases us greatly."[24] At least since the twelfth century Italian city-states had been agreeing among themselves to expel, extradite, or pursue their respective rebels. The object of such agreements was to keep fugitives in motion, flush them from strategic bases, and undercut their political connections. Here again, territorial consolidation had its transforming impact on the conscious tone and practical scope of this familiar policy. There were no biblical injunctions or references to Guelphs or Ghibellines in the instructions accompanying a Florentine ambassador on an antirebel mission to Siena in 1411. In order to persuade the Sienese to take action against the Florentine exiles operating in their territory, the ambassador was to appeal to mutual self-interest: "what we ask of them we must and shall do similarly for them." The rebels were to be portrayed as enemies of all "peace-minded, tranquil, and free states and peoples."[25] The ambassador's instructions seem to envision easy agreement, the Sienese already giving their assent to Renaissance oratory on the proposition that all rebels deserve severe punishment. This kind of consensus underlies a chapter in Machiavelli's *Discourses*. You should never trust exiles because their false hopes and deliberate deceptions will nearly always end "with shame or great damage" for the government unwise enough to support them.[26]

In 1436 exile intrigues figured again in the relations between Siena and Florence. Leonardo Bruni, then chancellor of Florence, wrote to Siena protesting the "scandal, sedition, and discord" caused by anti-Medicean exiles just across the Florentine border. Had the Sienese really believed that Medici agents attempted to assassinate Francesco Filelfo in Siena? Bruni's astonishment may have been disingenuous, though his contempt for his humanist rival Filelfo was probably genuine enough. The chancellor's chief complaint was that Florentines had been insulted on the streets and, worse, that the *podestà* of Siena, reportedly a hireling of the exiles, had condemned a Florentine citizen on trumped-up charges. The Sienese answered cautiously. Where they were able, they blamed some elusive troublemaker from Perugia. They vouched for the due process of what was after all their law to administer—but then promised more effective measures. Two months later, the exiles crippled a horse the Medici had entered in the Palio races and would have given the groom no better had he not escaped in time.[27]

These incidents suggest the possibilities, if also the limitations, of what one Renaissance state could expect from another against its exiles. There were limitations, of course. Despite the proximity of their larger neighbor, a nearness made more threatening by the recent history of Florentine expansion, the Sienese did not suppress the Florentine exiles altogether. Perhaps they did not suppress them at all. The realities and the self-conscious traditions of independence were at least as strong as pressures for cooperation with Florence. Apart from self-interest, inertia, or sheer inefficiency, ideals of hospitality and expectations of asylum may have moved the Sienese as much as they had the marquis of Ferrara in 1385, "because an exile asked me for bread in such a manner that I could not refuse him." It was the duty of princes, a humanist tract would remind the duke of Calabria, to welcome strangers humanely.[28] The fact remains that there were Florentine agents and a Florentine ambassador at work in Siena in 1436, even if Filelfo may have been exaggerating—as usual—about Medicean assassins. The Florentine chancellery was kept well informed. It demanded action against the *fuorusciti* through official channels and, no doubt, in secret, and the rulers of Siena did not ignore Florence or flaunt their independence as they might once have done. Under constraints such as these, exiles could be prevented from forming the old large-scale organizations and were more likely to surface from the underground, individually or in small groups, for scattered violence, minor diplomatic intrigue, and petty sabotage.

For their part, Renaissance states were able to send exiles with some confidence to more or less distant places where they might have been dreaded in the communal age. This policy too was traditional, but after the middle of the fourteenth century it was evidently more widespread than it had been, and it was undoubtedly more effective. In 1382, when the last traces of the Florentine woolworkers' revolt of 1378 were liquidated, eighteen men were sentenced to two-year confinements in exile from Florence—six in Bologna, two in Venice, two in Padua, two in Perugia; the others singly in the region of Lucania and the towns of Aquila, Pisa, Foligno, and Senigallia. Beginning in 1387, the Alberti of Florence were exiled in every direction with few variations on what had already been considered standard procedure in 1382; so were the Medici in 1433 and, when their turn as exiles came, the anti-Mediceans in 1434.[29] After the Guinigi took control of Lucca in 1392, leaders of the opposing faction were assigned fixed places of exile, from Rome and Perugia to Avignon and Toulouse.[30] From an early date maritime towns had confined their exiles to islands or to colonies overseas; Alfonso of Naples continued this practice as a Renaissance prince, sending outcasts to Mediterranean islands in self-conscious imitation of the Romans. At the other end of Italy the exile of Ludovico Sforza and his brothers to Pisa, Bari, and Perugia after the murder of Galeazzo Maria Sforza in 1476 was only the most conspicuous use of similar devices in Milan.[31]

When Palla Strozzi sent word to Florence after his exile in 1434 that "the hen is brooding," Cosimo de' Medici supposedly replied: "the hen cannot brood well outside the nest."[32] In putting down the taunt, Cosimo was also putting Messer Palla in a proper historical place. Exiles had once brooded quite well in the external communes, international alliances, ungoverned spaces, and welcoming towns of the older order. But as the likelihood of foreign intervention decreased, as the major Italian states pushed out their boundaries and stabilized their relationships, or localized their conflicts, exiles could be watched and contained to an extent perhaps as characteristically "Renaissance" as humanist readings of classical texts or artistic renderings of perspective in space. Messer Palla's contemporaries were pleased to compare him with the "good Romans" of antiquity. It would not be the least of resemblances to see in him and other *fuorusciti* of his time figures like Cicero's Marcellus, even in exile "still within the power of the conqueror."[33]

Internal Pacification and the Art of Accepting Exile

Internal changes accompanied shifts in the external relations among the Italian states after the middle of the fourteenth century. Jacob Burckhardt's phrases come to mind—"the state as a work of art" and "Renaissance individualism." With his searching eye for the details of the larger picture, Burckhardt included exiles in the panorama of *The Civilization of the Renaissance in Italy.*[34] Like other actors in the arena of Renaissance politics, he observed, they found it increasingly difficult to resort to the forms of collective violence and corporate organization that had been so characteristic of Italian life in the Middle Ages. They were especially vulnerable to the devices of political control and the demands for allegiance that Renaissance states could employ against them. Renaissance politics aimed at internal "pacification," and exiles were forced to adapt to the consequences.

A mid-fourteenth-century encomium of the Visconti by Galvano Fiamma contains an early agenda for the politics of pacification.[35] In a "most just and holy law" Azzo Visconti had ordered subject-cities of Milan to repatriate their exiles. For this measure alone, "now observed very diligently by our lords of Milan," Messer Azzo should "possess paradise." But there is much else that Fiamma wishes to praise in the Visconti. He goes on to salute the creation of a new official whose duties are to secure the countryside, to curtail vendettas and freelance military ventures, especially during harvest time, and to preserve, not destroy, the houses of bandits and rebels "for the common good." He further rejoices over the peace Milan had made with the Church after twenty-two years of war and tells how the Visconti have undertaken many other "worthy works of law and justice" to eliminate arbitrary taxation, to regulate the jurisdiction of local lords, to cut the public payroll, to punish extortion by public officials, to exact strict justice, to equalize impositions for the public granaries and military expenses, and to supervise the medical profession and the clergy. Fiamma associates these measures with the latest technological marvels—mills that run not by water or wind but with weights and wheels and other subtleties never seen before in Italy; boats which can transport five hundred or six hundred men from Venice to Lago Maggiore and the river Ticino; new processes for fermenting wine and for weaving cloths of silk and gold. "And so [the Visconti] introduced many praiseworthy laws and studied ways of extirpating evil customs." The good news, as Fiamma calls this programmatic proto-absolutism, has spread throughout Italy. He imagines that many more cities will soon be submitting to Visconti rule and to still another of his lists of Milanese accomplishments.

Since the first step toward pacification in Fiamma's account—recalling the exiles—was not limited to Milan, the place he assigned to Azzo Visconti in paradise must have been crowded. A Lombard poet had already given his blessing to similar measures on the part of the Della Scala of Verona.[36] In a republican context Leonardo Bruni linked the political stability of Florence in the mid-1380s to the reassimilation of exiles after the failed attempt of the Florentine woolworkers, the *Ciompi*, to win permanent representation in the government of the city. More than a century later Piero de' Medici tried to broaden a dwindling base of support by proposing to recall the *fuorusciti* just before his own exile in 1494.[37] Even historians reluctant to speak of any political coherence in the Romagna have noted a tendency to combine legislation for amnesty and administrative reform in Malatesta Rimini. Carlo Malatesta recommended just such a combination in the political testament he drafted in 1408 for the young duke of Milan.[38] After his own takeover of Milan in

1450, Francesco Sforza ordered his council to proceed with moderation against his fugitive opponents and congratulated his lieutenant in Alessandria for restoring émigrés to their homes. Two years later Borso d'Este celebrated his triumphal entry as lord of Reggio with a series of decrees which included the cancellation of sentences against exiles.[39]

There were long-standing precedents for measures such as these. Amnesties or "compositions" allowing fugitives, bandits, and rebels to satisfy fines and other penalties at a discount were familiar communal institutions. Rarely able to impose severe condemnations to the letter of the law, magistrates had often preferred token obedience to none at all. Permitting exiles to return was a dangerous expedient, but it was also a showy display of official magnanimity and, in any case, a practical lure to attract *fuorusciti* away from their companies abroad. The pardons offered by Black Guelph Florence in Dante's time were expedients of this sort, and it has been argued that, on the whole, justice was more lenient and hortatory than severe in Florence until the 1340s.[40] The inconsistencies of the Florentines were not exceptional. Between 1302 and 1354 the commune of Siena proclaimed no fewer than ten general amnesties benefiting well over five thousand people. By the fourteenth century "graces" reducing penalties and fines were a regular occurrence in Venice.[41]

Renaissance governments, then, continued earlier tactics of pacification, but they also tended to transform them into something like a coordinated political program. On the one hand, exiles were restored; on the other hand, new steps were taken—the second Visconti *podestà* mentioned by Galvano Fiamma was one of them—to suppress exiles and other sources of disorder. Prohibiting the private justice of the vendetta and such acts of public vengeance as the destruction of rebel property opened the way for exiles to return; these same openings to repatriation represented, and were also supplemented by, provisions for eliminating further unrest. First the carrot, then the stick. From Milan to Naples this combination of tactical concessions and invasive institutions was to be expected of territorial states intent on bringing as many levels of existence as possible within their purview.[42] Whenever possible, the new statecraft meant the large, aggressive, and more or less inviolable company of exiles to be as outmoded as the old technology, as anachronistic as the easy recourse to collective violence and corporate immunities in an earlier age.

A practical consequence was a gradual shift away from the traditional executive and judicial institutions. Since the twelfth and thirteenth centuries, "foreign" magistrates had ridden the communal office-holding circuit with a combination of executive, judicial, and police powers; as well as judges and notaries there were soldiers and bailiffs in their official entourages. The call for peace and justice had long been a favorite theme in the council halls where the *podestà* and the Captain of the People served out their terms of office. Lawyers, notaries, and theologians had expounded the virtues of just and peaceful rule in orations, treatises, books of advice, and sermons, and so had the painter Ambrogio Lorenzetti in his famous fresco (ca. 1337) for the Palazzo Pubblico at Siena, where the ratio between officials with police powers to the population had reached the impressive proportion of 1:145 early in the fourteenth century. Lorenzetti's allegory of Good Government was dominated by the stern personifications of Justice and the Common Good. Both figures, Lady Justice with her scales and the gray-bearded worthy symbolizing the *Ben Comune*, were shown linked by a cord passing between them through the hands of Concord and the Sienese citizens who filled the lower portion of the painting.[43] The fusion of prerogatives and the call for law and order remained standard features of Renaissance government, but just as diplomatic missions were placed on a regular footing after the middle of the Trecento, so too internal administration tended to pass from temporary officials imported from the outside to permanent institutions closely bound to the ruling regime. In this process the judicial and executive functions of government slipped from the control of the constitutional restraints and the legislative assemblies which foreign magistrates had been established to maintain and defend. Early in the fourteenth century Messer Cante Gabrieli of Gubbio had been a formidable figure as *podestà*, judge and executive arm of Black Guelph Florence; later in the century, tales by Boccaccio and Sacchetti had already begun to play on the joke of the powerless *podestà*.[44]

The newer sort of compact and often omnicompetent council or commission was no joking matter. The Secret Council that Giangaleazzo Visconti made regular and supreme for advisory and executive functions in Milan was also a tribunal with jurisdiction in all his territories, especially for political cases. The Estensi imitated the Milanese model in Ferrara, though their councils were less clearly defined and less fully developed. In the kingdom of Naples too similar institutions on a more or less continuous basis can be found under Alfonso of Aragon, and the protests—sometimes successful—of his barons are a measure of their relative efficiency. However "disinclined to institutional change," the Malatesta of Rimini also established or reformed small councils to extend what has been called "centralization without administrative unity" over their subject towns.[45]

There were republican parallels. Emergency commissions, or *balìe*, were granted nearly unlimited power in Florence for limited terms during the crises of the 1370s and 1380s; between 1393 and 1404 a Council of Eighty-One, a super-*balìa*, was the central clearinghouse of government in Florence. These institutions were responsible for exiling the leaders of the *Ciompi* and later the Alberti and their allies, just as emergency commissions in the 1430s presided over the exile first of the Medici and then of their opponents.[46] The Eighty-One were disbanded in 1404, and even the commissions of the Medici regime after 1434 were subject to renewal by constitutional means. This was a tribute to Florentine suspicion of any unchecked exercise of authority—and to the cautious style of Medici rule.[47] By 1434, however, centralizing principles had been institutionalized at other levels of administration in Florence and elsewhere.

The notorious examples were close-knit, flexible, and secretive boards on internal security. Marino Sanuto characterized the Venetian Council of Ten as an "extremely awesome magistracy," as "highly secret" and the central nerve of the state since "all state affairs are dealt with in this council."[48] Respectful praise had often been heard before, but in critical republican moods Venetian patricians also spoke of the Ten with a bitterness quite as telling as the complacent view of Domenico Morosini that Venice owed the "perpetual tranquility of our city and our long-lasting liberty in large part to this council."[49] An analogous Florentine institution, the Eight on Internal Security, inspired a similar aura of fear and respect in Florence. According to Francesco Guicciardini, "if the fear of this magistracy, which comes from its dispatch in discovering crimes and judging them, did not restrain spirits up to no good, one would not be able to live in Florence. . . ."[50] As the Venetian Ten were called into being between 1310 and 1355 to put down conspiracies against the state, so the Eight originated in Florence as a political police commission for the suppression of the *Ciompi* experiment in 1378. Both councils became permanent, and the competence of both soon went beyond limited and exceptional responsibilities in political cases to regular inquiry and prosecution in criminal cases of all descriptions.

When the newer institutions competed with traditional courts and law-enforcing agencies, it was an uneven contest. The Ten had their own police force and spies, and their interrogations were carried on behind closed doors, unlike the debates with a lawyer for the defense in the sessions of the Venetian *avogadori di comun* ("state lawyers"). Summary justice by the Ten and "bulletins" issued by the Eight could dispense with elaborate rituals, procedural formalities, and constitutional checks.

The expediencies of the Eight contrasted sharply with the more restricted jurisdiction of ordinary courts in Florence; the concentrated powers of the Ten overshadowed the dispersed authority of the quasi-judicial panels of Venetian patricians and the criminal and civil sections of the major Venetian tribunal, the *Quarantìa*. In institutions such as the Ten and the Eight, Renaissance states found ideal means to supplant (or disguise) old ideals of punishment by retributive vengeance with the utilitarian pursuit of social control.[51]

The politics of pacification depended on shared attitudes as well as institutional refinements. In Florence, with its republican tradition of political debate, discussions concerning exile as a form of punishment were especially intense. Much of the official rationale on questions of internal security comes to light in the records of the Florentine *Pratiche* between 1382 and 1430.[52] In these extraordinary assemblies, partly informal boards of directors, partly exclusive debating societies, important office holders and influential citizens met to voice their opinions on the political issues of the moment. Since civic justice and civic duty were, as one speaker put it, next to God among a citizen's obligations, few *Pratica* meetings were complete without touching upon alleged or actual offenses against public order.

True justice, the men of the *Pratica* commonly assumed (or said), was severe but fair. In 1387 Filippo Magalotti and other speakers demanded judicial surgery against the Alberti, who stood accused of treason, "like an infected member." Rinaldo Gianfigliazzi, Marco Strozzi, and Niccolò Davanzati urged all the rigors of justice in 1393, and Guccio Nobili likened clemency to a sin. So that the Alberti might never again find "the audacity to raise their heads," it was repeatedly suggested in 1411 that the Eight on Internal Security should be given free rein against them. But more moderate recommendations could also be drawn from ideals of stern justice and the public good. Filippo Magalotti was reminded in 1387 that the obligation to punish the guilty could not be met without a scrupulous investigation of the facts. No one should escape justice, agreed Vanni Castellani in 1400, and for that very reason punishment could only be proportionate to the fault. It was only just to distinguish leaders from followers and greater from lesser transgressions. Even in the tense political atmosphere of 1411 there were those who counseled the regime—it was almost a self-counsel, given the composition and quasi-official status of the *Pratica*—to proceed "deliberately and thoroughly," to exact no more punishment than the law allowed, and to protect the innocent. "Justice is the surety of the people," announced Maso degli Albizzi. While the words of the leader of the ruling faction may have been superbly hypocritical, they opened even the Alberti case to at least the show of due process.

Leonardo Bruni was thinking of exiles when he made an epigram out of attitudes such as these in his *History of Florence*: "For citizens ought to be hated in such a way that we still remember them to be citizens."[53] Bruni conceded that disorder was always a possibility, especially in republics; citizens could not be kept from rivaling and, if it came to that, from hating one another. But the headlong expulsion or exclusion of social groups and political factions had been counterproductive in Bruni's view. The traditional policy had only heightened the grievances underlying political factionalism and social strife. Unqualified clemency or laisser faire was not the only alternative policy. What the epigram of the humanist chancellor and historian envisaged was rather a world of citizens equal enough in their loyalty (and their vulnerability) to the state to accept the remedies of the state against disorder. The older order of corporate groupings had been loosened by demographic collapse, economic dislocation, social upheaval, and the pressures of political centralization. Authoritative citizens and aggressive institutions had set about the work of political reconstruction. Even exiles owed the political community their allegiance and obedience.[54] The old art of returning home thus became an art of accepting the terms of exile.

Long and plaintive letters which Donato Acciaiuoli sent to the government of Florence in 1396 suggest how exiles themselves could acknowledge the bonds of citizenship and subjection.[55] Acciaiuoli's confinement to Barletta on the Adriatic was one of the most clamorous cases of exile in the late Trecento, and in at least two letters he told his own exculpating version point by point. An informer's claim early in January 1396 that he, Donato, meant to raise his sword against the regime had been all "malice" and "impassioned ill will" and worse.[56] Despite the contrary advice of his friends, had he not presented himself voluntarily in the palace of the priors to confront his accuser and defend his innocence? No one could deny that violent voices had called for his skin from the piazza or the palace within. The *balìa* had welcomed him, then refused to hear him out, and in the end left him the choice of a false confession and exile or death. Chroniclers and judicial records add further charges—that Acciaiuoli was accused of planning to petition for the recall of exiles; that, if petitioning failed, he was ready to try political assassinations and a full-scale revolt.

The truth of these allegations remains uncertain though it is clear enough that Messer Donato had some share in a campaign to rehabilitate members of the Alberti family who were in exile and that, in his provoking, over-mighty style, he had opposed the war policy of the regime and the extension of emergency powers. Acting out what seemed to many a rabble-rouser's part, Acciaiuoli was fair game for what the authorities called a "merciful" confinement to Barletta on 12 January 1396.[57]

For all his injured protests, Messer Donato knew his duty and expressed it in tones reechoed by many later exiles. He suppressed hints of open opposition and did not renounce his citizenship or seek some higher justification beyond it. He omitted no sign of reverence before the "magnificent lords" of Florence, *padri dolcissimi della libertà*. To them he claimed to have turned "as, after God, princes and guardians of our country, ordained by God and the ordinances of the people to rule over all with justice. . . ."[58] He cited as proofs of loyalty his appearance in the palace against the advice of his friends, then his appeal as an obedient exile. At another level he recognized the power of the state disguised in his own high, if calculating, phrases and understood the limits of a citizen's defenses when "the will of the government . . . can de facto offend persons, their status, and their possessions."[59] The protective net of his relatives and friends, he granted, had not held, however dazzling his connections— the cardinal-cousin at Rome, the great offices held by his family in the kingdom of Naples, and, beyond the grave, the still-sustaining reputation of the Acciaiuoli dead. Messer Donato did remind the priors of these potential sources of resistance. But as he had presented himself alone in their palace, so he appealed for himself in his letters as "your most faithful citizen, *popolano* and Guelph, ever zealous [for the cause of] liberty." A faithful citizen he promised to remain, still ready in exile to serve "the state of our city with my person and possessions."[60]

Whereas Dante had transformed or transcended his exile in principles and poetry, Messer Donato was obsessed in prose with the details of his case. Dante continued to resist, but Messer Donato alternately accepted his exile and appealed through official channels. The anguish one senses in Acciaiuoli's account was that he hardly knew how to do otherwise. He felt himself to be in the power of authorities whose legitimacy his own words acknowledged and magnified. Ties of belonging, of duty, identity, and self-interest as a citizen, bound him to Florence, and neither greater causes nor complete companies of exiles beckoned to him from the outside. Messer Donato was left to put a good face on his downfall, to relive his disgrace and rehearse his reasons in a casuistry of submission, supplication, and muted bursts of protest. When he remembered the example of martyred saints and "the venerable spirit of Lucrezia of Rome," it was only for the lesson he needed to hear—that it was "allowed to everyone to flee the greater by the lesser evil, hoping for some remedy in God and the world." Time alone would be "the just remedy against violence."[61] In fact, he broke his confinement prematurely. In 1397 Messer Donato escaped to Venice, forfeiting the bond his relatives and friends had posted for him. It was already too late to salvage a principled resistance or perhaps even much sense of personal release.

The language and the logic of Acciaiuoli's letters were taken up by other Florentine exiles in any case. In 1400 Bernardo Velluti petitioned the priors for permission to return, alleging that during his eighteen years in exile on charges of treason "he had defended his city with words and deeds, and that he had cherished and supported the regime to the limits of his ability." In the same year Giovanni di Marco Strozzi fled to escape a death sentence for conspiracy, but in 1428 he appealed for the chance "to return to his native city with his wife and children . . . to live in peace and then to die there, so that he can pass on to his descendants the heritage of liberty that he received from his forebears."[62] Under the terms of a law providing for a kind of ostracism *contra scandalosos* Neri Capponi was ordered on 28 March 1432 to stay at least twenty miles from Florence for three years. Even in his private papers he did not complain. The sentence was soon canceled, and when the Medici were exiled in 1433, Capponi urged Averardo de' Medici to follow his example.[63]

Averardo replied as if the advice were hardly necessary. Ever since he could remember he had never been less than a good citizen and staunch defender of Florentine liberty, "which I know in all and for all to consist in obedience to that magnificent *signoria*." The priors might command as they would. "All their commands must be reputed just and honest and reasonable, and from them let us await pardon and readmission. . . . And so I bow to their pleasure. . . ."[64] In the end Averardo lost a waiting game in which failing health, irony, pride, and scrupulous devotion to duty were evidently mixed. Despite the goading of worried relatives and friends, he was too sick and perhaps too calculating to move fast enough for the authorities. Although they did extend the time for him to begin a term of confinement in Naples, they refused to extend the deadline long enough or to allow him to choose another place of exile. On 28 November 1433 they condemned him as a rebel for having resisted "willfully and with the intention of scorning and degrading the authority of the lord priors and the citizens of the *balìa* and of his whole native city of Florence."[65]

The most famous Florentine exile of the fifteenth century also refused to criticize openly the government that had expelled him. "He and his family have always defended their country with everything in their power," a sympathetic listener reports hearing him say in Padua, "and now, to regain it, he would rest content not only to stay in Padua but even at the top of the world, even until death itself."[66] Received by the Venetians "not as an exile but as an ambassador," the distinguished émigré played the good citizen to the point of exposing a plot by a member of his own family to launch a Milanese expedition against Florence. Official commendation and praise were sent to him and his brother as *nobiles viri et cives nostri dilecti*. To the end of his confinement, which shrewd strategy, genuine conviction, and the mistakes of his enemies cut short, he had no desire, he said, "to return by any other route other than that by which he had departed." For Cosimo de' Medici was quite as conventional and as artful in exile as he was to be when he became the unofficial ruler of Florence after his triumphant recall in September 1434.

Twenty-five years after Cosimo's return many leaders of the anti-Medicean opposition or their descendants were still in exile. When the sentences issued against them in the 1430s and the 1440s were prolonged or stiffened in 1458, Filippo di Marco Strozzi wrote from Rome that "these are only the fruits of this world." He resolved to be patient "since this has come about with the consent of those who govern." "I am certain," he explained, "that they have done it solely for the good and repose of the city as a whole. . . . I will not on that account lessen the respect I have for our leading citizens, or even the love I bear toward my fatherland." And then, as Messer Filippo's long-suffering mother confirmed from Florence, "there is no other remedy."[67]

But the art of accepting exile was not an exclusive Florentine skill. The assassination of Galeazzo Maria Sforza in 1476 ended in a failed uprising and another corps of obedient outcasts from Milan. For punishing him with confinement at Turin, Giacomino Olgiati not only thanked the regent-widow Bona Sforza and her ward; he also vowed that he had meant "a thousand times" to kill the assassin, his own son, "the archtraitor," with his own hands.[68] It would seem from the correspondence of Ludovico Sforza in exile at Pisa that there had never been a more faithful brother, vassal, or subject than the man who had raised the rebel cry

"Moro, Moro!" in the streets of Milan a few weeks earlier.[69] But necessity turned easily to virtue in Ludovico il Moro, and besides, Cicco Simonetta, chancellor of Milan, was following the exiles' every move. Perhaps, wrote Messer Cicco, obviously enjoying his omniscience, Ludovico was unaware that an agent whom the exile himself had commissioned for the purpose was raising money from the sale of Sforza holdings in Milanese territory? Well-placed friends, such as Ercole d'Este in Ferrara, counseled "great patience and submission." Ferrara could offer nothing better than bland advice and "one of our good falcons for taking a bit of recreation." Naples would send a musician. At court Agostino de' Rossi observed that Ludovico's reputation was improving day by day and added that he "should not cease to recommend himself and to write often. . . ." The flood of obsequious letters from Pisa rose higher. Ludovico sent presents. He spied on the Florentines for "his" government. For her part, Bona Sforza remitted his pension (under the seal of Cicco Simonetta) and graciously accepted gifts of stirrups and amateur intelligence. But Ludovico was left languishing in exile until a shift in the Italian balance of power made it possible for him to return in 1478.

In Rome, where plans for rebuilding a "most perfect paradise" included measures for strengthening police powers, Bernardino della Valle took his banishment by Sixtus IV in 1484 with something like gay desperation.[70] News of the sentence caught him in the act of writing, or so he informed his correspondent, Francesco Gaddi, papal agent in Milan. "Well now," he burst out midway through a rambling letter, "the pope at this point has just banned from the whole territory of the Church, in one way or another, the Margani, the Santacroce, and me and my brothers. I ask for peace, and I've always obeyed the orders of His Holiness and so must be off to exile. . . . In the beginning when I was writing I was a citizen, now I am an exile; it's a carnival mask this human condition and life of ours." Della Valle's most active resistance was to curry the favor of another prince and patron. In a letter written a month later, he begged Gaddi to tell the duke of Milan that "this little breath still remaining to me I have by the grace of *sua illustrissima signoria* and I live at his command." The next day he sent Gaddi another pleading note. He could think of nothing else to do. "Justice, life, and death," he wrote, lay in the hands of the duke, though the pope must never know it. "I do believe all the wiles of the world reside in Italy, so unfathomable are things. . . ."

Niccolò Vitelli was no stranger to the wiles of Italy. This petty tyrant ruled Città di Castello for thirty years until his expulsion by Pope Sixtus IV in 1474.[71] He had defied the popes before from his stronghold on the border between Florentine territory and the papal states. But Pope Sixtus mobilized an army against him, neutralized his potential allies, and tricked him into seeking pardon in Rome after admitting a papal garrison at home. Città di Castello fell to the Pope's ruse. Vitelli retreated as an exile to Castiglion Fiorentino. Contemporary observers report seeing him there exercising his falcons, cursing the pope, and rationalizing his fall with lines from Cicero on the unmerited fate of the just man in an unjust world.[72] All his attempts to return from exile came to nothing.

Resistance wore itself out easily in the depths and shallows of such a world, and in at least one significant instance where an open and principled spirit of opposition survived, it took the form of withdrawal and retreat. Eleutherus, Alamanno Rinuccini's spokesman in his dialogue *De libertate* (1479), is a voluntary exile from Florence at his countryhouse.[73] The dialogue opens with the arguments of his guest and counterpart Mitoxus for the old traditions of civic engagement and self-help. Put on the defensive by the doubts of the host, another guest, Altheus, intervenes with the Aristotelian and humanist case for an activist's conception of human freedom. Liberty, he maintains, is the highest good. True liberty is the ability to live within the limits of the law; implanted in man by nature, it must be perfected by study and by the active defense of free speech, equality, and justice. Rinuccini-Eleutherus is not convinced. When Altheus admits that liberty may be giving way to willful injustice and tyranny, Eleutherus goes on to say that he, for one, has failed to find any place for self-respecting virtue and disinterested service. "Therefore I turn often into myself in this solitude and speak frequently with those books which you now see and delight in that [wholly contemplative] liberty of which I approve." Like Rinuccini himself, "as it were, an exile from the city," Eleutherus can only disdain those "who, agitated day and night by endless care, tolerate shameful servitude and are unable, they say, to lift a finger except at [the ruler's] bidding."[74]

Ineffectual discontent was a fitting outcome of the politics of pacification and the art of accepting exile. In the later Quattrocento the elaborate, failed conspiracy of a few reckless individuals was a characteristic form of protest. Another was the gentleman's private disenchantment behind a facade of outward conformity.[75] There were exceptions of course, especially after the new siege of foreign invasions beginning in 1494 exposed the precariousness of the status quo. But with the Renaissance narrowing of political and psychological space, visions of open, organized, and righteous resistance in exile had already begun a long descent into the collective memory.

Rules for Inclusion

Changes in the rules were bound to changes in the facts of exile. Courts in the early fourteenth century, like the Florentine tribunal of Messer Cante Gabrieli of Gubbio, had founded their authority on the spectacle of force and the multiplication of technical distinctions. The would-be tenants of the imposing edifice of the law had often refused to enter it. Harsh, partisan proceedings had actually encouraged tactics of evasion, and when open spaces, willing allies, and whole communities of his own kind beckoned to the exile, he was not likely, as Dante put it, to lack his bread. In Renaissance Italy magistrates, lawyers, and notaries dispensed with many of the heavy-handed legal bluffs and administrative formalities of Dante's time. Wherever possible, they were dutiful bureaucrats and servants of the state. Their procedures, records, and reasoning tended to be more efficient and more discriminating because their chances of having their way had improved. The contrast between the older and the newer rules of exile can be explored in detail in the case of Florence. They are well documented there. But the Florentine case suggests directions and dimensions of change which can also be discerned in legal treatises and administrative manuals consulted by Renaissance magistrates elsewhere in Italy.

In Florence new emphases were given to old procedures for confinement to exile from the post-*Ciompi* settlement of the early 1380s through the formation of the Medici regime in 1434–1435. In 1382 the Captain of the People of Florence was instructed by an emergency commission "to proscribe and confine" twenty-five enemies of the regime, "observing such forms as are customary in similar matters."[76] The enabling legislation might have cited the authority of the Ordinances of Justice of 1293 for this, except that the *balìa* of 1382 was proposing the use of confinement as a regular punishment rather than as the more traditional preventative measure for removing potential troublemakers from the city. In the thirteenth century convicted enemies of the regime might not have got off so easily, nor would many earlier regimes have shared the apparent confidence of the *balìa* that their sentences would be heeded.

As issued in 1382, the sentences of the Captain of the People were very specific in provisions which were, in the event, quite flexibly applied. On 11 March the unlucky twenty-five were ordered to leave Florentine territory within two days of being notified. They were to remain for three years in designated places where they were obliged to present themselves daily before the local *podestà* or other officials. Eight days later these

10. *A Renaissance Consolation for Exile: "The Triumph of Cicero"* by Franciabigio.   Cicero is shown returning triumphantly to Rome after bearing up under the misfortunes of exile. Renaissance moralists often recommended the example of the ancients to the exiles of their own day; this scene was probably intended as an allegory on Cosimo de' Medici's return to Florence in 1434. Freco, Villa Medici, Poggio a Caiano, 1520–1521.

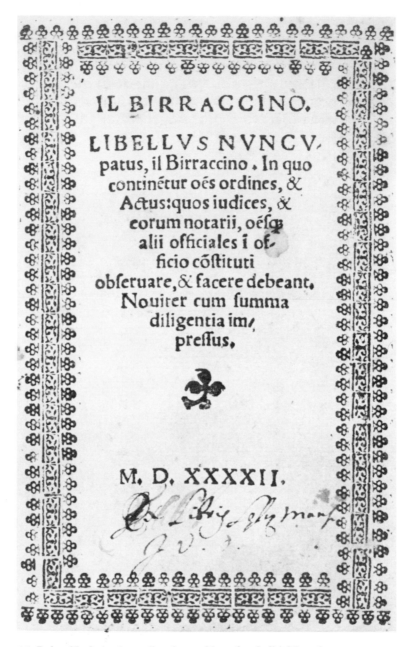

IL BIRRACCINO.

LIBELLVS NVNCV,
patus, il Birraccino . In quo
continétur oés ordines, &
Actus:quos iudices, &
eorum notarii, oéfc̄p
alii officiales í of-
ficio cóstituti
obseruare, & facere debeant.
Nouiter cum summa
diligentia im,
pressus,

M. D. XXXXII.

11. Rules of Inclusion from a Renaissance Manual on Judicial Procedure.
  a. Title page of *Il birraccino* by Ser Raffaello de' Cerchi, first published in 1497.

ſquartentur, ſiue propaginetur, vel in mare mer
gantur, vel aliam quācunꝗ morte violentā fece
rint. Nec mutatur aliud: niſi quando fit mentio
de morte ad quā condénatus eſt: vt infra oſten
dā: quando tractabimus de generibus, & qua
litatibus morti: ſecundum qualitatem deli
ctorum.

Videamus nunc primo de omnibus titulis
qui apponi poſſunt in ſententiis, & condemna
tionibus: videlicet in principio tibi.

❡ In Dei nomine amen. Hæc eſt quædā con
dénatio ꝛc. Poſtea videbimus de pœnis iponé
dis i ſingulis maleficiis cōprehēſis ſupra i ſupra
ſcripta inꝗſitione magna. Et primo videlicet.
❡ In Dei nomine amen. Hæc eſt quædā condé
natio corporis defectiua, ꝛ ſententia códénatio
nis corporis defectiuæ Lata, data ꝛc. Nos talis
ꝛc. Vbi dicitur ſimiles códénationes, dicatus:
Vbi ſimiles códemnationes corporis defectiuæ
ꝛ ſententiæ códénationū corporis defectiuarū,
dari legi ꝛc. ꝛ ſic de ſingulis.

In Dei nomine amen. Condemnatio cor
poris afflictiua, ꝛ ſententia corporis condemna
tionis afflictiuæ Lata, data ꝛ in his ſcriptis ſen
tentialiter pronuntiata ꝛc.

In Dei nomine amen. Hæc eſt quædam con
demnatio ad certum tempus, ſiue in perpetuū
relegatoria: et ſententia condemnationis ad
certum tempus, ſiue in perpetuum relegatoriæ
Lata, data etc.

Aliquando apponitur conditio certæ pœ
næ: et tunc dici debet. Hæc eſt quædam con
demnatio ad certum tempus, vel in perpetuū

b. Amidst formulas to be used in sentencing malefactors to various punishments by physical mutilation, *Il birraccino* gives the standard formula for sentences to relegation in exile.

12. Facts of Exile in Renaissance Italy: The Defeat at Anghiari. This seventeenth century drawing by Peter Paul Rubens after a fresco by Leonardo da Vinci shows four horsemen battling over the standard of the Florentine republic a Anghiari, where a combined army of Florence and the pope routed a force c

...lanese mercenaries and Florentine exiles on 29 June 1440. The original ...nting was commissioned in 1504 for the Palazzo Vecchio in Florence but ...s destroyed or painted over in the second half of the sixteenth century. ...uvre, Paris, Gabinet des Dessins.

Ritratto di Monte Alcino in quel di Siena, con l'assedio, e batteria. C
IAC CASTR.

E I L'anno predetto, ritrouandomi all'impresa di Mi n'Alcino, & ha
banda confiderato la difficulta, el fito, & il buon principio fatto per
luogo, come ianno tutti quegli Illustrissini Signori, che si si trouare
volendo conquistarlo, non era da perder tempo, ma da far subita risol
banerlo, e che doursie uoltar tutte il difegno inuerso quei gabbioni,
fatti uerso la porta, prima che fussero stati insieme con le cafe terrapienati, e con qu
tigliaria battere tanta cortina, che la gente potesse entrar dentro a quello spatio.

ITALIANI
PIAZZA

SPAGNOLI
PIAZZA

S Camillo Colonna

Conte santa fiora

13. *The Siege of Montalcino, 1553.* Engraving from Girolamo Maggi, *De*

tlieria nel lungo dimostrano per le lettere. O. a bruciare tutte le case per fianco , perche quelli di dentro farebbono fiui sforzi abbandonarle, Lo , e così si farebbe fatto qualche buono effetto, altrimenti sotterrebbero i detti Signori, e si farebbe perduto il tempo fatto acquistato o Irò

G I R O L A M O   M A G G I.

può dire, che quanto segui , fosse per esaltazione dello Illustrissima Signore gran mastro la guerra il gran Giordano Orsino , quale la mer prima nella sua più verde età in Puglia , in Africa, di in a' in luoghi dove gran segni del suo sommo valore, in qual era lungo ma aro al mondo, che l'opere , unito con l'animosità , e col valor militare, può facilmente salvarete Città , e i Rani . Costanza si vece in una renzo di Corsica . Donde oltre a' grandi honori che per tali prove egli merito appresso al Re Christianissimo , fu sempre padre di utili, lettera , e Signori stimato degno di stima , e di soprana me costante a quello del Re Decembio detto Riparatore della Città , e sopra quello fernatore di quelle .

tificazione della città (Venice, 1583), fols. 99v–100r.

14. Emblems of the Last Republic of Exiles at Montalcino, 1555–1559.
Drawings after coins minted by the *Repubblica Senese Ritirata in
Montalcino.* Adapted from *Corpus nummorum italicorum* (Rome,
1929), XI, Plate 16.

terms were reduced in a tactical modification that might well have seemed unacceptable under the more rigid procedures of Dante's generation. One group was simply forbidden to hold communal office for three years. Another eighteen citizens, including the *Ciompi* leader Michele di Lando, were confined for a two-year period in various locations, from Venice and Padua in the north to Lucania in the south. Four days were allowed for them to depart. Those confined within two hundred miles of Florence had one month, those beyond that limit two months, to certify their arrival at the place of exile in a notarized document which was to be sent to the palace of the priors at home. The signory also required official verification every four days that the terms of confinement were being observed. Anyone failing to meet these conditions was subject to beheading and confiscation.[77]

Later sentences refined the pattern of 1382, beginning with those issued against the Alberti family on charges of intrigue and conspiracy over a period of twenty-five years. The first Alberti condemnations of 1387 added (or pretended to add) provisions for self-imposed exile to the familiar formulas. Benedetto and Cipriano Alberti were not required to settle in specified places but were permitted to move at will anywhere beyond a one-hundred-mile limit so long as they steered clear of Lombardy, where the long reach of the lord of Milan was always dangerous. Thus, "for the sake of peace and concord," and "to placate" the Alberti brothers the *balìa* claimed to have "accepted" their petition to leave the city on business; the conditions were that, under penalty of a 2,000 *lire* fine and confiscation for noncompliance, they depart within eight days, pass the one-hundred-mile limit within fifteen, and give notice of their whereabouts every fifteen days over a two-year term.[78]

Three more sets of condemnations varied the pattern just enough to suit new situations. In 1393, after the discovery of an alleged plot between certain Alberti and their supporters in the Romagna, the *balìa* gave the Captain of the People powers similar to those of 1382. But for the more serious charges and the second offense the range, costs, and duration of confinement were extended. Messer Cipriano Alberti was ordered to pay a fine of 1,000 florins within two days and exiled for life to the island of Rhodes under penalty of decapitation and confiscation. Alberto di Bernardo was fined 2,000 florins and sentenced to twenty years in Brussels; his brother Nerozzo was given ten years in Barcelona. Piero di Bartolomeo and Messer Cipriano's son Giovanni could choose their place of exile, provided that they remained one hundred miles from Florence and sixty miles from one another. Although the confines of Alberto and Nerozzo were later changed to include all of Flanders, with five days allowed for embarcation from Genoa, the general disenfranchisement of all but one branch of the family remained in force.[79] Other variations followed yet another alleged plot in 1401, when a sentence to twenty years' exile beyond one hundred miles from Florence was decreed for Alberti males over the age of sixteen. The final blow came in 1412. Warned by an informer of Alberti intrigues with the Strozzi and other exiles in Bologna, a *balìa* declared seven members of the family rebels between 21 and 30 July 1412. Their property was to be confiscated and their *loggia* pulled down; their remaining relatives were ordered to leave town. Ties of marriage or business between the Alberti and people in Florence were forbidden, and bounty hunters were to be rewarded for hunting and killing any Alberti exiles found at large within two hundred miles of the city.[80]

The Alberti case was an ugly affair, but it was not the crude vendetta it has often been taken to be. To the contrary, it was a classic case of "political justice" in Renaissance style. The gradual escalation of the penalty of exile came about at the bidding of a quasi-executive institution. Sentences for rebellion which the early Trecento court of Messer Cante Gabrieli had enacted within a few weeks were produced at the instigation of emergency commissions only after a number of years and, ostensibly at least, a number of provocations. Degrees of exile intervened, each with its precisely defined requirements. If this procedure was calculating and supple in its options, it was also direct and, in the end, devastating. The commands of the *balìa* thrust aside the fiction of judicial independence in the courts. While the White Guelph defendants of 1302 were never in the power of the prosecution, the Alberti, for the most part, turned contumacious only after their initial obedience, and while the effect of Messer Cante Gabrieli's sentences was to mass an enemy force against the city, the proceedings against the Alberti attempted, not altogether unsuccessfully, to disperse the domestic enemy. In 1449 Francesco di Bivigliano degli Alberti drew up a necrology of the men of his family who had died since 1400. From London to Bruges, Paris, Montpellier, and Avignon, from Genoa to Friuli, from Brescia to Ancona and beyond to the island of Rhodes he counted forty-seven Alberti dead in twenty-four places abroad.[81]

Few variations on confinement were tried, or needed, after the Alberti case. As usual, the Medici regime took the practice as the Medici had found and experienced it. Under terms much like those of the second Alberti exile, eight members of the Medici family were themselves confined in 1433 to Ancona, Rimini, Fano, Rome, Venice, and Padua. The stipulation that bonds be posted—Cosimo's was set at an enormous 20,000 florins—was the most substantial, if not at all unprecedented, difference in form, and it was to be used by the Miceans when their turn at exiling came in 1434.[82] The Micean *balìa* and the Eight on Internal Security drew on the full repertory of familiar possibilities to confine ninety-three citizens between October and November 1434. Distances were either loosely set—"outside the walls" or "in that place that will be elected by him"—or places of exile were exactly indicated, from Udine to Palermo. Various deadlines were set for departure from Florence, arrival in confinement, and verification of observance; sentences ranged from one year to ten years, bonds from 500 to 10,000 florins. The penalty of death and confiscation was set in case of disobedience and, in 1435, was actually declared against more than twenty-five individuals.[83] The renewal of these sentences in 1444 and 1458 and the new wave of expulsions after a would-be oligarchical coup in 1466 were repeat performances so far as their procedures were concerned.[84]

These procedures, modular and routine, called for forms of record keeping quite different from the records of exile in Dante's time. There is no notorious name for the very ordinary register in which the notaries of the Eight took note of sentences of confinement or rebellion from 1434 to 1468.[85] It could easily have been misplaced (as the missing volume for the succeeding years may have been) among similar registers of bureaucratic business by some distracted official. No one could have lost the cumbersome, brass-and-iron studded *Libro del Chiodo* in which the sentences against the White Guelphs of the early Trecento had been transcribed—though it might have been tempting to deface it. The *Chiodo* was the property of the Guelph party, its enemies list, and in its own right a physically formidable monument of an independence which had checked any abstract assertion of public authority. The register of the Eight, defining public processes from the beginning, opens with a calendar of legislation from 1434 to 1466 which delegated official responsibilities to the Eight in paragraphs of written rules. Legal Latin gives way to the vernacular in the sentences that follow. Formulas meant to embody majesty in the person of a magistrate have disappeared, for, by 1434, the Eight could not only initiate proceedings but, with its "bulletins," also indicate the sentence to be imposed. Gone are the ritual review of inquisition and charges, the jargon of moments and conditions of sentencing, the formal attestation of witnesses, judges, and notaries. Instead, the monotonous single lines of compressed entries, two or three to a page, suffice to specify a place of confinement, deadlines, fines and other payments due, the names of bondsmen, verifications received, and sentences of rebellion issued against those who failed to comply.

Three successive registers of "incorporations" of rebel properties in Florence and its territories were kept by the notaries of the Officials of the Tower from 1365 to 1509.[86] Noting the wasteful inefficiency of scattering communal jurisdiction among separate offices, a legislative provision of May 1364 established this magistracy as a central clearinghouse for the rights of the fisc over gabelles, mills, ports and ships, streets, bridges, and walls—and the goods of rebels.[87] The notaries of the first register of incorporations wrote the centralizing intent and bureaucratic apparatus of the provision into the administrative record. They collated lists of rebel property dating back to 1343, correcting, updating, and even cross-referencing them. They also indicated, in bureaucratic verbs, how property had been inscribed on the public rolls, estimated in terms of rental value (units of grain in the countryside, money rents in town), rented (by force to the country communities where willing tenants were lacking), sold, assigned to the maintenance of rebel wives in consideration of their dowries, assessed for the forced loans to the commune which had been exacted regularly from holders of rebel property since the 1330s, or canceled from the books as a result of payment of fines or pardon.

Once set in motion, this recording mechanism ran on through changes in personnel, through wars, rebellion, and new regimes. The second volume was opened in 1376. The still active accounts from the first register were carried over to it and new entries were added in chronological order until 1431. Then the transfer was repeated for the third volume, where the record continued alphabetically until 1509. By the time of the second register, blanket condemnations of entire families—*De Migliorellis, De Agolantibus, De Gherardinis, De Circulis, De Ubertis*—were holdovers from a past when the commune had fought whole clans and companies in exile. The confiscations of Alberti property were recorded under the names of individual members of the family, not en masse.[88] This discriminating precision increased in other respects as the record advanced in time. Beginning in 1391, entries were regularly made after the rebel's name rather than according to the location of confiscated properties, and rebel goods were more carefully described. The third register includes an index in red letters and, by order of the Officials of the Tower, was written in the vernacular so that it might be plain to read. This volume carried the search for the assets of rebels into the tax records and inventoried their personal possessions down to the smallest detail—Antonio di Ghino's farm tools; the sixteen horses, weapons worth 245 florins, and six pawned silver cups of Forza da Ripomerrancio of Volterra; Gregorio Marsuppini's slave girl; a piece of marble sculpture Angelo Neroni had owned; account books of the Lamberteschi and the Neroni; widow Caterina's linens.[89] Notations of the cause, source, degree, and date of sentencing focused the record in still sharper detail after 1431. These were technical adjustments and refinements on official routine. It is easy to imagine the notary of the latest entries, warming the same bench as Ser Jacopo Ambrogio, who had begun them.

Statistical analysis is possible where good bureaucrats have been at work. Table 1 shows the number of entries of incorporations of rebel

TABLE 1

Incorporations of Rebel Property in Florence, 1365–1509

	1365–1376	1375–1431	1431–1509
Property of Individuals	386	311	169
	(74%)	(75.4%)	(70.7%)
Family Property	134	99	61
	(25.5%)	(24%)	(25.5%)
Communal Property	4	2	2
Uncertain	1	3	7
Total Incorporations	525	412	239

Source: Archivio di Stato, Florence, *Capitani di Parte* (numeri rossi), 51 (1365–1376), 50 (1375–1431), 65 (1431–1509).

property from 1365 to 1509. The totals are given by type of entry for single individuals, for more than one member of a single family, and for rural communes sentenced to incorporation or in which a group of individuals was sentenced collectively. The first series of figures suggests a direction of change. The decline in the number of entries is absolute: there are 525 entries for the first twenty years of the record and 239 entries for the last seventy-eight years. Although this decline may reflect differences in the style of record keeping or may conceal changes, even increases, in the value of incorporations, the simplest explanation seems the most probable. Fewer entries should mean fewer rebels, either because the Florentines resorted less frequently to confiscatory sentences of rebellion or because Florentine politics and society were progressively more settled. Both reasons are probably valid, and both suggest a kind of procedural restraint which the relatively steady percentage of "family" incorporations also seems to confirm. One would expect a different statistical profile for an earlier period—perhaps a greater number of wholesale incorporations to reflect the recourse of a relatively weak state to tactics of massive retaliation, perhaps a larger percentage of "family" sentences to register a higher incidence of collective action and the vendetta.[90] But then, one would not have such full and official figures at all from a world so riven by centrifugal forces and episodes of raw violence.

Table 2 summarizes the data on the disposition of rebel property in the

TABLE 2

Disposition of Rebel Property in Florence, 1365–1509

	1365–1376	1375–1431	1431–1509
Sales	172	108	48
Cancellations	37	32	27

Source: Archivio di Stato, Florence, *Capitani di Parte* (numeri rossi), 51 (1365–1376), 50 (1375–1431), 65 (1431–1509).

three registers. One of the most striking patterns here, the steady rise in the number of incorporations canceled, from less than 10 percent for the period 1365–1376 to more than 50 percent for 1431–1509, seems consistent with the general direction of change indicated by Table 1. A judicial system, and a society, less likely to impose drastic penalties of exclusion should be, after all, more likely to facilitate the reentry of those against whom such penalties had been imposed. A further corollary may be that rebels themselves were increasingly willing to take advantage of procedures for remission, to signal their obedience and pay for their reincorporation into the community. Indirect ties between rebels and their families at home often met with official approval in any case. Between 1375 and 1431 the Officials of the Tower recognized the claims of ninety wives of rebels to their dowries; between 1431 and 1509 they allowed thirty-seven claims. Either property which had been confiscated was returned or the amount of dowry portions was paid from the proceeds of confiscated property which had been sold; in the case of rental property, money payments were made in proportion to the share of the dowry involved. Sometimes the goods of rebel brothers, husbands, or sons were "recommended" to the keeping of their wives. Conceding still further, the tower officials also "recommended" rebel belongings to thirty-one male relations over the period of the record. With somewhat less regularity—in nineteen and eight cases for 1375–1431 and 1431–1509, respectively—families were permitted to buy the property of their rebels or paid fines to keep a family patrimony intact. It seems fitting that the guardian and beneficiary of corporate conformity and extended responsibility, the Guelph party, dropped from the record as early as 1401. In its last appearance the party had been reduced to buying rebel property like any other citizen.[91]

While the tower officials of Florence were tending their registers, lawyers and notaries in Florence and elsewhere were reinforcing the theoretical foundations and codifying the procedural routines of Renaissance rules for exile. The legitimacy of any particular regime could be called into question so long as a determined opposition could claim legal sanction beyond the jurisdiction of the city-state. The first task of the theorists, then, was to seal off the old routes of appeal to higher authority. Privileges, exemptions, and immunities asserted by families, factions, and corporate institutions within the state or in exile were a second major challenge for the theorists. The memory of whole companies of *fuorusciti*, with their own seals, banners, assemblies, and officials, was still fresh, and the conception of city-state sovereignty was incompatible with even the more limited opportunities of Renaissance exiles for well-organized and principled resistance. Many people and many aspects of life had successfully evaded the tutelage of civic statutes during the communal age; Renaissance specialists on the law set about remedying what seemed to them glaring defects in the arsenal of political power.

To defend the sovereignty of the city-state the lawyers could refine doctrines which had been advanced by the early fourteenth century.[92] In the 1340s Bartolus had already reasoned that "cities recognizing no superior" were their own legitimate masters, with good claims to the sovereign prerogatives of the people and the prince in Roman law. Later writers were as quick to take this position as they were to neglect the reservation admitted by Bartolus that, de jure at least, many Italian cities still recognized the formal superiority of the emperor or the pope. A more direct approach was to argue from the *fact* that cities made statutes binding upon their citizens and subjects to the *principle* that they had acquired sovereignty by virtue of custom and tradition. The exercise of sovereignty established the right to exercise it. The law, in another axiom propounded by Bartolus and elaborated by his successors, had to conform to the facts of the actual situation; the actual situation was that many cities in Italy had been wielding sovereign powers for a very long time. The emperor and the pope were thus left without secure legal defenses, and so were the citizens and subjects of the city-state. By 1455 the brothers of the Florentine rebel Giorgio Davanzati could not have expected satisfaction for their complaint that the government of Florence had "confound[ed] in itself every prior and posterior right" by confiscating Giorgio's property despite their own "better and more solid" rights to it. Messer Domenico Martelli, in a legal brief for the tower officials of Florence, hardly deigned to reply at length. It was enough for him to turn what was meant as an accusation into a statement of the regime's proper prerogative.[93]

Although magistrates such as the tower officials took advantage of academic pronouncements on the law, they were busy men with practical duties to perform and self-esteem to protect. What they needed were not scholastic disputations but manuals of approved formulas and authoritative arguments which could put the finish of legal respectability on their proceedings. "[D]isputation about names is to be left to the obstinate," declared the lawyer and diplomat Nello da San Gimignano in his treatise *De bannitis* (1424).[94] So much for the traditional speculation on the origins of the communal ban. Where legal opinion had strained after analogies between communal *banniti* and the *relegati*, the *deportati*, and the *hostes et transfugae* of Roman law or the *excommunicati* of the canonists, Nello was perfunctory: "since this discussion is of little consequence, I will not insist on it further."[95] Where Jacopo d'Arena, at the end of the thirteenth century, had addressed fifty questions *de bannitis* in the earliest treatise on the subject, Nello dealt with more than three hundred because he wanted to consider every eventuality that the working magistrate might encounter. Where earlier writers had proceeded more or less at random, Nello divided his work into three parts so as to give systematic treatment to the legal status of the *bannitus* before, during, and after the formal declaration of the ban. Nello examined virtually every technical requirement, each in its logical place, "so that I and others who deal with what occurs may more easily find whatever is necessary."[96] The layman could not be expected to share Nello's confidence. In 1464, after seeing the legal documents on her son's case, the mother of an exile could only report: "there is so much writing that I can't give . . . news of it for now."[97]

A pocketsize handbook on judicial procedure first published in 1497 is the perfect artifact of the bureaucratic spirit.[98] The one-hundred-odd pages of *Il birraccino*, Ser Raffaello de' Cerchi announces in the preface to his little book, contains everything judges, notaries, and all other officials with criminal jurisdiction need to know. "Note these things," Ser Raffaello advises, "and you will appear expert and able . . . and will be honored."[99] *Il birraccino* begins with formulas for use in ordinary registers of criminal cases—introductory formulas; formulas for delegating responsibility to collateral judges; formulas for general proclamations issued at the beginning of terms of office against blasphemy, curfew breaking, bearing arms, gambling, raids on convents, receiving fugitives, rebellion and banditry, adulterated weights and measures, black marketeering, official malfeasance, and bribery. Next comes protocol for books of inquisition and accusation on thirty-seven kinds of crime, complete with simulated dialogue and a check list of inquisitorial procedures for citation, notification, declaration, and registration of criminal bans. In the last stage of the judicial routine sentences of condemnation should be inscribed in a separate register. Ser Raffaello gives concise directions and offers examples of model sentences. Among bland decrees ordering maiming and mutilation or confiscation and whipping, he inserts, without comment, the standard formula for sentences relegating convicted offenders to exile.[100] No comment was apparently necessary. (See Figure 11.)

Even so, procedures which were finely tuned called for a correspondingly careful articulation of different degrees of exile. The criminal ban deserved especially close scrutiny not only because it was a standby of the courts and a subject of generations of legal speculation but also because the ban raised fundamental questions about the effective power of the magistrate. Declaring the ban in the absence of the alleged malefactor amounted to admitting that he could not be brought to justice in any other manner. Whereas earlier writers had searched for ways around, and in the process had obscured, this embarrassing admission, Nello da San Gimignano treated *bannitus* status accurately at last as a function of communal procedures against contumacy. On the other hand, Nello was reluctant to concede that the state could lose its hold over any of its subjects, even over those who were in exile. Taking issue with the earlier consensus of the lawyers that the ban entailed loss of citizenship, he argued that the *bannitus* was still bound by the laws of his city wherever he might go. It followed that the criminal ban could be looked upon with some plausibility as the "punishment by exile" that, de jure, it had never properly been.[101]

Further steps were taken in the late fifteenth and the sixteenth centuries to strengthen the hand of the magistrate. Influential lawyers such as Paolo di Castro and Filippo Decio extended his jurisdiction over vigilante justice carried out against *banniti* unfortunate enough to fall into the hands of bounty hunters or vindictive enemies. They prescribed severe punishments for wounding or killing anyone who had not been placed under ban according to the letter of the law; to be certain about the validity of a condemnation, one presumably consulted with the presiding officials. In what became the prevailing view Messer Paolo went on to grant a right of appeal to the *bannitus*, even though the statutes of his city, with the concurrence of earlier legal opinion, equated his contumacy with a full confession of guilt for the crime with which he had been charged. This was a concession of sorts, but it was not an unqualified concession. For if the possibility of appeal afforded protection to the *bannitus*, it also reinforced the position of the authorities, who could bargain for his submission to the court.[102]

In another gain for the magistrate the figure of the exile held and punished by the state came into focus in his own right. Confinement to exile had not been discussed systematically as a form of punishment in the thirteenth and fourteenth centuries; relegation and deportation in Roman law had been academic terms by and large, much discussed but beyond the ordinary means of communal government. In the fifteenth century, however, the Roman terms *relegatio* and *relegatus* appeared in judicial sentences because something like Roman practice had reappeared.[103] Sixteenth-century codifiers of legal experience acknowledged, classified, and subdivided the penalty of exile as a matter of course. According to Giulio Chiaro's practical handbook on judicial sentences, "exile [*exilii poena*] is indeed a penalty much in use among us, not simply against those guilty of contumacy, . . . but also as the penalty for crimes. Sometimes perpetual exile is imposed, sometimes it is for a set term, and sometimes according to the pleasure of the court, as we see every day. . . ."[104]

Arguments among historians over whether the law turned retrograde or relatively enlightened in the Renaissance miss the point of these developments. The lawyers did make qualifications and distinctions; they could also afford them, and not because of some liberal humanitarian concern. The cobeneficiary of qualifications and distinctions was, after all, the magistrate whose prerogative it was to apply them. And while lawyers were careful over procedures and degrees of exile, they were busy transferring the overpowering claims of Roman law against crimes of lese majesty to the state. Liberty, the speakers agreed in Bartolomeo Scala's dialogue *On Laws and Legal Judgments*, was "for the sovereign magistrate, not for the people."[105] These refinements, these powers of the magistrate over those he punished, stood an age apart from the court of Messer Cante Gabrieli of Gubbio.

Coda: Crisis and Confirmation After 1494

Fifty years after the formation of the Italic League diplomatic agents and ambassadors might once again have expected to meet bands of exiles in Italy and abroad. Tested by the foreign invasions beginning in 1494, the closed balance of power, the politics of internal pacification, and the administrative machinery of the Italian states failed either to keep out the foreigner or to withstand the pressures of internal opposition. In the twilight of Italian independence, conditions and styles of action reminiscent of earlier days sprang back into place to rival the terms of the fifteenth-century settlement. Old themes of Italian history were replayed over the short span of two generations—but only, in the end, to reconfirm the claims of the Renaissance state.

From 1494 to the Treaty of Cateau-Cambrésis in 1559 the sense of déjà vu in Italy is striking, at least as striking as the new beginnings contemporaries and later historians were to insist on finding there.[106] Advisers around the Habsburg emperor and king of Spain Charles V often thought of Christendom in thirteenth-century terms. Early in his reign Charles himself defined his mission in Italy and elsewhere in a haze of medieval aspirations toward universal rule. The new political, military, and fiscal capabilities of the French monarchy did not exclude the atavistic vision of a crusade against the Turks, a campaign over half-forgotten dynastic claims in Italy, and the old-fashioned imperatives of chivalric honor and the *beau geste*. In the presence of powerful foreign intervention the popes also revived old traditions. The propaganda of papal universalism which they clothed in Renaissance art and oratory had medieval roots, and the expansion of their power in the papal states was the fulfillment of a long-standing goal.[107]

With the reappearance of foreign invaders, the particularisms and fissures of the Italian environment broke through the veneer of the Quattrocento. The expulsion of Piero de' Medici from Florence and of the Aragonese from Naples in 1494 was only the first sign of a reversion to once-familiar patterns. To archaic slogans and battle cries, political factions chose sides, sought outside allies, and called for the removal of the opposing party.[108] Major and minor states were won or lost with the passage of a foreign army, a shift in alliances, or the moves of a coalition centered on or against the imperialists or the French. The quick tides of these political changes carried new waves of exiles to and from their homes. The most formidable of them, the anti-Medicean exiles from Florence, with their close ties to France, were a disruptive force for decades. Even after the republican opposition was overwhelmed by Cosimo de' Medici at Montemurlo in 1537, the "other Florence" joined *fuorusciti* from Siena, Naples, and Genoa for the last stand of an "external commune" at Montalcino in 1555.[109]

Yet the regression was not complete. The thrust of Renaissance statecraft survived Italy's loss of independence. Magistrates continued to refine the calculated and discriminating procedures of the Renaissance political style. *Fuorusciti* were watched by professional bureaucrats, diplomats, and spies, and treaties of mutual protection were concluded among territorial states against them.[110] The most celebrated exiles came to a bad end. Ludovico Sforza of Milan died composing rhymes on the vagaries of fortune in a French prison. Captured at Montemurlo in 1537, Filippo Strozzi was never to leave a Florentine dungeon alive. Lorenzino de' Medici, the "new Brutus" who assassinated his cousin Duke Alessandro of Florence in 1537, was the victim in turn of a Medicean assassin in 1548. In losing their independence under Spanish domination, the client-states of Italy actually gained allies for the containment and repression of opposition and dissent.[111]

When the *fuorusciti* of Lucca and Florence presented their grievances to Charles V in the mid-1530s, they were met by the well-rehearsed arguments of Italy's Renaissance experience.[112] The exiles claimed that justice was on their side, that they had been expelled in defiance of the emperor's promises of conciliation and compromise. In case after case they documented what they took to be the tyranny and injustice of their enemies at home. But who were these troublemakers to question "prudent and expert men," "the best and most qualified citizens"? asked the representatives of the duke of Florence. Exile was richly deserved by those who sought to disturb the imperial "quiet and security" of Italy. The authorities had done their duty "out of necessity and according to the laws . . . which had adopted similar forms of relegation many times in the past and under various governments." After hearing both sides, the emperor limited his arbitration to proposing reduced sentences for exiles who had not openly resisted and were willing to pledge submission. The Florentine exiles protested that they were being asked "to return in terms of servitude to that city they had defended as free men."[113] In such dark moments of recognition the victory of the Renaissance state must have seemed complete.

5

The Voices of Exile in
Medieval and Renaissance Italy

Exiles keep—or find—a voice through all their losses. Language may become a surrogate country for them; in words, they resist or rationalize or resign themselves to their condition. Where voices of (or about) exile have survived in the literature of medieval and Renaissance Italy, they have a dual origin and a double identity. They are more and less than merely documentary because they are amplified by literary conventions and channeled into literary forms; they also register the particular needs and the preferred modes of expression of those who deploy them over time. The result is a chorus of commentary, at once perennial and time-bound, on the facts and rules of exile exposed in the preceding chapters.

Exiles Without Consolation

> my lamenting voice is my future
> Ovid, *De Tristitia* IV, 24
> your cry will do as the wind
> Dante, *Paradiso*, XVII, 133

The muse of poetry was especially generous to her devotees in exile during the thirteenth and early fourteenth centuries.[1] Her inspiration was both timeless and cued to precedents such as Ovid's verse from Tomis or the lamentations of the Old Testament. It was also timely because there was room in medieval Italy for poetic as well as political campaigns from exile. The literary and the political campaigns were usually collective affairs. To speak out in exile was to voice shared concerns and causes, to bear the hurt, the longing, and the loss one's companions bore, to assert claims of justice, principle, or power against what were seen as the false claims of the enemy within the walls at home. In poetry, Latin and vernacular, exile-authors found the expressive force, the authority, and the resonance to represent displaced energies and aspirations. Their verse was a powerful witness and weapon, and it still conveys something of the original range and intensity of their voices.

A long narrative poem from Bologna tells how the Ghibelline faction of the Lambertazzi set out from home in the spring of 1274. They had lost the battle in the streets against their Guelph rivals, the Geremei. The anonymous poet picks up the sounds of a loud debate on the losing side. Messer Soldano and Messer Lambertino must shout to be heard—"A little peace now!" "Now listen to me without interrupting!" The two leaders of the Ghibellines call for a quick retreat. An angry protest—"Seems like a bad idea to me!"—from Magarotto de' Magarotti breaks in. He would have stood his ground but for the sobering words of one last speaker. "There's nothing more to say here," says Messer Righetto da Baexe, "except [that we must] save our skins as best we can." At this the crowd grows quiet, as the verse does, and without further talk the Lambertazzi abandon Bologna, *dolorosamente*.[2]

Once they had departed, exile-authors searched through real and figurative landscapes to find their bearings. The paths through alien territory seemed long and hard to follow:

> Provenzano, tell me true
> what will the exiles do?
>
> . . . .
>
> Ruggieri, truth to say,
> seems to me they've lost their way.[3]

This snatch of dialogue was written at Siena around 1261. A century or more later Antonio da Ferrara was still wandering in exile, "without striking any port / to put an end to my long suffering."[4]

At nearly every turn there were stretches of material and moral wilderness to contend with. In 1260 Brunetto Latini heard that his party had been driven from Florence and went astray in a dense forest, the forerunner of the *selva oscura*, the "dark wood" where the pilgrimage of the

Divine Comedy would begin.[5] Cecco Nuccoli, rusticating in exile outside Perugia, complains that he can only listen to frogs and toads croaking and watch lizards running on the rocks. The country is hostile and the fare bitter for the Lucchese exile Ser Pietro Faitinelli.[6] Experience and allegory were practically inseparable in this mapping of physical estrangement and spiritual desolation. Exile-poets knew the backcountry and the borderlands of the Italian peninsula; they also magnified and moralized their experience in keeping with long-standing literary traditions. The interplay between circumstance and convention is especially clear in the poetry of Giovanni Quirini. Although he may have been describing the actual setting of his own exile from Venice after 1310, he obviously imitated Ovid to do so in lines such as these:

> I am with barbarians now, cruel folk
> who live lawless by thieving
> and graze mountains white, freezing,
> feeling again and again the frosty cloak.[7]

Authentic or not, the harshness of the exile-poet's world *seemed* forbidding in proportion to the brilliance of the scenes he imagined at home. Like the prophets of the Old Testament or Ovid at Tomis, Cecco Angiolieri and Ser Pietro Faitinelli see in vivid detail the days of homecoming they long for. Cecco swears that a gouge in the eye would hurt like milk and honey, that he would feel like a dove and consider all the pains of purgatory pure gold, if only he were called back to Siena.[8] In his mind's eye, Ser Pietro returns to Lucca in time for ripe pears, his heart bursting, like them, with tears and joy. He licks the walls—candy-colored pink, green, and cream, one imagines, like towns in fourteenth-century paintings. On that glorious day he puts aside any thought of revenge and embraces those who had driven him away.[9] Pieraccio Tedaldi uses the same formula—"If I see the day"—to portray his return to Florence, "to the delightful space / of the noble city joyous and great." The "inflamed imagination" of Fazio degli Uberti pictures scenes of home that he, born in exile from Florence, had probably never seen.[10] The force and the anguish of these visions depends on an illusion of possession made palpably real and compelling.

Since families, factions, and whole companies of exiles actually possessed refuges abroad, their poets exploited tactical variations on the differences between home and exile. *O dolce terra aretina*, begins Guittone d'Arezzo in a poem from the 1250s. One expects yet another forlorn reminiscence. But Guittone goes on to project his "weeping and sorrow" into (and against) Arezzo: nothing is left there of the old pleasures and virtues, and it would be madness to return to the scene of so much evil.[11] Guittone drives his point home in another poem—*Gente noiosa e villana.* In Arezzo good people are poor, vile scum well off; envy, hate, and money have taken friendship's place. Instead of reason and good manners, instead of solace and diversion, there are falsity and wrong in Arezzo now, and the fox-bark of bad masters drowns out decent conversation. Such things, Guittone exclaims from his refuge in Bologna,

> make me, alas, hate my hometown
> and love this other I have found.[12]

Later poets devised an elaborate symbolism in order to gain ground on their enemies. In one of his greatest *rime* Dante meets three lady-symbols of Justice in exile and welcomes them to the throne of Love in his heart. "Don't my eyes make you feel sorry?" asks one of the dismayed and battered beauties. The obvious deduction lies somewhere between calculation and conviction: there will be no justice and no love in Florence until the poet returns. Only the last lines of *Tre donne* hint that pardon might be the Florentines' and not Dante's to give.[13] An allegorical Lady Florence in exile recites a lament written for her by Fazio degli Uberti. She can hardly remember the time when the river Arno and the flowering fields along its banks had been fair; nothing but weeds grow where her city should stand. In these dark days, she cries,

> Widows and orphans and innocents
> of my best blood roam
>   for their bread
> in some stranger's home,
>   with great shame and mortal dread.[14]

A grieving Lady Rome whom Bindo di Cione encounters on the roads of exile has a similar tale to tell. In the company of virtuous Romans she wanders abroad, for the hostile legions of Pride, Envy, and Avarice have expelled all true friends of virtue from the city.[15]

By the 1340s the Florentine *fuoruscito* Matteo Frescobaldi can compress these motifs into a single refrain: Avarice, Pride, and Luxury have *exiled* Prudence, Fortitude, Justice, Temperance, and their sisters.[16] So be it. Let Florence lie abandoned and desolate. In the world of Matteo's poetic reveries on life in exile, spring is greening to sounds of birdsong and shepherd's tunes.[17] From this idyllic setting it seems but a short distance back to the pastoral terrain of exiles in Virgil's *Eclogues*—or forward to Shakespeare's forest of Arden, where outlaws find "tongues in trees, books in the running brooks, / sermons in stones and good in everything." The outcast discovers sweet "uses of adversity"; the truly "wild folk" are those caged like dangerous animals within the walls at home.[18]

The boundary between home and exile remains intact in all these journeys through space and sensibility. It is defined by city walls and territorial frontiers which were closed to exiles. It follows the contours of political, social, or legal distinctions between "us" and "them" and runs deep to perceived contrasts between "center" and "periphery" which an ancient literature of exile had explored. In verse the exile-poet can return to old haunts he cannot enter in fact. Or he can deny that anything of value survives in his homeland and, through poetry, imagine that whatever is good and true lies before him in the lands of exile. In either case he is free to vent his feelings, high or low, and demand that his voice be heard.

By the early fourteenth century Niccolò Quirini expects no one to wonder at his "mourner's guise" in exile from Venice. It is the exile's lot to be "consumed," as the Florentine Sennuccio del Bene says of himself, in "sighs and lamentation" (*sospiri e pianto*).[19] Exiles already "cry like lambs" in the Bolognese poem on the Lambertazzi and the Geremei; they squeal like stuck pigs in the cruel verses of Brizio Visconti, an outcast from Milan after 1349.[20] The famous prophecy of Dante's own exile in the *Divine Comedy* sounds like chant or dirge—"Tu lascerai," "Tu proverai"; "quello strale," "sa di sale"; "duro calle," "per l'altrui scale."[21] Ser Pietro Faitinelli was a refugee from Lucca for fifteen years after 1315, and he too chants mourning refrains:

> Whence are pleasure and solace to come to me?
> Whence are jests to come to me with a smile?
> Whence, if not tortures of every style?
> Whence is anything but madness to come to me?[22]

The answers were seldom good enough for exiles in the thirteenth and early fourteenth centuries. As their sorrowful voices crack and come apart in anger, they change from connoisseurs of sadness into masters of malediction. Dante and Ser Pietro let their jeering taunts fly with a sure sense of target—proud Florence, home of a mongrel race mixed with the bad blood of backwaters beyond Galluzzo and Trespiano; fair Lucca, ruled by upstart artisans and country bumpkins of the likes of Nello, his mouth hanging open like a carp's.[23] This name-calling was one of the few obvious pleasures of exile. But sometimes it was also a self-flagellation of rage and (one supposes) of release. Simone Serdini—"having been, on account of faction, hunted out of Siena," according to a note in one of his manuscripts—wrote more than one hundred lines of verse which cry out self-contempt in a tradition going back to Ecclesiastes and the Book of Job:

> O curse of God with which I was born,
> cursed be the day that brought me here,
> a figure monstrous and strange!

Simone relishes the tortures he can invent for himself—his body dismembered, his limbs twisted, his heart fed to dogs. The frenzy of annihilation will cease only when he has taken all creation and its creator down with him:

> Cursed be the light, the splendor
> that to my eyes first rushed;
> would that whoever be their Maker
> were caught in these teeth and crushed.[24]

At these extremes of anger exile-poets become censors and prophets of retribution. Dante foretells terrible punishments for Florence. Niccolò Quirini, with far less force of character or language, predicts a "bitter and harsh sentence" against the pride of Venice.[25] The terrorist's *Schadenfreude* is Fazio degli Uberti's revenge in a poem addressed in 1336 to the Florentine ambassador at the court of Mastino della Scala. Fazio's opening lines make a mockery of politeness: how wise the ambassador is, a learned lawyer; how cunning, with his weapons concealed beneath his cloak and a fat purse to buy off enemies, just like a Florentine. Then the tone shifts in anticipation of apocalyptic changes the poet sees in store. For the Florentines have hurt too many; their victims are gathering even now to take vengeance. No worldly power can stay the wrath that must fall on Florence. Soon the black bird and the ladder of the Della Scala will appear at the head of an avenging host; soon gold in flames will be seen. All will burn soon in Florence as in the nightmare beauty of Fazio's image of destruction:

> You will see flame flare,
> tower upon tower seizing,
> and you will see looting and seizing
> and blood running in every pretty street
> and people fleeing through the street
> and fathers abandoning children and ground,
> dead, lying dead, on the ground.[26]

Hatred so all-consuming could not last—in part because exiles could not have hated so well what they did not also love and long for. Sooner or later the anger of exile-poets subsides, and when it does, love rallies and underwrites their verse. The voices of the lover and of the exile had been practically indistinguishable long before thirteenth-century poets, whether remembering the Old Testament and Ovid or not, renewed an old set of associations. In one Dugento variation on old themes, unrequited love becomes a kind of "banishment"; in another variation exile is the bitter fruit of love wasted on the hard hearts at home. In a whole genre of *poesia di lontananza*, to be distant from a loved one is to be homeless; to love or be loved is to come home again.[27] The greatest of Italian exile-poets brings several of these motifs together at the beginning of the fourteenth century. In at least three of the lyric poems which Dante seems to have composed in exile it is impossible to tell whether the object of the poet's longing is a lady or whether "she" is Florence.[28]

Not that exile-lovers were satisfied by purely poetic *patrias* or high-minded allegories of love. Carnino Ghiberti protests that his all too human passions are weighing him down like ripe fruit on the limb of a tree; he cannot settle for less than returning to his beloved "really, in the flesh."[29] Carnino was writing as a Florentine émigré during the 1260s. Fifty years later Sennuccio del Bene weeps for the White Guelph cause, and still more for the sultry lady—*donna di valenza*—whom he, cast out of Florence with the White Guelphs, has left behind. It is for the loss of his lady that he will never be consoled. Nature will never surpass the virtue in her beauty; of any beauty in her virtue Sennuccio has nothing to say. Still earthier and more irreverent, Cecco Nuccoli plots his exile-lover's return to Perugia as an erotic escapade with a berry-eyed whore sure to cost him plenty.[30] Even Dante, in an otherwise rather staid exchange of poems with his fellow exile Cino da Pistoia, confesses that talk of reason is like whistling in the wind where love is concerned. Dante's three lady-exiles in *Tre donne* may be symbols of justice, but he makes Love look hard at the bodies beneath their torn skirts when they appear before Love's throne in his heart.[31]

The exile-poet, then, claims to know the full force of love. From spiritual exaltation to lust, from tenderness to fierce obsession, his love ranges over great heights and depths of feeling. To him the passions of his enemies at home must seem by comparison complacent and amateur. But the exile-poet also calls the justice of his enemies into question precisely because, as Dante insists, it is unaccompanied by love. The justice of the "other side" can always be discredited as rigid and unfeeling in conflicts between groups sure of their own righteousness. In this *guerriglia* over principle, the exiles of medieval Italy were formidable opponents, all the more so because they often had their own statutes, institutions, elected officials, and other paraphernalia of legitimacy.

Cino da Pistoia expects no convincing reply to the question he asks the faction that had driven him into exile:

> So, cruel sect, why make me
> suffer for wrongs I did not commit? [32]

Ser Domenico da Gravina is unrelenting with this same line of questioning. In 1349 he had found himself on the losing side in one of the countless quarrels over the succession to the throne of the kingdom of Naples. He had fled Gravina at dawn with his defeated party after promising his tearful family that he would return for them. One attempt at rescue had brought him so close that he could hear the voices of his enemies and watch their movements from his hiding place. Far from Gravina, joined at last by his family after a series of narrow escapes, Ser Domenico conducts an inquisition in his own terms:

> Have I committed such crimes that, despoiled of everything, houses pulled down, ejected from my own country, I might be called traitor? And supposing my "crime" deserved all that, what did my poor brother Guglielmo deserve? What wrong did our mother, did my wife, did my sister commit? And . . . Gregorio and Cola, my sons, Boliarina, my little slip of a girl, and Filippo, hardly two months old . . . why have they been made exiles with me? [33]

The guiltless exile—*exul immeritus*, as Dante calls himself in an epithet borrowed from Ovid—was such a standard figure in the literature of exile that Ser Domenico did not need to waste words defending himself.[34] Against the injustices of those who presumed to condemn them, on the other hand, exile-poets could hardly say enough. In a Latin epic on the misadventures and eventual repatriation of the Milanese exiles of the 1260s and 1270s Fra Stefanardo da Vicomercato charges the home regime with every violation of reason and justice. "O how much license dare one put into words?" he has one exile-orator exclaim. A great deal of course: religion violated, laws trampled under foot, public property put to private use, private property put to public use, fellow citizens tyrannized, high towers built, family rights ignored, the poor stripped of their meager possessions, honors and offices usurped. "For crimes cry out," the orator concludes, "murmuring sorrow breaks out, and laws violated are not silenced. . . ."[35] As self-styled "herald of justice," Dante embroiders his own charges against the Florentines with biblical phrases and precepts drawn from history or philosophy. But the complaint is a familiar one: the *scellerati intrinseci* are dazzled by cupidity, seduced by poisonous whispers, corrupted by sin, rebels to the sacred laws of justice. "O people united by wickedness alone! O people blinded by the foulest passion. . . ![36]

It had not always been so. Once upon a time, in the days of Dante's ancestor Cacciaguida, even Florence had enjoyed a "sober and chaste" peace (*Paradiso*, XV, 97–99). Other exile-poets scale the heights of an imagined past to stand in judgment over the injustices of the present. Guittone d'Arezzo is certain that the virtues of Roman ancestors and the prowess of heraldic lions are only memories in Florence and Arezzo; the Florentine Chiaro Davanzati and the Pisan Panuccio del Bagno echo this indictment as they agonize over whether to go into exile.[37] According to Messer Niccolò del Rosso of Treviso, an Iron Age of executions and exiles had descended on Italy with the Hohenstaufen emperors—but once "all [was] gold, / and Saturn reigned under the shadow of Jove."[38] This complex mixture of political strategy and poetic nostalgia gave a special turn to that anxious perception of decadence and decline which was one psychological and literary response to the rapid pace and uncertain direction of change in the thirteenth and early fourteenth centuries. By improving imaginatively on the past, exile-poets were escaping the present and identifying their hopes for the future with the image of the good old days as if the troubles of the moment had no right to exist.[39]

With high hopes, with their sense of sorrow, anger, love, and justice fully exposed, exile-poets set about finding practical means of returning home at last. They could call upon popes and emperors or their representatives to intervene in their behalf. Even in the absence of higher authorities, regional rivals to every city-state and its ruling party were likely to listen to a neighbor's exiles and to support the causes they chose to hear for their own particular ends.

Exile-poets cultivated the borrowed force of their external accomplices in a whole genre of duels in rhyme, or *tenzoni*. Alternately in and out of exile from Florence around the middle of the thirteenth century, the Guelph stalwart Monte Andrea and his Ghibelline respondents spar in verse over the merits of French or German support. The object is to show that resistance is futile against one powerful champion or another. Weapons clatter in these verbal power plays; diplomatic pawns are won or lost; the one side's lions are the other side's goats.[40] In much the same spirit Guittone d'Arezzo belittles the Ghibelline *fuorusciti* who returned to Florence after the Guelph defeat of 1260 at Montaperti:

> To you who are now in Florence, I say . . .
> since you have the Germans at home,

serve them well, and be sure to make them show
those swords that broke heads in,
    killed fathers and children.
I'm so pleased that you will owe
them so much
    (they did such hard work to get you there)
of your fair coin.[41]

But exiles needed more than brute force from their outside supporters
to justify a right to repatriation. To project their interests above self-
interest and local circumstances, they represented their protectors as
saviors embodying overwhelming and mysterious, though never quite
secret, powers. Just judge, defender of the cause, deliverer—the external
accomplice was transformed into an agent of sublime ideals and great
missions. He would be righteous, legitimate, and invincible as surely as
the enemies of exiles were unjust, illegitimate, and ever vulnerable. Even
the rough *tenzoni* of the mid-thirteenth century refer to the high principles of the Guelph or Ghibelline standard-bearer as Light of Hope, Divine Messenger, and Guardian of the Church or the Empire.[42] Like Dante,
the exiled notary Francesco da Barberino summons Emperor Henry VII
to resume the roles of Old Testament patriarch, high priest, Roman
Caesar, and philosopher-king. "Hasten, hasten to my aid, o my hope and
my consolation!" cries Ser Francesco, imitating Psalms. "Liberate me, I
implore thee, and set me by thy side!"[43] When, with Trecento realism,
exiles seek aid from the despots of Lombardy or the Romagna, they still
endow those suspect patrons with the trappings of the idealism of the
Trecento. To exile-poets at least the soaring rhetoric of high causes,
triumphant justice, and resplendent virtue does not seem out of place in
the Scaligeri of Verona or the Visconti of Milan.[44]

    The joyous homecoming that lay at the end of so many flights of feel-
ing and imagination was seen as a welcoming festival for prodigal sons and
long-lost loved ones. In the 1270s Fra Rainieri de' Granchi calls for the
return of the exiles to Pisa to as many songs of peace as there are columns
in the buildings of the city.[45] For the ceremonies that must accompany
her exiles home Fazio degli Uberti's Lady Florence issues elaborate instructions. Let them be received (or else!), she commands,

with alms and sacred sacrifices,
with psalms and holy offices,
with fasts and penance sustained,
with war and discord restrained,
with scorn for cursed vices,

with scorn for all devices
that sow bad seeds among citizens.[46]

Still more exalted visions celebrate a kind of cosmic renewal and reconciliation. Fra Stefanardo da Vicomercato makes the goddess Astraea herself return to Milan in 1277 in the unlikely company of Bishop Ottone Visconti and his fellow exiles. Her reappearance after a long absence from earth is a long-awaited sign that the Golden Age is beginning again.[47] Dante dreams of worldly redemption at the highest levels of his heavenly journey. If Florence still seems cruel, she is also the *bell'ovile*, the "fair sheepfold" to which the poet can see himself coming home, called back, the lamb at the place of his baptism and of new life (*Paradiso*, XXV, 4–6).

But when would that great day come? Already in Dante's time the exile must struggle with doubt. The failures of the imperial cause and of communal liberty were closely interwoven in the life and work of Albertino Mussato. The Paduan poet and scholar was four times an exile during the losing battle of his commune with the Della Scala and Carrara despots. He was crowned poet laureate by Henry VII but after the emperor's death was left to write a tragedy and historical accounts on the theme of the inevitable misery and ruin of great men and noble causes.[48] Had Emperor Henry not died too soon, "the exile would have returned," declares an anonymous poet, probably one of several exile-poets who despaired over the emperor's death in 1313.[49] According to Cino da Pistoia, wisdom, valor, and justice had died in one man. Too good for the evil, animal earth, the emperor has risen to heaven.[50] In the next generation Fazio degli Uberti can only inflate the slightest hopes. Writing propaganda in verse for the Italian mission of Louis of Bavaria and later, though he came to regret it, for Emperor Charles IV, Fazio launches all the ritual appeals of an old Ghibelline, or rather of the new Ghibelline whose lines sound at once stale and shrill. The result is a poetry of superannuated props—favorable auspices, great forerunners (Charlemagne and Otto the Great), prophecies of the Apocalypse, Italy in disarray, the stink of the Guelphs, Ghibelline martyrs to avenge and rebirth for the Ghibelline cause.[51]

Despite outbursts of fitful enthusiasm, signs of disillusionment appear, and in the end some of the most passionate and willful exile-poets recognize that their expectations have been misplaced. Ser Pietro Faitinelli shows his loss of temper and patience in what begins as a poem of exhortation meant to goad Robert of Naples and the Guelphs of Florence into action. Wars are not won, complains Ser Pietro, in the only way

Florentines seem to fight them—with threats and slogans but tight purses, with napping and parades to delight pretty girls and jousts in fancy helmets. Ser Pietro calls for unity; he demands readiness for war, good strategy, and abundant provisions. He discerns nothing of the kind in Florence or in Naples. In 1317 King Robert made a diplomatic and compromising peace and left his allies in exile, including Ser Pietro, to fend for themselves.[52]

What seems to be Fazio degli Uberti's last political poem (1355) takes the form of a lamentation for a lost cause. Against Emperor Charles IV he makes Lady Italy speak, citing Ovid and sorrowing over yet another time of broken promises. For one hundred years or more, she says, the popes have been false pastors. This new emperor serves for hire at papal pleasure, and even then his sword is dull. More than ever, Rome despairs. Siena and Pisa lie despoiled, and Lombardy is no better than a slave. While factions multiply endless hatreds, the imperial eagle has become, owllike, blind and predatory. Near the end of her complaints Lady Italy strains after a hopeful denouement: surely the talons of the imperial eagle can still be sharpened to open the Temple of Janus for war. But this vision flickers out with the recognition that the truth, however unwelcome, must be told.[53]

The truth was that the facts and the rules of exile were not what they had been in the thirteenth and early fourteenth centuries. With the retreat of emperors and popes from the Italian peninsula, with the consolidation of ambitious and watchful territorial states, exiles had less room and rationale for their collective hope, their defense of principle, or the high and low dramas of rebellion. While the clamorous voices of their poets wore out with overuse, their relevance to historical circumstances also came into question. Exile-poets had spoken the language of an order of corporate groups organizing, clashing with their rivals, taking allies, and claiming superior honor and justice for themselves inside city walls or on the outside. As conditions changed, as Renaissance states extended their boundaries and their claims, the old voices of exile lost their cumulative force, were dispersed, resisted, suppressed, and all but silenced.

Petrarch's Remedies

> DOLOR: I am being sent to an unjust exile!
>
> RATIO: You would rather be sent to a just one then?
>
> *F. Petrarchae de Remediis utriusque fortunae libri II* (1366), Dialogue 67

Ratio has earned the little joke in Petrarch's *On Remedies Against Good and Bad Fortune*.[54] Tiresome *Dolor* has already asked for remedies to sixty-six kinds of misfortune, and there are still sixty-five to go. The touch of wit is a winning response. It breaks sorrow's self-absorption, eases a little—eases so much, perhaps, as to conceal how much is happening in the brief dialogue that follows. Although some critics have found little more than philosophical confusion, hackwork, or old man's petulance in his book of remedies, Petrarch is never more convincingly "the father of Renaissance humanism."[55] In the small scale of his exile dialogue the nature and significance of a kind of cultural revolution come into clear relief. Representing both a new voice and the voice of *Dolor*'s old rival, *Ratio* is prepared to resume, and to win, an ancient confrontation with adversity.

There is no place for the clamorous muse of the exile-poets of medieval Italy in Petrarch's manual of cures for the soul. When *Dolor* tries to dodge the opening sally, *Ratio* amasses an army of distinctions. If exile has been decreed by a king, the sentence is either just or the king is a tyrant; if by a tyrant, the victim should rejoice over his escape; if by a corrupt people, he will be reputed incorruptible; if by his enemies, better exile than something worse; if by free choice, to flee the tyrant or the crowd, he should glory in his honest virtue on the model of Pythagoras, Solon, and Scipio. But *Dolor* insists on its miseries again. Unimpressed, *Ratio* sees the rosy side. Many exiles have returned home more illustrious and prosperous for their absence. Let *Dolor* remember the example of exiled Roman heroes—Camillus, Rutilius, Marcellus, and Cicero.

Dolor still suffers. *Ratio* blames false opinion. The wise man is, like Socrates, a citizen of the world, at home everywhere and nowhere under this sun; heaven is his true fatherland. *Dolor* has been forced into exile? No, exile is a pilgrimage, involuntary only if the pilgrim is unworthy of the free will and spirit bestowed on the best of men everywhere. Under the mere appearance of misery lies the true happiness of repose from the distractions of civic life. *Dolor* has been expelled from the fatherland? Wrong again since the exile has been cast out by the wicked, who do not deserve his company. Not exile, but a test of virtue lies ahead. If the exile sets forth undaunted and serene, the long arms of the Lord will shelter him wherever he may go.

Closely read, *Ratio*'s remedy breaks into particular references and sources, like pieces of a philological puzzle. The opening ploy probably derives from Cicero's *Tusculans*. The penultimate line—"let us go forward undaunted and serene"—probably comes from Seneca's *Consolatio ad*

Helviam.[56] Between the borrowed beginning and ending there are more or less direct allusions to ancient authorities. Some sources are openly acknowledged, meant to show because their credentials vouch for the effectiveness of the remedy. This is the case when the examples of ancient heroes are cited or when *Ratio* quotes an arsenal of authorities by name.[57] Elsewhere there are echoes, adaptations, and imitations in familiar-seeming words and phrases, among them those from the key sources of the dialogue. *Ratio* does not reveal the source of the sentence "it is a paltry soul which fastens itself onto one little angle of earth." Nor are references given for the tales of Socrates and Metellus, for the definition of exile as "pilgrimage," or for the assurances that any country where the wicked expel the good does not deserve the name of fatherland. But then, the sources of the opening and closing lines are not identified either. The fact is that *Ratio* follows the same authorities throughout—the *Tusculans* of Cicero and the *De remediis fortuitorum* or the *Consolatio ad Helviam* of Seneca.[58]

Petrarch was cribbing, as usual—but, as usual, not altogether indiscriminately or superficially. Read for overall effect, his topics and turns-of-phrase converge and connect within a general framework of style and purpose absorbed from the key sources. Cicero had dropped a few hints on exile in a summary model of the consoler's art in the *Tusculans*, where Petrarch was to find them. There, too, turning pedagogical and drawing perhaps on his lost work *De consolatione*, Cicero had surveyed the various topics of a whole literature of consolation. He pointed out that certain expressions of solace for poverty, dishonor, conquest, slavery, injury, death, and for exile were matters of convention; they had already been tried, tested, and classified by the Greeks.[59] Although Cicero was tantalizingly brief, Petrarch could see what he meant in Seneca, whose full-fledged consolations were known to him. In the preface to his own book of remedies, Petrarch says that he wishes to do for Azzo da Correggio what Seneca had done to console his friend Gallio in *De remediis fortuitorum.* He borrowed Seneca's title accordingly and imitated Seneca's form of presentation as well—the catalogue of misfortunes, the exclamations of distress, and the consoling responses. He also took Seneca's sense of the consoler's task—to apply ancient disciplines for the soul to present needs—as his own.[60]

In this way, beginning with broad clues and small fragments of an ancient genre, Petrarch gained possession of the classical art of consolation.[61] There is little trace of the medieval preference for Boethius's *Consolation of Philosophy* in his remedies for exile. Among Christian authors he limits himself to citing St. Paul and does not dwell on the Christian theme that the human condition is itself a kind of exile from the heavenly Jerusalem. Neither sage nor saint, Petrarch's *Ratio* is, if anything, a descendant of the ancient orators who had been among the earliest practitioners of the consoler's art. Like the Sophists and a long line of their classical successors, Petrarch rationalizes more than he reasons; like them, he combines dialogue and didactic discourse in order to charm and edify at the same time. Using the eclectic and pragmatic tactics of the orator, he plays both the Stoic and the Peripatetic, with no apparent scruples about philosophical contradictions. He maintains, on one side, that exile cannot be an evil since it cannot affect the spirit, the true seat of virtue, one way or another; with the other side, he acknowledges the injury of exile but encourages the victim to make do with the many resources for a good and virtuous life still at his disposal. The title *On Remedies* itself recalls the conception of healing that the Sophists originally developed from Pythagorean precedents, and their confidence in the power of speech (and their speeches) returns in Petrarch's metaphor of arming the exile with words.

The little dialogue on exile, then, is a microcosm of that revival of classical rhetorical culture which some recent historians consider the most decisive feature of Renaissance humanism.[62] It is clear enough that the philosophical patchwork, the shifts in argument, and the conversational style were technically rhetorical in the traditions of ancient oratory. But these techniques implied in turn a network of broad assumptions about the possibilities and limitations of humankind. If people could be consoled by such devices, they could hardly be regarded as fundamentally rational creatures, capable of arriving unaided at a systematic understanding of the self and the world. For the same reason, their stormy emotions and self-important assertions of principle could hardly be taken very seriously. The rhetoric of consolation presupposed an audience of vulnerable and quite gullible individuals tossed by confused perceptions and shallow feelings. It was an audience to be swayed by half-reasons, arguments from authority, and appeals to self-interest, an audience needing to be flattered, entertained, enchanted or scolded in order to be brought up to respectable standards of decorum. The "dignity of man" depended on the willingness of the consoler to condescend to discipline his client.

The consoler was prepared for his task by the general attitudes and the special skills of the complete rhetorician. Strict constructions of what could be thought true were less important to the orator than what could be effectively said; what people at bottom *were* was less important than how their feelings and behavior could be manipulated. The essence of humanity was obscured by the conflicts and contradictions of human existence. And since people were so changeable and many-sided, they could not be reached in the abstract or moved by specialists' arguments. Pure logic or metaphysics could be left to the philosophers. The orator would find all the models he needed in literature, history, and moral philosophy; the longer the models had been handed down over time, the better the reason for believing in their authority. It was just such a curriculum and just such an accumulation of lore designed for speech to all men in all seasons that the classical rhetoricians had preached and professed to practice. By identifying himself with them, Petrarch recovered their role for himself and for the humanist movement. His dialogue on exile was one of the many single points in his writing which contained the seeds of something like a whole cultural program, its parts related less by any interest in logic than by his sure instinct for the interconnections.

Once drawn into dialogue, *Dolor* hardly had a chance. *Ratio* would argue with anguish, classify it, make it manageable, demean it, kill it with kindness. Petrarch's successors turned these same tactics against exile as against other misfortunes. The unreconciled, deeply moving voices of earlier generations of exiles would have shocked them, like loud noises in libraries or unwillingness at school.

Renaissance Consolations for Exile

> I decided to defeat your sorrow, not to dupe it.
>
> Seneca, *Ad Helviam matrem* III, 4

> What would you say if I prove exile . . . is not a great evil at all?
>
> Francesco Filelfo, *Commentationes Florentinae de exilio* (after 1434), fol. 13v

Petrarch arrived at a paradigm of consolation for exile when the time was ripe for it. *Ratio* drowned out *Dolor* just as exiles were being crowded out of spaces that had sheltered their outrage, principles, and protests. The retreat of international interests from Italian affairs left them without the support of powerful allies or ideal causes from abroad. Territorial states demanding, and increasingly able to command, authority and allegiance were absorbing the old maneuvering room. Rather than outright resistance, the new situation called for acceptance and resignation. So did *Ratio*. In the name of virtue Petrarch offered troubled individuals strategies of personal poise and emotional control. He turned the exile in on himself at a time when it was increasingly difficult for him to turn out against the world. *Ratio* substituted self-interest for collective concern, rationalization for resistance, safe and measured recreations in prose for outbursts of poetry. Interior battles at least the exile could win, whether or not he knew that the magistrate and the bureaucrat shared his victories over himself.

Some of these themes had already appeared in unexpected contexts during the fourteenth century. Dante, in a Stoic mood and metaphor, had warned away unruly feelings in the image of the unmovable self— the *tetragono* (*Paradiso*, XVII, 24)—he meant to be in the face of misfortune. To the Florentine friend who urged him to accept the humiliating terms of an amnesty, he replied with Seneca rather than Ovid that the whole world is home to the wise man.[63] Ser Bartolomeo di Ser Gorello's Arezzo chronicle in verse was old-fashioned in many ways by the 1380s. But he chose to speak in the voice of a weary old Father Arezzo, tired of all factions, and not through one of those fierce allegorical ladies of the earlier Trecento. Although Ser Bartolomeo had been an exile himself, he had little sympathy for the conduct, causes, or allies of his companions. The clearest conclusion he drew from his experience was that pacification is worth any cost, including the loss of Arezzo's independence to Florence in 1384, when at last "the old wolf [Arezzo] turned tame."[64] Protest and high feeling, Pieraccio Tedaldi had already suggested to an exiled friend in the 1340s, only made matters more desperate. In an unfamiliar turn for verse Pieraccio advised patient submission:

> Since Fortune's wheel has brought you low,
> Messer Simone, keep your courage up,
> and don't be crushed or build rancor up,
> and don't say "O alas!" "O woe!"
>
> . . . .
>
> If you will face your suffering with reason,
> you will return to Florence in good season.[65]

Despite these suggestions of change, the art of consolation did not so much adapt to older forms of expression as replace them. This is understandable: the muse of Ovid, the exiles of the Old Testament, and the exile-poets of medieval Italy had inspired a long tradition of disquieting or openly subversive song that the consoler aimed to suppress. The ancients and, following them, Petrarch and the Renaissance humanists wrote (or spoke) consolations in prose. With arguments to develop and persuasions to administer, they needed forms of discourse that could be at once routine and open-ended, both regulating and responsive to the case at hand.

In Latin letter writing Petrarch and his successors recovered an ideal medium of the consoler's art.[66] The author of a more or less formal epistle to an exiled friend or client confronted his correspondent person to person and yet wrote from a distance where he could observe the exile's condition and treat it with words. The learned and imitative Latin of the humanists was in itself a remedy for feelings that were awkwardly immediate or inelegant. As a vehicle for good classical precedent and a rhetoric of improving persuasion, the letter was less ephemeral, more studied and subject to study, than talk; it was also more versatile than a treatise could be. Whatever else they may have been, Renaissance humanists were expert letter writers, and letters of consolation for exile were one of their routine assignments.

When Petrarch edited his *Epistolae familiares*, he included several epistles to exiles which read like full-scale models of the motifs summarized in his manual of remedies. Consolation is a word game, logotherapy, from the first of his two long letters to a certain (perhaps fictitious) Severo Appenincola.[67] Petrarch begins not with experience but with definitions, a pedantic touch which converts exile at the start into a topic for learned discussion. If to go into exile is only "to exit" or "go outside," what is it but a form of travel? The exile, Petrarch suggests straight-faced, ought to thank the authorities for the opportunity. Having detached things from words, or rather identified them, the good consoler proceeds to detach the exile from himself, or rather to identify the true self with a self-inspecting and controlling superego. The point of all the variations and ornaments on the argument is the same: dependence on external things or the opinion of the crowd is the (avoidable) source of all suffering; misery is a "mistake" which self-reliance, moderation, and decorum can correct. It follows from this denaturing of the sufferer that human suffering can be denied any specific effects. Exile is no different from, say, poverty or death or any other misfortune falsely feared by humankind. The only revenge Petrarch allows the exile is the grudging appreciation of his enemies for a virtuoso performance of self-control. The virtuous exile is also an obedient one.

Once set in motion, the consoling machine could be operated at different stops and registers. Petrarch's first letter to Severo concentrates on the theme of hope. Variations on the theme are turned out as needed—the hopeful "traveler" (*sic* "exile"), exiles whose virtue and good fortune (Cicero, Metellus, Marcellus, Camillus, and, among the moderns, Matteo Visconti and Stefano Colonna) had brought them home in glory, and the promising fact that Florence rather than some dismal outpost is the victim's place of confinement. The best hope of all is unassailable virtue. The second letter to Severo grants the hopelessness of his case but only to introduce a kind of miracle cure.[68] Like a doctor reassuring his patient, Petrarch says that he will isolate the wound with soothing gentleness: "Never fear, my finger will not touch you where it hurts." The mild remedy (Bion of Borysthenes, Stilpon, Cicero, and Seneca all swear by it) is the knowledge that, even if the exile can never return to his home, many roads to virtue are still open to him. The consoler prescribes a fortifying diet of liberal studies, especially philosophy. He concludes by flourishing a list of ancient conquerors of the real world whose example the studious exile must dare to equal in conquering himself.

Petrarch's four letters to Giovanni Colonna, a member of the famous Roman family and an exile after 1331, are less obliging.[69] They are also a demonstration of the liberties a consoler could take with prominent people. But the strategy of consoling virtue is the same even though the tactics are the shock treatment of a presumptuous friend, or of crisis therapy:

> You've lambasted me again and again with your laments, and by now I am so annoyed at it that I won't put up anymore with this cowardice of yours. . . . Shame on you for growing old amidst lamentations; shame on you, old man that you are, for whining like a baby. . . . To old men, especially when they are learned, as nothing should seem new or unimaginable, so should nothing give cause for surprise or pain.[70]

By the early fifteenth century the consolatory letter on exile had become an established genre. When Cosimo de' Medici was exiled from Florence in 1433, Poggio Bracciolini offered disingenuous apologies for being so inadequate to the consoler's task—and then proceeded through a familiar series of consolations.[71] Unlike "dignities, dominion, honors, wealth and riches," which are all external things, prudence, magnanimity, constancy, probity, virtue, and faith are our own to command; let Cosimo take refuge in the fortress of his own reason and virtue. Studies are the true glory of the wise man in the theater of the world; let Cosimo continue to cultivate learning and learned men. Politics is the arena of trouble and ingratitude; let Cosimo enjoy the true freedom of the contemplative life as an approved list of Greek and Roman worthies had done. With the sham modesty of the successful impresario, Poggio concludes with farewells and excuses for the verbosity which Cosimo will surely forgive as a sign of his "great good will."

After manuals on letter writing began to appear later in the Quattrocento, there was no excuse for anything less than epistles polished to a high finish. Giovanni Mario Filelfo gives the user of his model letter book a brief introduction to the precepts of rhetoric. In his schematic instructions for various kinds of consoling letters, the *consolatoria* for an exile are classified according to their intended effect—"familiar," "most familiar," or "grave." For quick reference Filelfo provides an abbreviated guide to the entire repertory:

> That you should not take exile seriously.
> Bear with equanimity your exile.
> Lest you grieve over missing your homeland:
> > exile should not be difficult for you;
> > one is not outside home territory—which is virtue.
> Consider yourself not an exile but a citizen wheresoever.
> Only the wicked lack a home: you are indeed at home.
> It is tolerable to you because your enemies are envious and malign.
> Goodness is wherever you are: consider it home.
> You cannot go into exile anywhere since your virtue can never be exiled.
> Behave with a constant spirit so that, honored outside your city,
> > you may prevail within it.
> Inasmuch as you are an exile, you can live with fame and glory as
> > a private person.
> Your fatherland is heaven, to which virtue aims, from which
> > it descends.[72]

Francesco Negri had little to add. The definitions in his book of ready-made letters are more schoolmasterly. So, for example: "The genus of consolation is that by which solaces are composed for the ills of which we are informed by a friend either by letter or by messenger; we desire him to be consoled; and of this genus there are three species. . . ."[73] Then too, Negri's volume is even more stiffly symmetrical in organization than Filelfo's; to balance the usual customary *consolatoria* on exile, he includes a chapter of *lamentoria* in good Latin drawn wholesale from classical models. But either with Filelfo or with Negri, the letter writer could no more go wrong than could a judge or notary with contemporary handbooks of judicial protocol. By the end of the fifteenth century, first to sentence an exile and then to console him, there were faultless formulas available to screen out the embarrassments of anger or grief.

Formal dialogues composed by (or representing) exiles were another important branch of the Renaissance art of consolation. During the 1430s the humanist Francesco Filelfo completed four of the ten dialogues he planned to include in a book of *Florentine Commentaries on Exile*. Not a man to hold his tongue (and threatened with losing it by the authorities), Filelfo was expelled from Florence in 1432. After 1434, when he became a client, spokesman, and consoler of the exiled anti-Medicean opposition, he cast Palla Strozzi, Palla's son Onofri, Rinaldo degli Albizzi, and other prominent *fuorusciti* as the main protagonists of his dialogues. Members of Leon Battista Alberti's own family of exiles are the speakers in Alberti's *On the Family*, and the proper conduct of the exile is a topic they discuss at some length. By the time of Pietro Alcionio's *On Exile* (1522) the dialogue of consolation for exile was a genre as familiar and polished as the consolatory epistle on the same theme.

Although Filelfo's *Commentaries* have been characterized as a propaganda piece of the anti-Medicean opposition of the 1430s, Filelfo himself had much higher ambitions.[74] Waspish asides against the Medici were all in a day's work for the contentious humanist; what he wanted his book to be most of all was his great contribution to the literature of consolation. *De exilio* is the first dialogue and, as Filelfo announces in a dedicatory letter, a true test of skill since exile is so often regarded as the supreme example of misfortune. Filelfo professes to welcome the difficulties: the greater the challenge, the more impressive the "long and arduous and magnificent" achievement.[75]

The dialogue on exile unfolds as an exchange of "grave and useful and memorable pronouncements" in a conversation between Palla and Onofri Strozzi. From the beginning the younger Strozzi plays directly into the consoling paternal hand:

> *Palla*:   Why so sad, son? Why do you sigh? Why
> these groans? Why are you so afflicted?
> *Onofri*:   Is it not right to be sad, father, or
> to feel afflicted for good reason when I've been
> transformed from a happy into a most unhappy man through
> no fault of my own? Can I not, must I not, sigh and
> lament seeing that you yourself have been despoiled of
> your position and driven out of your house and home? And
> still worse, rewarded by the enemy with exile from the *patria*?
> Is anything more desperate or more miserable than exile? [76]

Palla-Filelfo has all the stock answers at his disposal. As predictably, Onofri—"I was ignorant before, father, but now that you have spoken so perceptively and fully, I have no doubts whatsoever"—is a polite and rather slow learner.[77] In this way Onofri and the reader are made to hear (and presumably to learn) a series of disquisitions on true happiness and all the standard *topoi* on exile, infamy, poverty, and ungrateful politicians. The only relief from the consoler's routine comes with the entrance of Poggio Bracciolini as a Medicean toady and immoral misfit who objects that the pleasures of the body, especially the distractions of drink and the well-laden table, are the only consolations of this world. Poggio's objections are quashed in short order. The high-minded speakers in the dialogue will not tolerate frivolity. Although Filelfo includes many Greek texts and cites a whole host of sources along the margins of the manuscript, the main line of argument he puts in the mouth of Palla Strozzi is always the same:

> Only the wise man is great, only he is powerful, only he is fortunate, only he belongs to himself. He knows that nothing can perturb him. . . . If you will contemplate this, you will not be downcast but rejoice that we are exiles despised by the unjust mob.[78]

The members of the Alberti clan who speak in Leon Battista Alberti's dialogues *On the Family* voice far more compelling opinions on exile than Filelfo's cast of wooden characters. The Alberti use the vernacular, and what they have to say seems as much a vehicle of experience as of humanist learning. There is genuine pathos in Lorenzo Alberti's deathbed speech on leaving his sons "in exile and fatherless, far from the *patria* and your homes."[79] The disillusionment of the crusty old model merchant Giannozzo Alberti is believable enough: "how could I have imagined more callousness toward our wounds . . . ?" When Giannozzo characterizes political life as a source of frustrations which the exile ought to be glad to do without, his remarks are not the pedantic reflections of someone with only armchair experience of politics:

> Now people want you to put taxes or expenditures in order, now get ready for wars, now confirm or renew laws; all these things are so bound up together that you can't handle anything all by yourself, and you are not allowed to do as much as you want with anyone else. Everybody thinks what he wants is right, his judgment praiseworthy, and his opinion better than others'. Following some error of ordinary people or the arrogance of a few, you acquire infamy for yourself, and if you put yourself up for service, you please one man and displease a hundred.[80]

Plausible and direct as this kind of talk may sound, the dialogue often falls into a more conventional mold. The self-administered but perfectly paradigmatic remedy for Lorenzo's sadness is virtue: "He who has virtue in himself, to him very few external things will be necessary." The response to Giannozzo by Lionardo, one of the family literati, is a demand for more self-discipline: the wise man who rules himself "with virtue, with study, and with every art" should have no difficulty ruling others.[81] With a sidelong glance toward the authorities in Florence, the Alberti go on to offer their virtue and profess their lasting allegiance to their native city. Piero Alberti tells how, even at the court of the duke of Milan, he spoke up for the regime that had expelled his family.[82] Lionardo admits that there is nowhere else to turn because the individual depends for the recognition of his individuality on "public experience" and "public piazzas," where "fame is born" and "glory rises up."[83] The implication is that neither the solaces of the family circle nor the consolations of virtue will suffice for leading the good life. Even in exile the Alberti also do tribute to the state, like the citizen-saints who pay Caesar's taxes in the nearly contemporary Florentine fresco by Masaccio.

The tradition established by Filelfo and Alberti culminates in Pietro Alcionio's two dialogues *On Exile*.[84] The year is 1512; the setting is a Medici palace in Rome. In a quiet library and a walled-in garden, Giovanni, Giulio, and Lorenzo de' Medici—the future Leo X, Clement VII, and duke of Urbino—take consolation for their exile from Florence since 1494. Cardinal Giovanni, the main speaker, looks back for support to examples from family history and the ancient authors. The career of Cosimo de' Medici should be enough to disprove the three reasons of the vulgar crowd for considering exile the greatest of calamities. Foolish people may believe that exile deprives its victims of their native land, strips them of honors at home, and leaves them in many cases without the bare necessities of life. But Cosimo transcended such adversities and returned within a year as "father of his country." (See Figure 10.) This should silence the chattering multitude. If not, there are the *consolatoria* of the ancients, Latin and Greek, which the cardinal elaborates with ponderously bookish eloquence. For, of course, the true sages of antiquity taught that the wise man takes the whole world for his city, knows his fatherland to be wherever virtue and liberal studies are valued, and maintains his dignity wherever he may go.[85]

Alcionio's command of the consoler's repertory is sure. So sure that he can meander through literary excursuses in the conversation without supposing that he has lost the train of argument. Through Cardinal Giovanni he treats his own scholarship to self-serving praise. He drops the names of literary lions—Ermolao Barbaro, Giovanfrancesco Pico, Jacopo Sadoleto, and Paolo Giovio—and makes room besides for set pieces on the three kinds of friendship, on the analogies between oratory and painting, and on the supposed flaws in Plutarch's literary style.[86] Alcionio could afford the discursive pace and complacent tone because the Medici had made their victorious return to Florence and seen Cardinal Giovanni elected pope nearly ten years before the dialogue was published. But the redundancies and the pedantry were also mannerisms of a High Renaissance mastery of the genre.

It was not only in the fictional present of the humanist dialogue that history was revised according to Renaissance standards. Unsettling voices of exiles from the past were a standing challenge to the rules of decorum. Loyalist history written on commission or out of conviction had somehow to come to terms with the apparent disloyalty of the *fuorusciti*, who had been in any case too numerous in Italian history to be ignored. Even exiles long dead had to be censored or at least discredited if the triumph of the consoler's art was to be complete. The authorities went so far as to circulate grotesque historical laments supposedly uttered by exiles but actually composed to mock them.[87] If every generation rewrites history, it does not do so for pure pleasure; it is also a question of managing the present by manipulating the past.

Court writers consulted their options carefully. Pier Candido Decembrio chose to forget that Francesco Sforza had been exiled to Mortara by Filippo Maria Visconti.[88] After all, the official version was that Sforza had always been honored and accepted as the rightful heir to Milan by his most reluctant and devious father-in-law. A confrontation between Ferdinand of Naples and his rebel barons becomes a display of perfect princely virtue as Giovanni Pontano tells it. Unflinching, Pontano's ruler "never used a single harsh or injurious word against those same rebels"; he is allowed no more than a mild expression of regret that men of good family could be so unworthy of their ancestors.[89] If one could believe Giovanni da Ferrara, no prince had ever triumphed more magnanimously over the past than Borso d'Este. According to his historian, the duke of Ferrara wished to extend his grace and pardon to all the exiles of the previous regime. The triumphal floats paraded before Borso at Reggio in 1452 inspire the historian to reflect that the dazzling light of justice has been embodied in the duke so as to cancel out all the dark dissension and violence of earlier times.[90]

As historian of the Florentine republic, Leonardo Bruni sets the distance of historical perspective between his present and the exiles of the past. He describes the collective actions of the *fuorusciti* "by common consent" and appreciates how much they had once depended on foreign intervention.[91] The lesson he obviously wishes to teach is that things are different in his own day. When he puts orations in the mouths of insiders, it is to indict exiles for concealing purely partisan designs, opportunism, and violent intentions behind the pretense of just grievances. Stepping forward on his own, he editorializes over the terrible consequences that follow from the "illness" of exiles.[92] Granting, as the historian does, that past regimes were mistaken to exclude their real or imagined enemies, he leaves little doubt as to whose side he is on. One of the high points in his *History of the Florentine People* is a speech by Farinata degli Uberti after the rout of the Guelphs at Montaperti (1260). The Ghibelline chieftain argues for moderation and devotion to Florence, even in exile and even when he would have been able to take revenge. In another speech censuring the exiles from Bruni's native Arezzo in 1354 perhaps one hears something like Bruni's own voice: "no citizen who has marched against his *patria* is worthy of praise."[93]

There is no more striking instance of the victory of the dutiful present than the domestication of Dante by humanist biographers and critics. A few decades after Dante's death, Boccaccio was still echoing the poet's own passionate indignation in exile. "O evil thought! O dishonest deed! O miserable example, manifest cause of future ruin!" An "unjust and furious damnation" was the tribute of Florence to Dante, "the marble statue made for him." If all the other iniquities of the Florentines could be hidden from the sight of God, that injustice alone would still condemn them.[94] Fifteenth-century writers repudiate Boccaccio to a man. The first and most influential of Dante's humanist biographers was Leonardo Bruni, and he ridicules Boccaccio's tone and his picture of a poet outraged or amorous and contemplative by turns. Bruni's Dante is the good citizen, moralist, and well-rounded man of letters—a good sort of proto-humanist *malgré lui*. Coming to the time of the poet's exile, Bruni concedes that a "perverse and iniquitous law" had been responsible; he had done, he says, research in the archives on it. And so Dante's exile remains for Bruni, a research problem or an example of the whims of fortune, the obvious risks of politics, and the need for the consolations of virtue. Dante should have kept his initial resolve to earn pardon by "good works . . . and good behavior" rather than by menacing Florence with ill will and the specious claims of an emperor. Yet with Petrarch, the son of Dante's fellow exile, the divine poet must still be reputed "to belong to the glory of our city."[95]

The problem was that the Florentines could not vaunt the glory of their literary tradition under censure from their greatest poet. Hence their emphasis on Dante's virtuous resistance against misfortune rather than against Florentines, his loyalty to the city and not his contempt for it, his language as *letterato* rather than its disturbing political content. By

1373 the descendants of the Black Guelph regime that had excluded Dante had already begun to reclaim him. First they sponsored public readings of the *Divine Comedy*; then, in 1396, they sought—unsuccessfully—to have the poet's remains, like relics, returned to Florence. Nearly a century later Cristoforo Landino dedicated his commentary on the poet's greatest work (1481) to the signory of Florence, "so that by the hands of the magistracy which is supreme in the Florentine republic it [the *Divine Comedy*] may be after long exile restored to its fatherland and recognized as neither Romagnol or Lombard nor of the idiom of those who have commented, on it, but as pure Florentine. . . ."[96] Landino's work was to be the major commentary for at least a century, and if the poet's condemning voice could not be totally forgotten, it was dismissed as mere calumny by the early sixteenth-century author of a discourse on language once attributed to Machiavelli.[97] Dante's bones, which still rest in Ravenna, escaped the profanation.

Cinquecento moralists continued to administer their consolations.[98] So far as exiles were concerned, they were no longer urgently needed because the old, tumultuous voices of exile had long since been subdued or dispersed. Wistfulness, disappointment, and irony at his own expense were the most expressive forms of protest that the greatest Italian exile of the sixteenth century would show openly in his letters from Sant' Andrea in Percussina. Ready even "to roll a stone for these Medici *signori*," Machiavelli masked his pain in compulsive study and writing, in flights of fantasy, comedy, or calculation. Fortune, he declares, may sometimes yield to the young or the bold, especially if they happen to be princes. For the rest, she "wishes us to leave her alone, to be quiet and not to give her trouble, and to wait until she allows us to act."[99]

The submissive, Machiavellian anticlimax was a genuine but not an unqualified victory for the disciplines of Renaissance culture and the Renaissance state. The imperatives of state power could be exalted over and against the individual; losers and victims might be given over to the comforts and controls of the consolatory routine. But as the reach of the authorities widened, so did the range of conflicting interests with which they had to come to terms. The dangers of disaffection were thus placed in an intimate relationship with an established order which was anxious to be rid of the opposition but reluctant to let it go. For their part, the exiles who were creatures of the half-century of foreign invasion and political upheaval in Italy after 1494 rarely expressed their grievances in poetry, but the more articulate among them did produce a great outpouring of political speculation, proposals for constitutional reform, and historical writing.[100] The style of dissent tended to change in part because the political order which had emerged as the encompassing subject of history had become at the same time an accessible object of critical inspection and analysis. Assigned a place on the margins of official schemes of political and social relations, the opposition learned to voice its reasons against the domestic enemy.

The individual personality on which Renaissance moralists had lavished so much attention was unexpectedly troublesome in its own right. The utopian vision of a dutifully dignified and restrained model of humanity was constructed by isolating the individual in the sensitive web of his own self-consciousness. The consoler's prize pupil was likely to be a lonely and restless figure beneath the surface finish of decorum. Denied direct expression, sorrow could still turn devious to carry on a discourse of internalized alienation in place of the old external chorus of complaint. Despite all their practiced words of consolation, Petrarch and his successors recognize as an unrelieved kind of exile the nagging sense of dissatisfaction that individuals bear within themselves. For that affliction *Ratio* has no real remedies.[101]

Epilogue

The Senses of an
Ending at Montalcino

> To sum up all, there are archives
> at every stage to be looked into,
> and rolls, records, documents, endless
> genealogies. . . . In short, there is
> no end of it.
>
> Laurence Sterne, *Tristram Shandy*

The hilltown of Montalcino overlooks what was once the medieval Via Francigena halfway between Siena and the mass of Monte Amiata to the south. Viewed from a distance across a scarred landscape of volcanic outcroppings and pale, eroded hills, the town shapes itself to its ridge on the solid geometries of Etrusco-Roman foundations. The highest points in profile suggest no more than a modest history. A slender tower rising from the *palazzo comunale* near the center of town marks the brief independence of the commune during the thirteenth century. More impressive are the dark battlements of a fortress which the Sienese imposed on their new provincial possession in 1361.

One imagines Renaissance statesmen poring over their maps to find this unlikely arena of high politics around the middle of the sixteenth century.[1] In 1553 Montalcino withstood a siege by an imperial army of Spanish, Italian, and German troops in a campaign to outflank the rebellious Sienese republic. (See Figure 13.) In April 1555, after the fall of Siena, a group of refugees formed a government in exile there. For the Habsburg emperor-king of Spain Charles V these *fuorusciti* were one of the few remaining obstacles to Spanish domination of the peninsula, and there were old scores to settle with the exiled antiimperialist and anti-Spanish opposition. Cosimo de' Medici meant for his part to deliver the *coup de grace* to those Florentines who rallied to the defense of Mon-

148

talcino after keeping a dogged resistance alive in exile for more than twenty years. As duke of Florence, he was determined to round out the southern boundaries of his Tuscan state. The court of France supported the republic of exiles against its powerful enemies. Montalcino was the last ditch of a long and losing campaign which had begun with the French invasion of Italy in 1494. But French inability, or unwillingness, to match the resources of Spain and Florence became increasingly evident in a flurry of pitched battles, guerrilla raids, and diplomatic maneuvers.

The defenders of Montalcino were outnumbered from the start. Their outlying strongholds were eventually taken one by one. But even though they were alternately promised mercy and threatened with all the punishments for rebellion the sixteenth century could devise, the exiles managed to hold out for four years. Then, by the terms of the Treaty of Cateau-Cambrésis (April 1559), Henry II of France abandoned his beleaguered allies altogether. When Duke Cosimo advanced an occupying force toward an exhausted and starving town in the summer of 1559, further resistance was impossible. On 4 August 1559, dressed in mourning, representatives of the exile republic of Montalcino finally surrendered.

The republic of exiles which fell at last in 1559 was a successor to the old "external communes" of medieval Italy. By the middle of the sixteenth century, however, the once-familiar community of exiles with its own institutions, officials, and collective sense of legitimacy was relegated to the margins of great power struggles among Renaissance princes and confined to the backwaters of the Italian peninsula. The fall of Montalcino was decisive; there were no more Montalcinos for the contrary commonwealth of exile in Italian history. The developments which this book has traced seem thus to reach a logical conclusion and a dramatic climax in the exiles' last stand in the fortress where their banner still hangs, faded brown and torn so that the motto *Libertas* and the image of the Virgin protectress can hardly be made out.

But then, any finale can be drawn out or cut short so as to appear climactic, anticlimactic, circumstantial, or foreordained.[2] Depending on the story being told, the same event can serve as a conclusion, as a transition, or as the beginning of a tale. Although it is not hard to understand why the republic of Montalcino fell in 1559, the significance of Montalcino's brief time in the sun is not at all easy to assess. The tragedy or even the farce of the contrary commonwealth's last stand will seem from another perspective only an incident in a long struggle between the state and the outsider which is far from over in our own day. If there is a single truth

to the end of the exile republic at Montalcino, it is that the story is open-
ended.

The tragic motifs in the story are clear enough: so, for example, the
"flaw" of the exiles' pride and short-sightedness in the face of overwhelming odds; the clash of the great powers, the "gods," whose rivalries over
Italy determined the exiles' "fate"; or the "inevitability" of Spanish supremacy and Florentine territorial consolidation. The most prominent
leader of the *fuorusciti*, the Florentine exile Piero Strozzi, was a tragic
figure in his own right. His father had been one of the richest men in
Europe and an exile himself before his suicide, or murder, in a Medici
prison in 1538. While Piero was at one time or another a favorite of the
French court and marshal of France, he was also a loser in the war of
Siena and in many other failed causes of the Florentine *fuorusciti*. One
chronicler pictures him as a new Catiline or Brutus, translating Latin clas-
sics into Greek on the eve of hopeless battles.[3] As tragedy, the affair of
Montalcino even has its "catharsis" in the black-robed surrender of
August 1559.

In one form or another the tragic scenario has long been accepted as
the standard version of the affair. Historians have objected, it is true, to
what they regard as sentimental effusions "on the setting sun of communal
liberty saluting the bastions of Montalcino."[4] The systematic archival
research and careful reconstructions of modern historiography should be
concerned, we are told, with the objective historical realities of the case—
internal conflict and foreign entanglements; the superior political, financial, and military capabilities of the Florentine state and its ruler; the
underlying dynamics of Habsburg and Valois intervention in Italian affairs. But the historians go on to tell us that the "fate" of Siena and Montalcino was already "sealed" from the time of the first foreign invasions
of Italy. Italian independence, they say, remained "forever circumscribed
within the ambience of the protectorate of some outside power." Failing
to understand the true situation, the remnant republic at Montalcino
plummeted toward "the fatal day of surrender," only then "resigned to
the ineluctable, but with much dignity, without acts of servility. . . ."[5]

According to the literary critic Northrop Frye, tragedy seems intel-
ligible and true "because its catastrophe is plausibly related to its situation"; tragedy explores the relation to society of its protagonists and
exposes the constraints governing their actions.[6] The aims of much historical inquiry are similar, whether or not the historian employs the
specific dramatic and rhetorical devices of the tragic mode. It is, after

all, a common task of the historian to relate events to plausible conditions and contexts and, like the playwright, to reveal the significance and direction of human actions in the unfolding of some crucial situation. Plotted as tragedy, the struggle of the exile republic against Spanish imperialism and Duke Cosimo's territorial state becomes one last confirmation of the terms of a long-standing historical conflict. At Montalcino old forms of protest range themselves against the new power of Renaissance states ruling over the physical, political, and psychological spaces where the opposition had once organized and operated on a large scale. "Plausibly related to its situation," the catastrophe of Montalcino reveals once again the incompatibility of old and new forms of political action and, this time, draws the confrontation to a close. The tragic failure of the embattled exiles to learn the lessons of Italy's Renaissance experience brings the historical truth to light "in the end."

To ask whether this version of events—and of an ending for this book—is true or false would be beside the point. Clearly, the story can be, and has been, told as a kind of tragedy. It is also clear, however, that the tragic denouement is not the only possible interpretation of the fall of Montalcino. It is at least as plausible and as revealing "in the end" to read the history of the exile republic as a comedy in which subjects play at being master and fancy themselves able to relive the good old days when whole communes of exiles were formidable opponents in many parts of Italy. The folly of Montalcino is that it fell too late to be taken altogether seriously. The behavior of the French accomplices and the Habsburg enemies of the exile republic looks at times like a parody of some medieval chronicle, and there is something grotesque and absurd about Duke Cosimo's resounding triumph over an anachronism. One thinks of Marx's dictum that history repeats itself not as tragedy but as farce.

The elements of farce can hardly be missed at Montalcino. The French adopted the exiles' cause with fine disregard for a consistent record of French and exile losses in Italy. Henry II's claims to be defending the Angevin inheritance in Italy were arrogant and empty. Henry's queen, Catherine de' Medici, fanned her foolish enthusiasm for the *fuorusciti* with a loathing for Duke Cosimo that went back to the falling out between another set of Medici cousins two generations earlier. Charles V brought a brutal war to Tuscany in the name of imperial justice and peace. Pope Paul IV, a great friend of the exile republic, revived the most extreme temporal claims of the medieval papacy—and was soon chastened by the Spanish as thoroughly as Boniface VIII had been humiliated by the French at the beginning of the fourteenth century. To Cosimo de' Medici the rebels, though hostile to the emperor, were still imperialist by nature because they always had been. There was even talk of Guelphs and Ghibellines.[7]

With its own backward glances, the *Repubblica Senese Ritirata in Montalcino* proclaimed itself the true republic of Siena.[8] In the style of the old external communes, it legislated an oath of fidelity, created a governing council of five members, and provided for a sheriff, ambassadors, and a territorial administration divided into four regions. The exile republic also had its own seal—or rather the seal of Siena, which the fugitive Captain of the People had carried off to Montalcino—and it stamped its own coins with the image of the Virgin protectress, the she-wolf of Siena, and the motto *Libertas*. (See Figure 14.) Like the old company of exiles, Montalcino was dominated by an elite, descendants for the most part of the parties of the *Popolari* and the *Riformatori* which had fought for control of Siena since the fourteenth century. Merchants and bankers stood out in this ruling group, just as they always had. And just as they always had, the exiles counted on support from the countryside and, still more widely, on the sympathies of émigrés in more distant parts of Italy and abroad, including refugee aristocrats from Spanish rule in the kingdom of Naples, the Fieschi of Genoa, and, above all, the anti-Medicean exiles from Florence.[9] In their quixotic dreams of revenge and a republican restoration the defenders of Montalcino had forgotten little and learned less from the past.

So strong is the sense of déjà vu that plain truths register as comic distortions or embarrassments. After less than a year the republic of Montalcino became officially what it had been from the beginning in fact —not a truly independent state but a "royal republic," as dependent on France as the Sienese at home were upon their new Spanish and Medicean rulers. A year later a French governor passed on candidates for office, approved or vetoed their decisions, and even paid their salaries. The exile defenders were forbidden to enroll in the army and so to fight many of their own battles. All the while the French garrison protected the town in sixteenth-century fashion, consuming its supplies and terrorizing the inhabitants. Eventually, the French governor edged away from Montalcino to the port of Grosseto, where an escape by sea was still possible. Piero Strozzi, courtier and condottiere rather than Florentine patriot at his end, had already gone his stormy way toward his death in French service at the battle of Thionville (June 1558).

For all the fine coins minted at Montalcino, scarcely enough money remained to send one last embassy to France in the fall of 1558. When the ambassadors finally realized that Henry II had betrayed them, they burst into tears, reportedly to the shock or amusement of the court. According to English dispatches from Paris, they said they would rather kill themselves than submit to Cosimo de' Medici—whose gracious disposition "to embrace the penitent" was soon accepted by other representatives of the exile republic in the summer of 1559.[10] Once what Florentine court historians insist on calling the madness, folly, and childishness of Montalcino were over and done with, many former exiles became obedient subjects of the Medici state.[11]

In farce as in tragedy, then, the ordeal of Montalcino confirms the failure of the old-style company of exiles to withstand Renaissance imperialism and the territorial state. But in tragedy the contrary commonwealth of exile must fall from great heights whereas in farce it stumbles toward a more human end. Tragedy compels the submission of its victims to higher authority; farce allows underdogs, scapegoats, and fools the revenge of telling truths out of season and looking wiser than their betters, even in defeat.[12] If the case of Montalcino had not been all too human, if the victory of the established powers had been complete, the exile republic might be consigned to a pure and simple tragic finale. In fact, claims of historical necessity at Montalcino have a hollow ring. Despite the crushing advantages of the attacking force, the exile republic survived for four years. There were miscalculations on both sides of the walls, and the delusions of the exiles seem relatively innocent compared with the hypocrisy and cruelty on the Spanish and Medicean side. In defending their liberty, honor, and independence, the exiles were defending a vital and dynamic legacy of the communal age which some recent historians contrast with the creeping economic and social stagnation, political subservience, and courtly or clerical brittleness of Italian culture in the later fifteenth and the sixteenth centuries.[13] In the farce of Montalcino it is the contrary commonwealth that has the last laugh.

The endings of tragedy and farce at Montalcino fit Aristotle's definition of a narrative climax by bringing the case of the contrary commonwealth to a point beyond which the account need not go.[14] Each version helps to endow the story with a meaning and a moral and to establish our distance from what each version construes as a completed sequence of events. By putting the past behind us, both tragedy and farce invite us to read history as a commemoration of *temps perdu* bearing only remotely on our own experience. This sense of closure has its satisfactions—and its distortions too.[15] There are, after all, continuities to be considered.

Long after the Tacitean peace of 1559 the wide arc of harsh country swinging from Montalcino and Monte Amiata west to the swamps of the Maremma and east toward Umbria remained a no man's land of back-country rebels.[16] By 1580 at least three bands of outlaws, each with its own chieftain, were operating along the southern borders of Tuscany. The most notorious of these bandits, Alfonso Piccolomini, duke of Montemarciano, made a profession of outmaneuvering or outrunning the agents of the grand duke of Tuscany and the pope. It might have been otherwise but for the fact that the noble bandit was a wayward but sometimes useful relative whose family tree included two popes and a long-suffering wife from the ruling house of Urbino. After much hesitation, Grand Duke Francesco de' Medici, a not-so-secret friend of the troublemaker thanks to his designs on the border baronies in southern Tuscany, decided that something had to be done. To the delight of the court at Florence, Piccolomini was persuaded in 1583 to set off for honest fighting in France to kill many Huguenots or be killed himself. Within three years the renegade was back in his old haunts. His band of five hundred men attracted new recruits after he joined forces with the restless mountaineers above Pistoia; there was talk of an uprising on a large scale, especially in Sienese territory. Not until the better part of the Tuscan army was mobilized together with troops from the papal states, Ferrara, and Mantua was Piccolomini finally captured. On 16 March 1591 he was hanged from a window of the Bargello's palace in Florence.[17]

The Venetian ambassador was satisfied. Tuscany, he reported, is "completely accustomed to life under the dominion of an absolute prince" and "now enjoys a continuous peace and a most happy tranquility."[18] Scipione Ammirato knew better, though that erudite gentleman of letters and comfortable familiar of the Medici court was not one to let natural or manmade calamities ruffle his dignity or disturb his pleasures. Still, the *banditi, masnadieri, bravi, malandrini*, and other plagues of public enemies at large under different names were worrisome to him. They seemed to have taken the place of the serious conspirators and the *fuorusciti* of earlier times. Strict measures for prevention and punishment only seemed to multiply their number. At least, in a well-run state, they had lost the appearance of a real political opposition and were no better than assassins and thieves. Ammirato conceded nevertheless that brigandage was perhaps an incurable affliction that would have to be tolerated somehow, like boils and vermin. For the next two hundred years historians of the grand duchy would have many exploits and many legends of *banditi* to recount.[19]

In the same swath of country around Montalcino where others had found worldly hideaways, Davide Lazzaretti founded a republic of spiritual exiles.[20] The career of the messiah of Monte Amiata developed in counterpoint to the progress of the Risorgimento. While the patriots of 1848 were fighting for the New Italy, Lazzaretti was having his first prophetic vision at the age of thirteen or fourteen; in 1868, when the occupation of Rome and the final unification of Italy were only months away, he was converted once and for all from his life as an unregenerate muleteer on the mountain. Visions of the saints and a mysterious visitor came to him in the cave where he did penance; stigmata appeared on his body, and he was born again with all his senses heightened and a mission to fulfill. In the fullest accounts of his teachings, Lazzaretti's descent from a sixteenth-century French king was revealed to him. He was told to announce, amidst terrible tribulations, the arrival of the third and last age of the world—the Kingdom of Justice and Reform of the Holy Spirit. The Lord would erect seven sacred cities, beginning with one on Monte Amiata, where Lazzaretti and his followers built a tower over a grotto and a church consecrated by the bishop of Montalcino. Gathered together in a Society of Christian Families and sharing their work and means of livelihood in common, the faithful awaited the great days that had been promised.

The *Lazzarettisti* were a religious cult, a social movement, a utopian community, and a political action group. Their little world was as complete as the old communes of exiles had been. The initial reactions of the authorities ran from condescension and benign neglect to active support by Catholic clergy and laity in search of a crusade against the secular state of usurpers at Rome. Lazzaretti went to and from the mountain, taking his message as far as Lyon and even London. In 1877 he was forced to take it to the Vatican where charges of heresy had finally been pressed against him. By the time he returned, the Church of the Faithful lay under interdict. His response—it was early in 1878, the eve of the deaths of both Pius IX and King Vittorio Emanuele—was to proclaim the Era of the Law of Right. One of his sermons during his last days on Monte Amiata conveys something of the range and the urgency of his movement as well as some sense of the increasingly radical turn it had taken:

What do you want of me? I bring you peace and compassion.
    Is this what you want? (*Responses*: Yes, peace and compassion.)
Are you willing to pay no more taxes? (*Response*: Yes.)
But don't think it will be the republic of 1849. It will be the

Republic of Christ. Therefore all cry with me: "Long live the Republic of God!"[21]

The long-promised descent from the mountain began in the dawn of 18 August 1878. Lazzaretti wore a close-fitting gown of gray and red, a blue mantle lined in scarlet, and a blue headdress with three drooping feathers. Seven Princes of the Crusading Militia of the Holy Spirit accompanied him in much the same dress, and they were followed by the Twelve Apostles in blue mantles and the Disciples in red. Then came the Hermit Priests and the Matrons and Sisters of Charity; then the Maidens and Daughters of the Canticles, robed in white, with flower wreaths on their heads; then groups of Levites and legionaries. Banners of the Virgin and the Republic of God flew above and hymns were sung as the faithful made their way around the mountain and down to the village of Arcidosso. A crowd of three thousand had gathered there. At half-past nine the marshal of the carabinieri advanced to meet the procession with nine or ten of his men and the mayor. Beckoning to Lazzaretti, the marshal read aloud three times the official order commanding him to turn back in the name of the law. The answer came in the hush that had fallen over the crowd: "I go forward in the name of the Law of Right. . . . If it is peace you desire, I bring it to you; if compassion, here it is; if blood, here am I."[22] A confused scuffle broke out. Stones began to fall on the official party, the marshal brandished a gun, the carabinieri fired, and Lazzaretti was killed.

There was no resurrection. The leading apostles were tried on charges of civil violence and conspiracy to commit plunder and theft. Every spring for years afterwards red flowers appeared on Lazzaretti's grave in the cemetery of Santa Fiora, but by 1943 the last original member of the sect was gone. Failure was only to be expected of a movement which, like other failed outbursts of "primitive rebellion," spoke to such cross-purposes and pieced together in action a crazy quilt of forms of popular protest—the millenarian tradition, the peasant conventicle, the republican cortege, and a touch of carnival. Or so one would think, except for a remarkable sequel. In 1948, after an assassination attempt against the Italian Communist party leader Palmiro Togliatti, there was a minor uprising in Arcidosso, as in many other places where it was believed that the sign for the revolution had come. This was not in the party's script, and every effort was made to put an end to the untimely exuberance of the rank and file. Some time later, however, an orator speaking at Arcidosso on the party's lecture circuit gave in to the temptation to praise the revolutionary credentials of the region and recalled the massacre of 1878. A number of people reportedly approached him after the speech to say that they were *Lazzarettisti* and so naturally on the Communist side out of opposition to the state. It had come as a surprise that the party, too, appreciated the prophet's great mission.[23]

With the bandit-duke of Montemarciano and the messiah of Monte Amiata we have moved far from exiles into company that has achieved, as Richard Cobb says, "almost alarming respectability" among historians —the company of "the deserter, the mutineer, the primitive rebel, the rural bandit, the market rioter, the urban criminal, the pickpocket, and the village prophet [who] have been taken in as honoured, pampered members of Senior Common Rooms."[24] But this motley crowd has some claim, at least a figurative or a typological claim, to descend from the exiles of Montalcino. Every society seems to project its fears (and surely many hidden desires) on the figure of the "outsider" whose guises may change while his functions remain more or less the same. As the connoisseur of conflict between the police and the people in early modern Europe points out, what may look like solo performances of social or political misfits usually turn out to be *pas de deux*; the misfits fit only too well.[25] True to type, Italian exiles during the Middle Ages and the Renaissance shared the styles of action, the forms of organization, and the prevailing values of their enemies inside the walls at home. In a similar way, Alfonso Piccolomini was well connected by birth and marriage, a duke by title, a guest at the best of courts, and a protégé at one time or another of the authorities that eventually turned against him. In the case of the *Lazzarettisti*, the grain, oxen, tools, and costumes of the faithful were contributions to a common pool that utterly dispossessed and destitute people could not have made. Small peasants, sharecroppers, and artisans were the mainstays of the movement, which depended besides on the support of the clergy, well-to-do donors in Italy and France, and the friendly disposition of the prefect of Grosseto.[26]

Then too, Piccolomini's bandits, like Lazzaretti's disciples, depended on the same divided and fragmented Italian landscape, with its "inside" and its "outside" spaces, that the existence of medieval and Renaissance exiles had once presupposed. And this physical environment was repeatedly perceived and valued in terms of moral contrasts. It was as natural that one of the notorious bandits of the 1580s should hole up in the swamps of the Maremma as it was fitting that he should be known to respectable society only as *l'uomo salvatico*, the wild man. Monte Amiata was not only remote in fact; it was as lawless and Godforsaken in the eyes of hostile authorities as it was uncorrupted in the visions of the *Lazzaret-*

tisti.[27] Far from Italy, Daniel Defoe insisted on seeing "banditti" issuing from their "infernal regions" to stalk English highways and the streets of London itself in the eighteenth century. "Dangerous classes," mobsters, and minorities have filled their places in turn in the slums and ghettoes of modern cities and minds—and their ultimate refinement, the prison.[28] The battleground and the cast of characters change, even as the clash between established authority and its intimate enemies goes on.

It is important to distinguish of course. If the old confrontation between the ruling powers and the outsider continues, its terms and its costs are transformed over time. But even this transformation can bring us back to Montalcino "in the end," for one site selected for a state penitentiary in the eighteenth century was none other than the old fortress of the exile republic.[29] From the fortress where the "external commune" made its last stand to the "carceral archipelago" of Kafka, Solzhenitsyn, or Foucault a figurative genealogy can thus be made to run through a single setting.[30]

But there is at least one more line of continuity that can be traced through Montalcino. A speaker at the ceremonies commemorating the four-hundredth anniversary of the fall of the exile republic hinted at it.[31] The exiles, he said, had held out for the expression of political belief and conscience. The important fact was not that their republic had been defeated but that it had managed to exist at all. Montalcino was one of those communities of refuge—Geneva in the sixteenth century; Amsterdam in the seventeenth; Paris, London, or New York at a later date—where political or religious refugees struggled to salvage their lives, opinions, traditions, and institutions. This line of descent cuts through dead ends and points instead to an escape, however temporary and precarious, from the futilities of tragedy and farce.

Although an ending in this sense is possible, it can hardly be a confident celebration of the "torch of liberty" passed down through Montalcino.[32] We know too much about the exile republic and its predecessors for easy optimism. The political franchise at Montalcino remained narrow and restrictive, as it had always been in the city-states and external communes of Italy. The very existence of the exile republic was due in part to the accident of a temporary political stalemate among greater powers. To the limited extent that the *fuorusciti* could preserve their liberty as they understood it, they were forced to become clients of France and tools of French political interests.

We also know too much about the uprooted and displaced victims of political and social upheaval since the sixteenth century to be especially optimistic. The state has not surrendered any real power to dispose of its subjects. If anything, the descendants of the victors at Montalcino have brought the old clash over political and moral space more firmly under their control. "Release into exile," in Solzhenitsyn's biting phrase, has become only too familiar as a grudging alternative to the incarceration or extermination of political dissidents and religious or ethnic minorities.[33] Outside their own countries, many exiles have been thrust into a world of "reluctant havens" in the well-documented view of a writer who is not unsympathetic to the problems of all concerned.[34] Organized relief efforts began only late in the nineteenth century and primarily through the private initiative of such men as Henri Dunant, founder of the International Red Cross, and Fridtjof Nansen, the first High Commissioner for Refugees under the auspices of the League of Nations. The charters of the League and then of the United Nations did not make explicit provisions for agencies to deal with refugees and exiles. Effective international institutions to aid them were not established until the years immediately after World War II, when the problem could hardly be ignored.[35]

The fact remains that the Geneva Convention and the Statute of the United Nations High Commissioner for Refugees (1951) offer limited protection at best. These documents grant the status of refugee to any person unwilling to return to the country of his origin or "to avail himself of its protection" in the case of "well-founded fear of being persecuted for reasons of race, religion, nationality, or political opinion."[36] Although a liberalizing protocol was added in 1967, significant restrictions have been maintained. Refugees who retain their first nationality or accept a new one are excluded, as are those claiming economic reasons or "personal convenience" as grounds for exile. Many states have insisted on the further reservation that persons "engaged in subversive activities against their country of origin, their country of asylum, or another country" cannot be considered genuine refugees.[37] These excluding provisions have created another category of exiles officially known as asylum seekers whose situation is especially difficult. In all cases the determination of eligibility for refugee status remains entirely in the hands of the country in which asylum is being sought.

And yet an international body has acknowledged the existence and the integrity of those who choose or are forced to go into exile "for reasons of race, religion, nationality, or political opinion." A former High Commissioner for Refugees has saluted this achievement as a great victory for the cause of human rights. He has also declared that the rights of exiles to asylum, to material assistance, to naturalization, and, where possible, to repatriation will need to be reasserted again and again.[38] According to René Cassin, joint author of the Universal Declaration of Human Rights and Nobel Peace Prize laureate in 1968, there will be exiles so long as there is injustice in the world. *Faire reculer l'injustice* is the endless task of those striving to ease their condition—and, it may be added, of exiles themselves.[39] Only in a just world will it be possible to bring the story of the contrary commonwealth to a definitive close.

NOTES

ABBREVIATIONS USED IN NOTES

MGH—Monumenta Germaniae Historica . . . Hannover and other locations, 1820–

RIS—Rerum italicarum scriptores ab anno aerae christianae quingentesimo ad millesimum quingentesimum . . . , ed. Ludovico Antonio Muratori. 25 volumes. Milan, 1723–1751.

RIS, n. s.—*Rerum italicarum scriptores; raccolta degli storici italiani dal cinquecento al millecinquecento ordinata da L. A. Muratori. Nuova edizione riveduta, ampliata e corretta* . . . , ed. Giosuè Carducci *et al.* 32 volumes in 119. Città di Castello and other locations, 1900–1975.

CHAPTER ONE

1. Paolo Paruta, *Opere politiche*, ed. Cirillo Monzani (Florence, 1852), I, 203, 205. Except where indicated otherwise, all translations are my own.

2. *Isidori* . . . *etymologiarum sive originum libri*, V, xxvii, 28, ed. W. M. Lindsay (Oxford, 1911).

3. See *Paulys Real-Encyclopädie der classischen Altertumswissenschaft*, ed. Georg Wissowa, VI.2 (Stuttgart, 1909), s.v. "exilium"; Theodor Mommsen, *Das römische Staatsrecht*, 3rd ed. (reprint Basel, 1952), III, 47–50; James Strachan-Davidson, *Some Problems of the Roman Criminal Law* (Oxford, 1912), II, 23–24, 60; Giuliano Crifò, *Ricerche sull'exilium nel periodo repubblicano* (Milan, 1961), I; and Crifò's entry in *Enciclopedia del diritto* (Milan, 1966), XV, s.v. "esilio."

4. Albericus de Rosate, *Dictionarium iuris tam civilis quam canonici* (Venice, 1581), s.v. "exilium"; and Nicolaus Antonius, *De exilio, sive de exilii poena antiqua et nova* (Antwerp, 1659), Bk. I, chap. 2 ("De exilij orthografia, etymo, diffinitione"), p. 5.

5. *Grande dizionario della lingua italiana* (Turin, 1968–1970), V–VI, s.v. "esule," "fuoruscito," "estrinseco."

6. Cf. *Paulys Real-Encyclopädie*, VI.2, s.v. "exilium"; Michel J. A. Bréal and Anatole Bailly, *Dictionnaire étymologique Latin*, 2nd ed. (Paris, 1886), s.v. "exul" (a derivation from *sedere* on the analogy of *consul* or *praesul*); and Strachan-Davidson, *Roman Criminal Law*, II, 33 (*eiectum ex civitate* as terminology already used by Cicero). On the theory and practice of the communal ban, see pp. 77–80 above and the references cited on p. 178, n. 32, esp. Desiderio Cavalca, *Il bando nella prassi e nella dottrina giuridica medievale* (Milan, 1978), pp. 17–22. With the problems of modern political refugees in mind, Paul Ta-

bori has discussed "the semantics of exile" more generally in *The Anatomy of Exile: A Semantic and Historical Study* (London, 1972), pp. 23–38.

7. Julio Caro Baroja, "The City and the Country: Reflexions on Some Ancient Commonplaces," in *Mediterranean Countrymen*, ed. Julian Pitt-Rivers (Paris, 1963), pp. 27–40; and Fernand Braudel, *The Mediterranean and the Mediterranean World in the Age of Philip II*, trans. Sian Reynolds (New York, 1963), Pt. 1 ("The Role of the Environment").

8. Donald S. Walker, *A Geography of Italy* (London, 1958) is a brief, comprehensive introduction. For the physical and historical geography of Italy, there is, as always, much of interest in Braudel's *Mediterranean* and in the relevant chapters of the Einaudi *Storia d'Italia*, I (Turin, 1972) by Luigi Gambi ("I valori storici dei quadri ambientali," 5–60), Giovanni Haussmann ("Il suolo d'Italia nella storia," 63–132), and Corrado Vivanti ("Lacerazioni e contrasti," 869–948).

9. Paul Morand, *Méditerranée, mer des surprises* (Tours, 1938), p. 7.

10. A point well made by André Siegfried, *The Mediterranean*, trans. Doris Hemming (London, 1948).

11. See Emilio Sereni, "Agricoltura e mondo rurale," and Ruggiero Romano, "Una tipologia economica," in the Einaudi *Storia d'Italia*, I, 175ff., 273–298; cf. Ronald Abler, John S. Adams, and Peter Gould, *Spatial Organization* (Englewood Cliffs, N.J., 1971), pp. 379–381. For a case study of geographical interplay in one commune (notorious, it might be added, for its exiles), see David Herlihy, *Medieval and Renaissance Pistoia: The Social History of an Italian Town, 1200–1430* (New Haven/London, 1967), pp. 34–54.

12. For exiles as *peregrini*, see Strachan-Davidson, *Roman Criminal Law*, II, 57 (citing Ulpian); and Cavalca, *Il bando*, pp. 29, 80 (citing Cicero and Placentinus). For subsequent usage, see J. Gaudemet, "L'étranger au bas empire," *Recueils de la Société Jean Bodin*, 9, pt. 1 (1958): 208–210.

13. Carlo Cattaneo, "La città considerata come principio ideale delle istorie italiane," in *Scritti storici e geografici*, ed. Gaetano Salvemini and Ernesto Sestan (Florence, 1957), II, 383; cf. for more recent perspectives, which have reemphasized the importance of the land, Giovanni Cherubini, "Qualche considerazione sulle campagne dell'Italia centro-settentrionale tra l'XI e il XV secolo," *Rivista storica italiana*, 79 (1967): 111–157.

14. *Ottonis et Rahewini Gesta Frederici Imperatoris*, ed. Georg Waitz (Hannover/Leipzig, 1912), pp. 116–117.

15. Giovanni Tabacco, "Problemi di insediamento e di popolamento nell' alto Medioevo," *Rivista storica italiana*, 79 (1967): 67–100; Vivanti, "Lacerazioni e contrasti," 878–893.

16. Eugenio Dupré-Theseider, "Vescovi e città nell'Italia precomunale," in *Vescovi e città nell'Italia precomunale (sec. X–XIII). Atti del II Convegno di Storia della Chiesa in Italia* (Padua, 1964), p. 89.

17. Leandro Alberti, *Descrittione di tutta l'Italia et isole pertinenti ad essa* (Venice, 1581), p. 8.

18. For especially good surveys, with extensive bibliography, see Edith Ennen, *Die europäische Stadt des Mittelalters* (Göttingen, 1972); Gina Fasoli

and Francesca Bocchi, *La città medievale italiana* (Florence, 1973); and Sergio Bertelli, *Il potere oligarchico nello stato-città medioevale* (Florence, 1978).

19. *Novelle* 27 and 101, in Franco Sacchetti, *Opere*, ed. Aldo Borlenghi (Milan, 1957), pp. 112–113, 322–328.

20. Heinrich Peyer, *Stadt und Stadtpatron im mittelaltlichen Italien* (Zurich, 1955); Alba Maria Orselli, *L'idea e il culto del santo patrono cittadino nella letteratura latina cristiana* (Bologna, 1965).

21. So, e.g., *Tractatus super constitutionem ad reprimendum*, V, 5–6, in *Bartoli opera omnia* (Venice, 1615), X, fols. 103v–104r; for the Viterbo inscription and Barbarossa: Bertelli, *Potere oligarchico*, p. 43.

22. Alfred von Martin, *Sociology of the Renaissance*, trans. W. L. Luetkens (New York/Evanston, 1963), pp. 5–46, drew the classic picture of "modernity" in the Italian urban setting; on the problem of anachronism in sociological studies of urban development, see, e.g., Charles Tilly, *An Urban World* (Boston, 1974), pp. 45–50.

23. Wolfgang Braunfels, *Mittelaltliche Stadtbaukunst in der Toscana* (Berlin, 1953); Giulio Carlo Argan and Maurizio Fagiolo, "Premessa all'arte italiana," in the Einaudi *Storia d'Italia*, I, 737–739 *et passim*; and Juergen Schulz, "Jacopo de' Barbari's View of Venice: Map Making, City Views, and Moralized Geography Before the Year 1500," *Art Bulletin*, 60 (1978): 425–474.

24. David Lowenthal, "Research in Environmental Perception and Behavior: Perspectives on Current Problems," *Environment and Behavior*, 4 (1972): 333–342; *Image and Environment: Cognitive Mapping and Spatial Behavior*, ed. Roger M. Downs and David Stea (Chicago, 1973); and *Geographies of the Mind: Essays in Historical Geosophy in Honor of John Kirtland Wright*, ed. David Lowenthal and M. J. Bowdin (New York, 1976).

25. Yi-Fu Tuan, *Topophilia: A Study of Environmental Perceptions, Attitudes, and Values* (Englewood Cliffs, N.J., 1974), p. 27.

26. Ibid., pp. 13–29.

27. See Yi-Fu Tuan, "Geopiety: A Theme in Man's Attachment to Nature and Place," in *Geographies of the Mind*, pp. 11–41; and Marc Fried, "Grieving for a Lost Home," in *The Urban Condition*, ed. L. J. Duhl (New York, 1963), pp. 154–171. My own analysis on the following pages owes much to the work of anthropologists on these themes, esp. Mary Douglas, *Purity and Danger: An Analysis of the Concepts of Pollution and Taboo* (New York/Washington, D.C., 1966), pp. 94–113; and Victor Turner, *The Ritual Process: Structure and Anti-Structure* (Chicago, 1969), chap. 3.

28. For the examples in this paragraph, see Douglas Frame, *The Myth of Return in Early Greek Epic* (New Haven/London, 1978); Theognis, *Elegies* 1197–2000, ed. J. M. Edmonds, in *Elegy and Iambus*, I, Loeb Classical Library (London/New York, 1931); Euripides, *Bacchanals* 1368–1370, ed. T. E. Page et al., *Euripides*, III, Loeb Classical Library (Cambridge, Mass./London, 1950); *Aeneid* III, 4; and R. J. Dickinson, "The 'Tristitia': Poetry in Exile," in *Ovid*, ed. J. W. Binns (London/Boston, 1973), pp. 153–190.

29. Hayden White, "The Forms of Wildness: Archeology of an Idea," in *The Wild Man Within: An Image in Western Thought from the Renaissance*

to Romanticism, ed. Edward Dudley and Maximillian E. Novak (Pittsburgh, 1972), p. 11.

30. George H. Williams, *Wilderness and Paradise in Christian Thought* (New York, 1962), pp. 10–64; and Gerhard Ladner, "*Homo Viator*: Medieval Ideas on Alienation and Order," *Speculum*, 42 (1967): 233–259.

31. Stephen Owen, *The Poetry of Meng Chiao and Han Yü* (New Haven/London, 1975), p. 282. More than a millennium earlier, Chu Yuan had wandered in exile over the region of Tung-t'ing Lake in northern Ho-non, where he found "dark and interminable forests, the habitation of apes and monkeys / And mountains wet with rain mists, so high that the sun was hidden": *The White Pony: An Anthology of Chinese Poetry*, ed. Robert Payne (New York, 1960), p. 89.

32. See Werner Vortriede, "Vorläufige Gedanken zu einer Typologie der Exilliteratur," *Akzente*, 15 (1968): 556–575; and the references in n. 91 below.

33. Of particular interest here are three poems, including *Die Landschaft des Exils*, in Brecht's *Selected Poems*, ed. and trans. H. R. Hays (New York, 1947), pp. 165–171; and Aleksandr Solzhenitsyn, *The Gulag Archipelago, 1918–1956*, trans. Harry Willetts (New York, 1978), III, 369–372, 440ff.

34. Czeslaw Milosz, *Bells in Winter*, trans. by the author and Lillian Vallee (New York, 1978), p. 12.

35. See Niccolò Machiavelli, *Tutte le opere*, ed. Mario Martelli (Florence, 1971), pp. 257, 1160; *Epistola* XIII, 4, in Dante, *Opere*, ed. Manfredi Porena and Mario Pazzaglia (Bologna, 1966), p. 1382; and Chapter Five of this book.

36. Emile Durkheim, *The Division of Labor in Society*, trans. George Simpson (Glencoe, Ill., 1947), p. 84.

37. "Considerations on the 'Discourses' of Machiavelli," in Francesco Guicciardini, *Selected Writings*, ed. Cecil Grayson (London, 1965), p. 81.

38. Antonio Gramsci, *Gli intelletuali e l'organizzazione della cultura* (Turin, 1966), p. 112; cf. Ettore Passerin d'Entrèves, "Il cattolicesimo liberale in Europa ed il movimento neoguelfo in Italia," in *Nuove questioni di storia del Risorgimento e dell'unità d'Italia* (Milan, 1961), I, 565–606.

39. *Maxims and Reflections of a Renaissance Statesman* (*Ricordi*), trans. Mario Domandi (New York, 1965), p. 122.

40. Jacques Heers, *Family Clans in the Middle Ages. A Study of Political and Social Structures in Urban Areas*, trans. Barry Herbert (Amsterdam/New York, 1977), esp. chaps. 2–3.

41. Ibid., pp. 20–31. F. W. Kent, *Household and Lineage in Renaissance Florence: The Family Life of the Capponi, Ginori, and Rucellai* (Princeton, 1977) has shown how fragmenting *and* consolidating phases were experienced in the "life cycles" of Florentine patrician families; see, too, the results of the massive quantitative analysis of the Florentine Catasto of 1427 by David Herlihy and Christiane Klapisch-Zuber, *Les toscans et leurs familles* (Paris, 1978). For a good case study of persisting family ties (and a dramatic exile resulting from them), see Marino Berengo, *Nobili e mercatanti nella Lucca del Cinquecento* (Turin, 1965), pp. 83–92.

42. Franco Niccolai, *Contributo allo studio dei più antichi brevi della Compagnia genovese* (Milan, 1939), pp. 12–17.

43. *Il libro di buoni costumi di Paolo di Messer Pace da Certaldo*, ed. S. Morpurgo (Florence, 1921), p. lviii; cf. Pietro Sella, *La "vicinia" come elemento constituivo del comune* (Milan, 1908).

44. J. Plesner, *L'émigration de la compagne à la ville libre de Florence au XIIIe siècle* (Copenhagen, 1934); and Cinzio Violante, *La società milanese nell'età precomunale* (Bari, 1953) are fundamental here; but cf. more recently Jacques Heers, *Parties and Political Life in the Medieval West*, trans. David Nichols (Amsterdam/New York, 1977), pp. 79–89. For interesting analyses of Florentine decentralization, see Samuel K. Cohn, *The Laboring Classes in Renaissance Florence* (New York, 1981); and Ronald F. E. Weissman, *Ritual Brotherhood in Renaissance Florence* (New York, 1982), chap. 1; cf., however, Richard C. Trexler, *Public Life in Renaissance Florence* (New York, 1980), pp. 12–13.

45. Quoted by Lauro Martines, *Power and Imagination: City-States in Renaissance Italy* (New York, 1978), p. 79.

46. Ibid., pp. 79–86—an especially searching analysis of the impact of money on communal society and politics.

47. See Franco Niccolai, *I consorzi nobiliari e il comune nell'alta e media Italia* (Bologna, 1939); Franco Valsecchi, *Comune e corporazione nel medioevo italiano* (Milan, 1943); G. M. Monti, *Le confraternità medievali nell'alta e media Italia*, 2 vols. (Venice, 1926); and Bertelli, *Potere oligarchico*, pp. 17–20.

48. Heers, *Parties and Political Life*, pp. 28–39.

49. P. S. Leicht, "*Communitas* e *comune* nell'alto Medio Evo," in P. S. Leicht, *Scritti vari di storia del diritto* (Milan, 1943), I, 377–380.

50. A. R. Scarsella, "Il comune dei consuli," in *Storia di Genova dalle origini al tempo nostro* (Milan, 1942), III, 129–131; and Vito Vitale, *Il comune del Podestà a Genova* (Milan/Naples, 1951), pp. 3–40.

51. Walter Ullmann, "The Medieval Theory of Legal and Illegal Organizations," *Law Quarterly Review*, 60 (1944): 285–291; cf., for lawyers' arguments against particularism, Julius Kirshner, "*Civitas sibi faciat civem*: Bartolus of Sassoferrato's Doctrine of the Making of a Citizen," *Speculum*, 48 (1973): 694–713.

52. For orientation and bibliography in a large literature, see Nicola Ottokar, "Il problema della formazione comunale," in *Questioni di Storia medievale*, ed. Ettore Rota (Milan, 1946), pp. 355–384; and Gina Fasoli, "Le autonomie cittadine nel medioevo," in *Nuove questioni di storia medievale* (Milan, 1969), pp. 145–176. For a fresh synthesis, see Martines, *Power and Imagination*, pp. 7–71.

53. "Il 'Chartarum dertonense' ed altri documenti del Comune di Tortona (943–1346)," ed. Ferdinando Gabotto, in *Biblioteca della Società Storica Subalpina*, 31 (1909): 5, quoted with many similar examples by Ottavio Banti, "*Civitas* e *comune* nelle fonti italiane dei secoli XI e XII," *Critica storica*, 9 (1972): 568–584.

54. For a useful outline of this process, with bibliography, see J. K. Hyde, *Padua in the Age of Dante* (Manchester, 1966), pp. 7–26.

55. *Istorie fiorentine*, III, 1, in *Tutte le opere*, p. 690; Bertelli, *Potere oligarchico*, pp. 106–108, discusses the many forms of exclusionary provision in

the legislation of the communes. For legal attempts (largely unsuccessful) at compromise among factions, see Antonio Marongiù, "Il regime bipartico nel trattato sui guelfi e i ghibellini," in *Bartolo da Sassoferrato: Studi e documenti per il VI centenario* (Milan, 1962), II, 335–343.

56. Beneditto Yesu Cristo / omne parte ha probato / Che è gire de fore, / da poi che è cacciato / . . . / ognuna è gita fore, / E cescasuna ha probato / che è rentrare a furore": Buccio di Ranallo, *Cronica aquilana*, ed. Vittorio De Bartholomaeis (Rome, 1907), p. 139.

57. Giulio Vismara, "Struttura e istituzioni della prima Lega Lombarda (1167–1183)," in *Popolo e stato in Italia nell'età di Federigo Barbarossa, Relazioni e communicazioni al XXXIII Congresso Storico Subalpino* (Turin, 1970), pp. 293–332; Gina Fasoli, "La legislazione antimagnatizia a Bologna," *Rivista di storia del diritto italiano*, 6 (1933): 10–11; and Fasoli, "Ricerche sulla legislazione antimagnatizia nei comuni dell'alta e media Italia," *Rivista di storia del diritto italiano*, 12 (1939): 86–133, 240–309.

58. *De regimine civitatum*, II, q. 19, in *Bartoli opera omnia*, X, fol. 153r; for chroniclers, see Heers, *Parties and Political Life*, p. 56, quoting, among others, Giovanni Villani, *Cronica*, ed. F. G. Dragomanni (Florence, 1849), IX, xxvii. The practical effects of exclusionary procedures were, to be sure, often more limited than pronouncements about them would suggest.

59. Durkheim, *Division of Labor*, p. 4.

60. See the suggestive essays by William J. Bouwsma, "Lawyers and Early Modern Culture," *American Historical Review*, 78 (1973): 303–327; and Julius Kirshner, "Some Problems in the Interpretation of Legal Texts *Re* the Italian City-States," *Archiv fur Begriffsgeschichte*, 19 (1975): 16–27.

61. *Corpus Iuris Civilis*, ed. Paul Krueger et al. (Berlin, 1892–1895), D. XLVIII, 19 (*De poenis*), 22 (*De interdictis et relegatis et deportatis*). See, in general, Wolfgang Kunkel, *Introduction to Roman Legal and Constitutional History*, trans. J. M. Kelly (Oxford, 1966), pp. 152–164; and Fritz Schultz, *History of Roman Legal Science* (Oxford, 1946), pp. 262–299.

62. *Corpus Iuris Civilis*, D. XLVIII, 22, 5; cf. Ugo Brasiello, *La repressione penale in diritto romano* (Naples, 1937), pp. 272–275.

63. See Strachan-Davidson, *Roman Criminal Law*, II, 51–74, for an especially clear account emphasizing the linkage of *interdictio, exilium*, and *deportatio*.

64. Theodor Mommsen, *Römisches Strafrecht* (Leipzig, 1899), p. 965.

65. *Tristitia* V, 2, 56; Pietro Nocito, *I reati di stato* (Turin, 1893), pp. 463–465, is a good, brief guide to the differences between relegation and deportation.

66. See, e.g., Crifò, "Esilio," pp. 715–720; and Cavalca, *Il bando*, pp. 22–28.

67. Here I mainly follow Strachan-Davidson, *Roman Criminal Law*, II, 51–74; cf., however, Crifò, *Ricerche sull'exilium*, pp. 69–70, 125ff., 311–312.

68. Velleius Paterculus, *Compendium of Roman History* CXXVI, 3, ed. Frederick W. Shipley, Loeb Classical Library (Cambridge, Mass., 1955); and *Epistola* I, 11, in *Q. Horatii Flacci Opera*, ed. F. Klingner (Leipzig, 1950).

69. Brasiello, *Repressione penale*, pp. 45–49; and Erich S. Gruen, *Roman Politics and the Criminal Courts, 149–78 B.C.* (Cambridge, Mass., 1968), pp. 6–7, 248–287.

70. See, e.g., *Corpus Iuris Civilis, Novellae* VI, 1, 9; VII, 7, 1; XIII, 6, 1; LX, 2, 2; CXII, 2, 1. Cf. Mary V. Braginton, "Exile Under the Roman Emperors," *Classical Journal*, 39 (1943–1944): 391–407; Kunkel, *Introduction*, pp. 61–71; and A. N. Sherwin-White, *The Roman Citizenship*, 2nd ed. (Oxford, 1973), pp. 425–444.

71. *Epistulae ad familiares* IV, 7, 4, ed. W. G. Williams, Loeb Classical Library (Cambridge, Mass., 1965).

72. For a useful survey, with extensive bibliography, see Marco Scovazzi, *Le origini del diritto germanico: Fonti, preistoria, diritto pubblico* (Milan, 1957); for the classic formulation of this contrast, cf. Otto von Gierke, *Das deutsche Genossenschaftsrecht* (Leipzig, 1881), esp. III.

73. Following an influential thesis of Heinrich Brunner, "Abspaltungen der Friedlogiskeit," reprinted in Brunner's *Forschungen zur Geschichte des deutschen und französischen Rechtes* (Stuttgart, 1894), pp. 444–481.

74. The best of the older and of the more recent accounts are by Pietro Del Giudice, "Diritto penale rispetto all'Italia," in Enrico Pessina, *Enciclopedia del diritto penale italiano* (Turin, 1906), I, 438–439, 511; Hinrich Siuts, *Bann und Acht und ihre Grundlagen im Totenglauben* (Berlin, 1959), pp. 143–144 *et passim*; and M. Jacoby, *Wargus, Vargr, Verbrecher, Wolf: Eine Sprach- und Rechtsgeschichtliche Untersuchung* (Uppsala, 1974).

75. This conclusion has the support of Cavalca, *Il bando*, pp. 40–42, 58–77; Siuts, *Bann und Acht*, pp. 78–79; T. F. T. Plucknett, "Outlawry," in *Encyclopaedia of the Social Sciences* (New York, 1937), VI, 505–507; and Maurice Keen, *The Outlaws of Medieval Legend* (London, 1961), pp. 192–194. Cf., however, Georg Dahm, *Das Strafrecht Italiens im ausgehenden Mittelalter* (Berlin, 1931), pp. 98–104; and Ghisalberti, "La condanna al bando," p. 15.

76. A proposition brilliantly invoked in another context by Michel Foucault, *Discipline and Punish: The Birth of the Prison*, trans. Alan Sheridan (New York, 1978), esp. pp. 78–82.

77. *MGH, Leges*, V, cap. 97, 155.

78. Quoted, among many other examples, by Antonio Pertile, *Storia del diritto italiano* (Turin, 1892–1903), V, 310. See the discussion of late imperial and Germanic statutes by Siuts, *Bann und Acht*, pp. 19–28; and Wilhem Eckhardt, "Die Decreto Childeberti und ihre Überlieferung," *Zeitschrift der Savigny-Stiftung für Rechtsgeschichte, Germanistische Abteilung*, 84 (1967): 1–71.

79. Cf. A. M. Enriques, "La vendetta nella vita e nella legislazione fiorentina," *Archivio storico italiano*, 91 (1931): 85–146, 181–223.

80. Quoted by Siuts, *Bann und Acht*, pp. 52–53.

81. Paul Hinschius, *System des katholischen Kirchenrechts mit besonderer Rücksicht auf Deutschland* (Berlin, 1893; reprint Graz, 1959), V, 1–85—still the most thorough survey on canonical censures. Cf. Willibald Plöchl, *Geschichte des Kirchenrechts* (Vienna, 1953), II, 305–354; and F. E. Hyland, *Excommunication: Its Nature, Historical Development, and Effects* (Washington, D.C., 1928).

82. *Corpus Iuris Canonici* (Leipzig ed. 1879; reprint Graz, 1959), *Decretum*, II, C. XI, q. 3, c. 107.

83. Hinschius, *System*, V, 1–3n.
84. Ibid., 16ff.; Hyland, *Excommunication*, pp. 2–4; Siuts, *Bann und Acht*, p. 138.
85. Siuts, *Bann und Acht*, pp. 80ff.; and P. Huizing, "Alcuni testi sulla scommunica ingiusta e l'esclusione dalla chiesa," in *Etudes d'histoire de droit canonique dediées à Gabriel Le Bras* (Paris, 1965), II, 1251–1253.
86. *Corpus Iuris Canonici, Decretal-Greg. IX*, II, tit. 1. de iudiciis, c. 10; and Emmanuel Le Roy Ladurie, *Montaillou: The Promised Land of Error*, trans. Barbara Bray (New York, 1978), p. 335.
87. As quoted by Ghisalberti, "La condanna al bando," pp. 40–41.
88. Julius Ficker, *Forschungen zur Reichs- und Rechtsgechichte Italiens* (Innsbruck, 1868), I, 174.
89. Ibid., pp. 171, 218ff.; *Die Konstitutionen Friedrichs II. von Hohenstaufen für sein Königsreich Sizilien*, ed. Hermann Conrad, Thea von der Lieck-Buyken, and Wolfgang Wagner (Cologne/Vienna, 1973), pp. 174–185 (Bk. II, rubs. 1–6); and F. S. Lear, *Treason in Roman and Germanic Law* (Austin, 1965).
90. Francesco Calasso, *Medio Evo del diritto* (Milan, 1954), I, 409–452.
91. For classical literature, see Alfred Giesecke, *De philosophorum veterum quae ad exilium spectant sententiis* (Leipzig, 1891); H. M. R. Leopold, *Exulum trias, sive de Cicerone, Ovidio, Seneca exulibus* (Utrecht, 1905); and esp. Crifò, *Ricerche sull'exilium*, pp. 50–70. On exile in Christian writers, cf. Hans von Campenhausen, *Die asketische Heimatslosigkeit im altkirchlichen und frühmittelalterlichen Mönchtum* (Tübingen, 1930); and the many suggestive hints in Ladner, "Homo Viator." The "stranger" and the "refugee" have been examined as ideal types in historical experience and in literature; see, e.g., the essay on "the stranger" by Georg Simmel, in *On Individuality and Social Forms*, ed. D. N. Levine (Chicago, 1971), pp. 143–149; the papers in *Recueils de la Société Jean Bodin*, 9, Pts. 1–2 (1958); and K. Cirtautas, *The Refugee: A Psychological Study* (Boston, 1957). Tabori, *The Anatomy of Exile*, and Vortriede, "Typologie der Exilliteratur," give the nearest equivalents for "the exile." For further discussion and bibliography, see *Exile und innere Emigration*, ed. Reinold Grimm and Jost Hermand (Frankfurt am Main, 1972); Thomas A. Kamla, *Confrontation with Exile: Studies in the German Novel* (Bern/Frankfurt am Main, 1975), pp. 7–17; and Lola Sladits, *Beneath Another Sun: Literature in Exile* (New York, 1977).
92. *Controversiae* II, 2, 1, ed. M. Winterbottom, Loeb Classical Library (Cambridge, Mass./London, 1974).
93. See the recent essay by Dickinson, "The 'Tristitia': Poetry in Exile," in *Ovid*, ed. J. W. Binns, pp. 154–190; for the problem of extracting the "historical Ovid" from his writings (and a spirited attempt to overcome it), see Ronald Syme, *Ovid in History* (Oxford/New York, 1978).
94. E. K. Rand, *Ovid and His Influence* (Boston, 1925), pp. 93–94; Anacleto Cazzaniga, *Elementi retorici nella composizione delle lettere dal Ponto* (Varese, 1937); and Gordon Williams, *Tradition and Originality in Roman Poetry* (Oxford, 1968), p. 510.

95. *Tristitia* I, 3, 60–68; I, 8–9; III, 46, 47–78; III, 12; IV, 10; and *Epistulae ex Ponto* I, 3, 49–56; III, 8, 13–16.

96. *Epistulae ex Ponto* III, 7, 21–26; cf. I, 3; and *Tristitia* II, 145–146.

97. *Tristitia* II, 205 et seq.; III, 6, III, 7, 45–52; IV, 9, 11–14, 21–28; and *Epistulae ex Ponto* II, 7, 17–20; III, 6.

98. *Tristitia* III, 3, 74; IV, 1, 5–16.

99. *Seneca*, ed. C. D. N. Costa (London/Boston, 1974), esp. pp. 9–11.

100. A context (see n. 104 below) easily missed, it seems, when Seneca's works are read as historical or biographical "documents"; see, e.g., Arthur Ferrill, "Seneca's Exile and the *Ad Helviam*: A Reinterpretation," *Classical Philology*, 61 (1966): 253–257. Cf. *Ad Helviam matrem* I, 1–2, ed. J. W. Basore, in L. A. Seneca, *Moral Essays*, II, Loeb Classical Library (Cambridge, Mass., 1951).

101. Cf. Karlhaus Abel, *Bauformen in Senecas Dialogen* (Heidelberg, 1967).

102. *Ad Helviam* VIII, 4–5.

103. Ibid., XIII, 1, 3.

104. Conrad Buresch, *Consolationum a Graecis Romanisque scriptorum historia critica* (Leipzig, 1891) was the pioneering work on the genre. See Berthold Häsler, *Favorin über die Verbannung* (Bottrop, 1935); M. E. Fern, *The Latin Consolatio as a Literary Type* (St. Louis, 1941); and Rudolf Kassel, *Untersuchungen zur griechischen und römischen Konsolationsliteratur* (Munich, 1958).

105. *Epistulae morales* LXIV, 8, ed. R. M. Gummere, Loeb Classical Library (Cambridge, Mass., 1925); cf. *Ad Helviam* I, 2.

106. Cf. Cicero, *Tusculan Disputations* III, 75, 77, 81, ed. J. E. King, Loeb Classical Library (Cambridge, Mass./London, 1960).

107. Kassel, *Untersuchungen*, pp. 17–39.

108. Ibid., pp. 40–48; and André Oltramare, *Les origines de la diatribe romaine* (Lausanne, 1926).

109. "On Exile," in *Plutarch's Moralia*, VII, 518–571, ed. P. H. Lacy and Benedict Einarson, Loeb Classical Library (London, 1959); for other Greek consolations on exile, see Häsler, *Favorin über die Verbannung*, pp. 7ff.

110. *Dio's Roman History*, XXXVIII, 18, 2, ed. E. Cary, Loeb Classical Library (London, 1914).

111. Charles Favez, *La consolation latine chrétienne* (Paris, 1937), pp. 15ff.

112. *Synonyma de lamentatione animae peccatricis* I, 15, in *Patrologiae Latinae*, ed. J.-P. Migne (Paris, 1862), LXXXIII, 831A. Cf. *Select Letters of St. Jerome* (*Epistola* XIV, 10), ed. F. A. Wright, Loeb Classical Library (Cambridge, Mass., 1954), pp. 48–51; and St. Augustine, *City of God*, I, 8–9; III, 16, ed. G. E. McCracken, Loeb Classical Library (Cambridge, Mass., 1957).

113. *The Consolation of Philosophy* I, 5, ed. Irving Edman [New York, 1943], p. 27:

> While I grieved thus in long-drawn pratings, Philosophy looked on with a calm countenance, not one whit moved by my complaints. Then she said, "When I saw you in grief and tears I knew thereby that you were unhappy and in exile, but I knew not how distant was your exile until your speech declared it. But you have not been driven so far from

your home; you have wandered hence yourself. . . . For if you recall your true native country, you know that it is not under the rule of the many-headed people, as Athens was of old, but there is one Lord, one King, who rejoices in the greater number of his subjects, not in their banishment. To be guided by His reins, to bow to His Justice, is the highest liberty."

114. See Giorgio Brugnoli, "Ovidio e gli esiliati carolingi," *Atti del Congresso Internazionale Ovidiano* (Rome, 1959), pp. 209–216.

115. *Theodolfus Modoino . . . de suo exilio*, lines 15–18, in *MGH, Poetae Latini Aevi Carolini*, ed. E. Duemmler, I, 563; cf. *Tristitia* I, 1, 17–19; III, 7, 6.

116. *Rescriptum Modoini Episcopi ad Theodolfum Episcopum*, in *MGH, Poetae Latini*, I, 569–573.

117. Cf., e.g., *Carmen Nigelli Ermoldi exulis in laudem Gloriossimi Pippini regis*, in *MGH, Poetae Latini*, II, 79–85. See Wilfried Stroh, *Ovid im Urteil der Nachwelt* (Darmstadt, 1969); Winfried Trillitzsch, *Seneca im literarischen Urteil der Antike*, 2 vols. (Amsterdam, 1971); and Pierre Courcelle, *La Consolation de Philosophie dans la tradition littéraire: Antécédents et postérité de Boèce* (Paris, 1967).

CHAPTER TWO

1. The legates can be followed through the extracts from their report and related documents in Robert Davidsohn, *Forschungen zur Geschichte von Florenz* (Berlin, 1908), III, 287–321.

2. Ibid., 295.

3. See, in general, the bibliographical essays by Paolo Brezzi, "I comuni cittadini italiani e l'impero medioevale," in *Nuove questioni di storia medioevale*, pp. 177–207; and Nicolai Rubinstein, "Studies on the Political History of the Age of Dante," in *Atti del Congresso Internazionale di Studi Danteschi* (Florence, 1966), pp. 225–247. One of the best older syntheses is Emile Jordan, *L'Allemagne et l'Italie aux XIIe et XIIIe siècles* (Paris, 1939); one of the most recent is by Giovanni Tabacco, in the Einaudi *Storia d'Italia*, II.1, 5–274.

4. Cf. Machiavelli's *Discorsi sopra la prima deca di Tito Livio*, I, 12, in *Tutte le opere*, pp. 95–96; and "Considerations on the 'Discourses' of Machiavelli," in Francesco Guicciardini, *Selected Writings*, p. 81.

5. *Ottonis et Rahewini Gesta Frederici Imperatoris*, pp. 116–117, 120; and "Dantes Alagherii . . . scelestissimis Florentinis intrinsecis," in *Opere*, ed. Porena and Pazzaglia, p. 1358.

6. Cf., e.g., the most recent syntheses by Heers, *Parties and Political Life*, pp. 50–54; and Martines, *Power and Imagination*, pp. 12–21, 45–46.

7. Robert Davidsohn, *Geschichte von Florenz*, II.1 (Berlin, 1908), 325–335, 504ff.; many other examples are documented in Davidsohn's *Forschungen*, IV, 8–67.

8. Villani, *Cronica*, ed. Dragomanni, V, xxxviii; and Heers, *Parties and Political Life*, pp. 27–39.

9. Davidsohn, *Forschungen*, IV, 29ff., is still the fundamental study of Guelph and Ghibelline origins; an excellent brief account is given by Daniel Waley, *The Italian City-Republics* (New York/Toronto, 1969), pp. 203–218.

10. Bonifacio de Morano, *Chronicon mutinense*, anno 1329, in *RIS*, XI, col. 117; and *Annales placentini Gibellini*, anno 1270, in *MGH, Scriptores*, XVIII, 542–543. Heers, *Parties and Political Life*, pp. 281–290, has a good chapter on rites and symbols of political allegiance. *Bartholomaei de Neocastro Historia sicula*, ed. Giuseppe Paladino, in *RIS*, n.s., XIII.3, 7, conveys in a single sentence something of the air of intense expectation which greeted a foreign champion in Italy: "Surgunt praeterea Regni magnates, anno decimae indictionis [1267], exules et Italiae partes Gibellinorum in Alemanniam protendunt; Conradinum hortantur ad Regni fastigia, quod, sublato jure, ad alterius [Charles of Anjou] posse devectum est."

11. Davidsohn, *Geschichte*, II.1, 470–471, 516–518.

12. Cf. the Ghibelline version in *Gli atti del Comune di Milano fino all'anno MCCXVI*, ed. Carlo Manaresi (Milan, 1919), no. 69, par. 2; and the Guelph statement of similar policy in Charles of Anjou's letter, 27 March 1271, "Potestatibus, Capitaneis, Consiliis et Communitatibus per Tusciam constitutis," in *Documenti delle relazioni tra Carlo I d'Angiò e la Toscana*, ed. Sergio Terlezzi (Florence, 1950), no. 302. A fourteenth-century example is the Black Guelph alliance of 5 April 1306 with provisions "ad conculationem, depressionem, exterminum et mortem perpetuum Ghibellinorum et alborum": Davidsohn, *Forschungen*, III, 319. See *Popolo e stato in Italia nell'età di Federigo Barbarossa*, esp. Giulio Vismara, "Struttura e istituzioni della prima Lega Lombarda (1167–1183)," pp. 293–332; and Emile Jordan, *Les origines de la domination angévine en Italie* (Paris, 1909).

13. Jordan, *L'Allemagne e l'Italie*, pp. 347–348; Jordan, *Les origines*, pp. 431ff.; and G. M. Monti, *La dominazione angioina in Piemonte* (Turin, 1926).

14. Davidsohn, *Forschungen*, IV, 157–158; Giovanni Gozzadini, *Delle torre gentilizie di Bologna e delle famiglie alle quali appartenero* (Bologna, 1875), p. 355; and Umberto Dorini, *Notizie storiche sull'Università di Parte Guelfa a Firenze* (Florence, 1903). Other examples are in Heers, *Parties and Political Life*, pp. 179–185.

15. *Cronica fratris Salimbene de Adam*, anno 1247, ed. Oswald Holder-Egger, in *MGH, Scriptores*, XXXII, 189–190.

16. E.g., in Florence and Romagna; see Nicola Ottokar, *Il comune di Firenze alla fine del Dugento*, 2nd ed. (Turin, 1962), 3–9; and Gina Fasoli, "La pace del 1279 fra i partiti bolognesi," *Archivio storico italiano*, 91 (1933): 47–75.

17. See esp. Gino Masi, "Il nome delle fazioni fiorentine de' bianchi e de' neri," *Studi medioevali*, 3 (1927): 123–134.

18. *Cronica di Dino Compagni*, II, xxxi, ed. Isidoro Del Lungo, in the second vol. of Del Lungo, *Dino Compagni e la sua Cronica* (Florence, 1879).

19. Cited by Waley, *Italian City-Republics*, pp. 206–207.

20. The documents and letters are in *Codice dantesco*, ed. Renato Piattoli (Florence, 1940), nos. 90–93; and *Opere*, pp. 1364–1373. See Carlo Cipolla, " 'La compagnia malvagia e scempia,' " *Archivio storico italiano*, ser. V, 49 (1912): 245–281; and Chapter Three of this book.

21. Davidsohn, *Forschungen*, III, 289–299.

22. See, e.g., Giovanni Arnaldi, *Studi sui cronisti della marca trevigiana*

nell'età di Ezzelino da Romano (Rome, 1963), *passim*; *Liber de laudibus civitatis Ticinensis*, ed. R. Maiacchi and F. Quintavalle, in *RIS*, n.s., XI.1, xxvii; *Rolandini Patavini cronica Marchie Trevixiane*, ed. Antonio Bonardi, in *RIS*, n.s., VIII.1, 41–43; Giuliana Giannelli, "Un governo di fuorusciti senesi," *Bulletino senese di storia patria*, 56 (1949): 80–92; and Heers, *Parties and Political Life*, pp. 35, 186–187.

23. Ludovico Savioli, *Annali bolognesi* (Bassano, 1784–1795), III, 214–221, 233–236; and *Documenti delle relazioni tra Carlo I d'Angiò e la Toscana*, no. 17.

24. The letters and legatine acts cited on these points are in Davidsohn, *Forschungen*, III, 307–314; cf. Emilio Orioli, "Documenti bolognesi sulla fazione dei Bianchi," *Atti e memorie della R. Deputazione di Storia Patria per le Provincie di Romagna*, ser. III, 14 (1896): 1–13; and Ubaldo Pasqui, *Documenti per la storia della città di Arezzo* (Florence, 1920), II, nos. 693, 695, 697–698.

25. See the analysis of the Florentine *Libro del Chiodo* by Isidoro Del Lungo, "Una vendetta in Firenze il giorno di S. Giovanni del 1295," *Archivio storico italiano*, ser. IV, 17 (1886): 400–409; and the parallel conclusions for Prato in Renato Piattoli, "I ghibellini del comune di Prato dalla battaglia di Benevento alla Pace del cardinale Latino," *Archivio storico italiano*, 88 (1930): 229, 235, *et passim*.

26. Hans Spangenberg, *Cangrande I. della Scala* (Berlin, 1892–1895), II, 12.

27. Davidsohn, *Forschungen*, IV, 191.

28. Demetrio Marzi, *La cancelleria della repubblica fiorentina* (Rocca S. Casciano, 1910), pp. 121–122, 272–273.

29. Davidsohn, *Forschungen*, III, 309.

30. Heers, *Parties and Political Life*, pp. 127–132, 187–188.

31. Villani, *Cronica*, VI, xxxiii; and Waley, *Italian City-Republics*, pp. 214, 218.

32. Giovanni da Prato, *Il Paradiso degli Alberti*, ed. Alphons Wesselofsky (Bologna, 1867), I, 100–101; and Renato Piattoli, "I ghibellini di Prato," *Archivio storico italiano*, 89 (1931): 247.

33. Michael Mallett, *Mercenaries and Their Masters: Warfare in Renaissance Italy* (Totowa, N.J., 1974), pp. 28–31, 46–47.

34. For one of the most influential and one of the most recent statements of this "revisionist" position, cf. Ottokar, *Il comune di Firenze*, pp. 99 *et passim*; and Bertelli, *Potere oligarchico*. For renewed emphasis on the importance of class conflicts, however, see Martines, *Power and Imagination*, pp. 45–56ff.; and, in a particular case, Sarah R. Blanshei, *Perugia, 1260–1340: Conflict and Change in a Medieval Italian Urban Society*, in *Transactions of the American Philosophical Society*, n.s., 66, Pt. 2 (1976): 8–10, 52–53.

35. Davidsohn, *Geschichte*, III, 212–217; Gino Arias, "Il fondamento economico delle fazioni fiorentine de' Guelfi bianchi e de' Guelfi neri," in *Studi e documenti di storia del diritto* (Florence, 1901), pp. 101–118; Gino Masi, "I banchieri fiorentini nella vita politica della città sulla fine del Dugento," *Archivio giuridico*, 105 (1931): 57–89; and Masi, "La struttura sociale delle fazioni politiche ai tempi di Dante," *Giornale dantesco*, 31 (1928): 3–28.

36. As noted by Berthold Stahl, *Adel und Volk im florentiner Dugento*

(Cologne/Graz, 1965), pp. 1–9; the Cerchi connections are traced by Masi, "I banchieri," pp. 60–66.

37. *Cronica di Dino Compagni*, II, xxix.

38. Davidsohn, *Forschungen*, III, 295ff.

39. Vito Vitale, *Il dominio della parte guelfa in Bologna, 1280–1327* (Bologna, 1901), pp. 13–17; *Chronica parva Ferrariense*, in *RIS*, VIII, col. 485; and *Storia di Milano* (Milan, 1954), IV, 101–115.

40. Davidsohn, *Geschichte*, II.2, 94, 160; III, 218–219.

41. *Cronica di Dino Compagni*, II, xxii; cf. Davidsohn, *Forschungen*, III, 300ff.

42. *Chronica parva Ferrariense*, col. 485; and Savioli, *Annali bolognesi*, III, 491n.

43. Giovanni Sforza, "Castruccio Castracani e i lucchesi di parte bianca," *Atti e memorie della R. Accademia delle Scienze, Lettere e Arti*, ser. II, 42 (1889): 345; and Luigi Frati, "Graziolo de' Bambagliuoli esiliato a Napoli," *Giornale dantesco*, 1 (1894): 212–216.

44. *Novella 1*, in *Tutte le opere di Matteo Bandello*, ed. Francesco Flora (Milan, 1934), I, 8–9.

45. *Enciclopedia dantesca* (Rome, 1970–1976), I, s.v. "Alighieri"; Ernest Hatch Wilkins, *Life of Petrarch* (Chicago/London, 1961), pp. 1–16; and *Epistolario di Coluccio Salutati*, ed. Francesco Novati (Rome, 1891–1916), IV, 149.

46. Villani, *Cronica*, VI, lxxxvi; IX, clxxxviii.

47. See Chapter Three of this book.

48. As recorded by doc. 4, in Piattoli, "I Ghibellini di Prato," pp. 256–257.

49. Renato Piattoli, "Vanni Fucci e Focaccia de' Cancellieri alla luce di nuovi documenti," *Archivio storico italiano*, 92 (1934): 93–115.

50. Davidsohn, *Forschungen*, III, 287ff.; and Villani, *Cronica*, IX, clxxxviii.

51. *De bannitis pro maleficio*, ed. Hermann Kantorowicz, in Kantorowicz, *Albertus Gandinus und das Strafrecht der Scholastik* (Leipzig/Berlin, 1926), II, 133–135; and Piattoli, "I ghibellini di Prato," pp. 236–237.

52. *Annales placentini Gibellini*, pp. 516–521.

53. *Cronica fratris Salimbene*, anno 1267, p. 474.

54. Robert Brentano, *Two Churches: England and Italy in the Thirteenth Century* (Princeton, 1968), pp. 145ff., gives telling concreteness to the theme of partisanship in arbitration "most of the time in most places in both Church and State in the thirteenth century" (p. 171). For European-wide movements and institutions of pacification, see, with bibliography, Heers, *Family Clans*, pp. 105–107, 120–121.

55. Antonio Di Stefano, "Le origini dei frati gaudenti," *Archivum Romanicum*, 10 (1926): 305–350.

56. Villani, *Cronica*, VII, xiii.

57. Jacopo della Lana, *Commento dantesco*, ed. I. Scarbelli (Bologna, 1866), I, 383.

58. Spangenberg, *Cangrande I. della Scala*, II, 93; for a similar example, see Emilio Cristiani, *Nobiltà e popolo nel comune di Pisa. Dalle origini del podestariato alla signoria del Donoratico* (Naples, 1962), p. 257.

59. *Cronica di Dino Compagni*, II, ii–iv; Guido Levi, "Bonifazio VIII e

le sue relazioni col comune di Firenze," *Archivio storico della Società Romana di Storia Patria*, 5 (1882): 365–374.

60. Villani, *Cronica*, VIII, xix.

61. I follow Compagni's description (II, ix–xx), and the reconstruction by Isidoro del Lungo, *I bianchi e i neri*, 2nd ed. (Milan, 1921), pp. 158ff.

62. Villani, *Cronica*, VIII, xlix.

63. From a letter of the Black Guelph *signoria*, in Del Lungo, *I bianchi e i neri*, pp. 254–255.

64. *Cronica di Dino Compagni*, III, iv.

65. Ibid., vii.

66. Raoul Manselli, "Ezzelino da Romano nella politica del secolo XIII," in *Studi ezzeliniani* (Rome, 1963), pp. 35–68; cf. Giovanni Battista Verci, *Storia degli Ecelini* (Bassano, 1779), III, docs. 200, 245, for the general understanding that many of Ezzelino's followers lived under ban "in . . . terra, seu districtu" and the particular case of Dominus Aldryhetum de Castrobarco. On the Visconti case, see *Storia di Milano*, IV, 297ff.; and pp. 56–57 above.

67. Cristiani, *Nobiltà e popolo nel comune di Pisa*, pp. 249–252; Friedrich Bock, "I processi di Giovanni XXII contro i ghibellini delle Marche," *Bulletino dell'Istituto Storico Italiano per il Medio Evo*, 57 (1941): 19ff.; and John Larner, *Lords of the Romagna: Romagnol Society and the Origins of the Signorie* (Ithaca, 1965), pp. 23–39 *et passim*.

68. Thanks again to the accounts in Villani, *Cronica*, VIII, xlix; and *Cronica di Dino Compagni*, II, xxviii–xxxvi; see, too, Del Lungo, *I bianchi e i neri*, pp. 282ff.; and Davidsohn, *Geschichte*, II.2, 245ff.

69. *Annales placentini Gibellini*, pp. 499–500; Villani, *Cronica*, VI, lxxxvii; IX, cvii; Axel Goria, "Le lotte intestine in Genova tra il 1305 e il 1309," in *Miscellanea di storia ligure in onore di Giorgio Falco* (Milan, 1962), pp. 261–263; and Daniel Waley, *Medieval Orvieto: The Political History of an Italian City-State, 1157–1334* (Cambridge, 1952), pp. 123–124, 127–128.

70. Davidsohn, *Forschungen*, IV, 157ff.; and Piattoli, "I ghibellini di Prato," pp. 235–240.

71. Spangenberg, *Cangrande I. della Scala*, p. 31, gives a close account of the incident.

72. Cf., e.g., the case of Ser Domenico da Gravina on p. 128 above; or the intrigues of *fuorusciti* inside Milan during the 1260s and 1270s in *Storia di Milano*, IV, 297ff.

73. Pertile, *Storia del diritto italiano*, V, 317–321, lists many examples.

74. *Annales placentini Gibellini*, pp. 565–566, citing "certain letters" on these events. For a modern account, see *Storia di Milano*, IV, 328–330, with references to other contemporary sources.

75. *Cronica di Dino Compagni*, III, x–xi; cf. suggestive interpretations of biblical symbolism in the narrative (but also the exotic conclusion that Dante authored it) by Elisabeth Von Roon-Bassermann, *Die Weissen und die Schwarzen von Florenz* (Freiburg, 1954). Interestingly similar elements appear in a nearly contemporary account of the return (July 1303) of Ghiberto da Correggio's party to Parma: *Chronicon parmense*, ed. Giuliano Bonazzi, in *RIS*, n.s., IX.9, 85.

76. I draw heavily in what follows on William M. Bowsky, *Henry VII in Italy: The Conflict of Empire and City-States, 1310–1313* (Lincoln, Neb., 1960).

77. Ibid., pp. 17–53.

78. *MGH, Constitutiones et acta publica imperatorum et regum*, IV.1, ed. Jacob Schwalm, no. 509 (27 December 1310).

79. *Acta Henrici VII*, ed. Francesco Bonaini (Florence, 1877), II, no. 16 (January 1311).

80. *Historia Iohannis de Cermenate*, ed. L. A. Ferrai (Rome, 1899), p. 39.

81. Davidsohn, *Geschichte*, III, 413ff.; *Dizionario biografico degli italiani*, s.v. "Buonsignori"; *Storia di Milano*, V, 56; and Bowsky, *Henry VII*, pp. 56ff.

82. Bowsky, *Henry VII*, pp. 70–71, 90.

83. *MGH, Constitutiones et acta publica*, IV.1, no. 359; IV.2, nos. 1273–1274.

84. Bowsky, *Henry VII*, pp. 61ff.

85. Francesco Petrarca, *Epistolae familiares*, II, iii, ed. Vittorio Rossi (Florence, 1933), II, 69.

86. *Historia Iohannis de Cermenate*, p. 33.

87. Ibid., p. 36.

88. *Storia di Milano*, V, 28–30.

89. *Cronica di Dino Compagni*, III, xxvi.

90. *Storia di Milano*, V, 32ff.; and Bowsky, *Henry VII*, pp. 78–95.

91. Cermenate (*Historia de Iohannis de Cermenate*, pp. 51ff.) is the principal source.

92. Giannina Biscaro, "Benzo da Alessandria ed i giudizi contro i ribelli dell'impero a Milano nel 1311," *Archivio storico lombardo*, ser. IV, 7 (1907): 281–316.

93. The *relatio* and *inquisitiones* of the imperial emissaries are in *Acta Henrici VII*, ed. Wilhelm Doenniges (Berlin, 1839), I, 123–178.

94. *MGH, Constitutiones et acta publica*, IV.2, no. 915; P. S. Leicht, "Cino da Pistoia e la citazione di re Roberto da parte d'Arrigo VII," *Archivio storico italiano*, 112 (1954): 313–320.

95. *Acta Henrici VII*, I, 125–139 (Brescia); 139–152 (Verona and Vicenza); 152–164 (Mantua and Modena).

96. Ibid., 176.

97. Ibid., 167.

CHAPTER THREE

1. The documents are collected in *Codice dantesco*, ed. Renato Piattoli (Florence, 1940), nos. 90 (sentence of 27 January 1302), 91 (sentence of 10 March 1302), 106 ("reform of Baldo Aguglione," 2 September 1311), and 115 (sentence of 6 November 1315). Throughout this chapter, I refer to and quote the record from this edition without citing every instance. Since some points of interpretation are still controversial, the reader may want to examine the texts along with me and also to compare Eugenio Barsanti, *I processi di Dante* (Florence, 1908); Bernardino Barbadoro, "La condanna di Dante e le fazioni politiche del suo tempo," *Studi danteschi*, 2 (1920): 5–74; Giovanni

Cuboni, "Le condanne di Dante," *Convivium*, 11 (1939): 1–45; and *Il processo di Dante*, ed. Dante Ricci (Florence, 1967). Isidoro Del Lungo, *Dell'esiglio di Dante* (Florence, 1881) is brief and more general; the five volumes of the *Enciclopedia dantesca* (Rome, 1970–1976) are convenient and richly authoritative, with entries and bibliography on most related questions.

2. Archivio di Stato, Florence, *Capitani di Parte*, 20 (numeri rossi). Excerpts appear in *Delizie degli eruditi toscani*, ed. Idlefonso di San Luigi (Florence, 1770–1789), X, no. 93; the best discussions and analyses are in Isidoro Del Lungo, "Una vendetta in Firenze," pp. 355–409; and Davidsohn, *Forschungen*, III, 263–321.

3. The most useful guides I have found to the *mare magnum* of Italian legal history are Calasso, *Medio Evo del diritto*, I; Pertile, *Storia del diritto italiano*; Georg Dahm, *Das Strafrecht Italiens im ausgehenden Mittelalter* (Berlin/Leipzig, 1931); Enrico Besta, *Fonti del diritto italiano dalla caduta dell'impero sino ai tempi nostri*, 2nd ed. (Milan, 1950); and *Novissimo digesto italiano* (Turin, 1968–1975).

4. *Paradiso*, XVI, 52–57; cf. Roberto Abbondanza, "Baldo d'Aguglione," in *Dizionario biografico degli italiani* (Rome, 1963), V, 506–510.

5. L. Cantini, "Dell'ufizio del potestà di Firenze," in *Saggi istorici d'antichità toscane*, II (Florence, 1796); G. Hanauer, "Das Berufspodestat im 13. Jahrhundert," *Mitteilungen des Instituts für Österreichische Geschichtsforschung*, 23 (1902): 374–426; Fritz Hertter, *Die Podestàliteratur Italiens im 12. und 13. Jahrhundert* (Leipzig/Berlin, 1910); and Angelo Sorbelli, "I teorici del reggimento comunale," *Bulletino dell'Istituto Storico Italiano*, 59 (1944): 31–136.

6. Hertter, *Podestàliteratur*, pp. 7, 78.

7. Sorbelli, "I teorici," p. 134; and Gino Masi, *Il sindicato delle magistrature comunali nel secolo XIV* (Rome, 1930).

8. Giuseppe Inizitari, "Cante de' Gabrieli," in *Enciclopedia dantesca*, II, 81.

9. It is interesting to compare Carlo Angeleri, *Il problema religioso del Rinascimento* (Florence, 1952), with its emphasis on the institutional and intellectual history of religion, and the fresh work of Donald Weinstein, Marvin Becker, Richard Trexler, and others represented in *The Pursuit of Holiness in Late Medieval and Renaissance Religion*, ed. Heiko Oberman and Charles Trinkaus (Leiden, 1973).

10. See Richard C. Trexler, "Ritual Behavior in Renaissance Florence: The Setting," *Medievalia et Humanistica*, ser. II, 4 (1973): 125–144; and now Trexler's full-scale study, *Public Life in Renaissance Florence* (New York, 1980), esp. pp. 19–33.

11. Josef Kohler and Giovanni degli Azzi, *Das florentiner Strafrecht des XIV. Jahrhunderts* (Mannheim/Leipzig, 1909), p. 50.

12. There are stimulating remarks on these themes, as on all questions of "political justice," in Otto Kirchheimer, *Political Justice: The Use of Legal Procedure for Political Ends* (Princeton, 1961); and Foucault, *Discipline and Punish*, esp. pp. 48–54.

13. *Codice dantesco*, p. 107; on the sources and instruments of judicial authority in Florence, see Lauro Martines, *Lawyers and Statecraft in Renaissance Florence* (Princeton, 1968), pp. 119–129.

14. Especially useful on these developments are the works by Francesco Calasso, *I glossatori e la teoria della sovranità*, 3rd ed. (Milan, 1957); Ugo Niccolini, *Il principio di legalità nelle democrazie italiane*, 2nd ed. (Padua, 1955); and Mario Sbriccioli, *L'interpretazione dello statuto: Contributo allo studio della funzione dei giuristi nell'età comunale* (Milan, 1969). It will be apparent by now that Max Weber's analysis, if not his historical account, of types of legitimacy has deeply influenced my own; cf. Weber's *The Theory of Economic and Political Organization*, ed. and trans. A. M. Henderson and Talcott Parsons (New York, 1964), pp. 124–130.

15. Angelo Solerti, *Le vite di Dante, Petrarca e Boccaccio scritte fino al secolo decimosesto* (Milan, n.d.), p. 103; cf. *Codice dantesco*, pp. 106, 133, 156; and the incisive comments by Carlo Dionisotti, "Dante nel Quattrocento," *Atti del Congresso Internazionale di Studi Danteschi*, I, 350–352.

16. *MGH, Constitutiones et acta publica imperatorum et regum*, IV.1, ed. Jacob Schwalm, nos. 715–716; Bowsky, *Henry VII*, pp. 178–192, reviews the imperial condemnations in Italy, the controversies surrounding them, and their outcome.

17. *Tre donne intorno al cor mi son venute*, in *Opere*, ed. Porena and Pazzaglia, pp. 1067ff.; cf. Chapter Five below.

18. Eduard Will, *Die Gutachten des Oldradus de Ponte zum Prozess Heinrichs VII. gegen Robert von Neapel* (Berlin/Leipzig, 1917); and Bowsky, *Henry VII*, p. 183.

19. Kantorowicz, *Albertus Gandinus*, I, has made the procedures and record keeping of communal courts tangibly precise; so, too, for ecclesiastical courts, has Brentano, *Two Churches*, pp. 106–173.

20. John H. Langbein, *Prosecuting Crime in the Renaissance* (Cambridge, Mass., 1974), pp. 129–139, neatly summarizes the results; for a clear guide to the workings of the process, see Giuseppe Salvioli, *Storia della procedura civile e criminale* (Milan, 1927), pp. 356–362.

21. F. A. Biener, *Beiträge zu der Geschichte des Inquisitionsprocesses und der Geschworengerichte* (Leipzig, 1827), pp. 8–9, quoted by Langbein, *Prosecuting Crime*, p. 137.

22. See Langbein, *Prosecuting Crime*, p. 133, citing Eberhard Schmidt, *Inquisitionsprozess und Rezeption* (Leipzig, 1940); and Roberto Celli, *Studi sui sistemi normativi delle democrazie comunali, secoli XII–XV* (Florence, 1976), p. 124.

23. John W. Baldwin, "The Intellectual Preparation for the Canon of 1215 Against Ordeals," *Speculum*, 36 (1961): 613–636; and Gina Fasoli, "Giuristi, giudici e notai nell'ordinamento comunale e nella vita cittadina," *Atti del Convegno Internazionale di Studi Accursiani* (Milan, 1968), I, 25–39.

24. *Codice dantesco*, p. 104; cf. excerpts from the statutes and the accompanying discussion in Kohler and Degli Azzi, *Das florentiner Strafrecht*, p. 133 *et passim*.

25. *Codice dantesco*, p. 105; and Barsanti, *I processi di Dante*, pp. 19–25.

26. Carlo Ghisalberti, "La teoria del notorio nel diritto commune," *Annali di storia del diritto*, 1 (1957): 403–451; and Celli, *Studi*, p. 101.

27. *Codice dantesco*, pp. 105–106.

28. See the exculpating discussions of the evidence by Barbadoro, "La condanna di Dante," pp. 30–45; and Dante Ricci, in *Il processo di Dante*, pp. 113–145.

29. *Codice dantesco*, pp. 95–96.

30. Kirchheimer, *Political Justice*, pp. 6–7.

31. Cuboni, "Le condanne di Dante," p. 9, carefully reviews the statutory legislation on citation.

32. Three recent studies make it possible to trace the theory and operation of this important but difficult and much-misunderstood institution: Anthony M. C. Mooney, "The Legal Ban in Florentine Statutory Law and the *De Bannitis* of Nello da San Gemignano," Ph.D. dissertation, U.C.L.A., 1976; Peter R. Pazzaglini, *The Criminal Ban of the Sienese Commune, 1225–1310*, Quaderni di "Studi Senesi," 45 (Milan, 1979); and Cavalca, *Il bando*. These works correct and supersede Carlo Ghisalberti, "La condanna al bando nel diritto comune," *Archivio giuridico*, ser. IV, 27 (1960): 3–75. Although some aspects of the ban remain controversial, I have pieced together what seem to me well-established points in the following paragraphs. I am grateful to Dr. Pazzaglini for sharing his work with me.

33. Mooney, "The Legal Ban," pp. 32–35.

34. See Kohler and Degli Azzi, *Das florentiner Strafrecht*, p. 171; Giovanni Corazzini, "Cenni sulla procedura penale in Firenze," in *Miscellanea fiorentina di erudizione*, ed. Iodoco del Badia (Florence, 1902), I, 21; and Mooney, "The Legal Ban," pp. 62–64. Pazzaglini, *The Criminal Ban*, pp. 23–34, gives an account of Sienese terminology and practice (the *relatio* of messenger to notary; the *cridatio in bannum*), which does much to clarify analogous procedures in Florence.

35. *Codice dantesco*, p. 106; Mooney, "The Legal Ban," p. 53, adopts the terms *bannum comminatorium* and *bannum diffinitivum* from Nello da San Gimignano's fifteenth-century treatise; cf. Pazzaglini, *The Criminal Ban*, pp. 23–34, who uses language more expressive of actual practice.

36. With Mooney and Pazzaglini, see Cavalca, *Il bando*, pp. 173–174.

37. Ibid., pp. 175–187.

38. *Codice dantesco*, pp. 106–107.

39. Ibid., p. 107; cf. Pazzaglini, *The Criminal Ban*, pp. 34–38, for the so-called *formatio* or *esemplatio* of the sentence.

40. Bernardino Barbadoro, *Le finanze della repubblica fiorentina* (Florence, 1929), pp. 219–221.

41. *Codice dantesco*, pp. 201–203; cf. Barbadoro, *Le finanze*, pp. 217–238, on the administration of rebel property generally. Similar communal provisions are found in Archivio di Stato, Perugia, *Banditi e condannati*, fols. 6–11v ("Ordinamenti per rebelles et confinati," December 1378).

42. *Codice dantesco*, pp. 204–212 (a settlement between Francesco Alighieri and Dante's sons Piero and Jacopo, 16 May 1332); cf. Michele Barbi and Renato Piattoli, "La casa di Dante," *Studi danteschi*, 32 (1938): 72–76.

43. Cf. *Codice dantesco*, pp. 231–233; and Umberto Dorini, "Dei beni rurali confiscati a Dante," *Bullettino della Società Dantesca Italiana*, n.s., 12 (1905): 34–39.

44. *Codice dantesco*, pp. 204–212; and Dorini, "Beni rurali," pp. 39–41.

45. See Cuboni, "Le condanne di Dante," p. 9; and on the status of the *citatus*, Mooney, "The Legal Ban," pp. 64–65.

46. Mooney, "The Legal Ban," pp. 68–69, underscores the role of contumacy—to the exclusion of the punitive component, which is kept in focus by Pazzaglini, *The Criminal Ban*, pp. 44–49 *et passim*.

47. As discussed esp. by Ghisalberti, "La condanna al bando," pp. 15 ff.; and now by Cavalca, *Il bando*, pp. 175 ff. *et passim*.

48. *Accursii Glossa in Digestum vetus* (Venice, 1488; facsimile ed. Turin, 1969), ad D. XLVIII, 19, 5; for Roman practices and glossators' opinions, see Cavalca, *Il bando*, pp. 78–83.

49. *Tractatus de maleficiis*, rub. *Quid agendum reo absente et contumace*, ed. Kantorowicz, in *Albertus Gaudinus*, II, 129–130.

50. *Tractatus de bannitis*, no. 1, in *Tractatus Universi Iuris* (Venice, 1584), XI.1, fol. 355 (*Bannitus quis dici possit, et cui aequiparetur*); it should be noted that the attribution of the treatise to Jacopo has been disputed (inconclusively) by A. Marcello, "Opere giustamente e ingiustamente attribuite a Jacopo d'Arena," *R. Istituto Lombardo di Scienze e Lettere, Rendiconti*, ser. II, 61 (1928): 851, 856. For contemporary discussions of the Accursian parallel, see Cavalca, *Il bando*, pp. 86–88.

51. Alberico da Rosciate, *Commentarium de statutis*, IV, q. 1, 1, in *Tractatus Universi Iuris*, II, fol. 2r.

52. *Tractatus de bannitis*, nos. 1–2, fol. 355.

53. *Quaestiones statutorum*, q. 1, 9, ed. Arrigo Solmi, in *Bibliotheca Iuris Medii Aevi*, III (Bologna, 1901); for some of those difficulties, see Chapter Two above.

54. *Tractatus bannitorum*, in *Bartoli opera omnia*, X, fols. 129v–130v. Cf. Cavalca, *Il bando*, pp. 94–100, for what seems to me the rather strained argument that Bartolus had altogether "solved" the problems; among other things, the relationship between imperial and communal jurisdictions and the procedural differences under the *Lex Iulia de maiestate* and communal statutes remained problematic. Nor do the terms *hostes* and *transfugae* actually appear in many of the communal sources cited to support the aptness of the analogy. See also Carlo Ghisalberti, "Sulla teoria dei delitti di maestà nel diritto comune," *Archivio giuridico*, ser. VI, 15 (1954): 100–177.

55. *Commentarium de statutis*, q. 1, 6.

56. Marcel David, "L'hégémonie impériale dans le doctrine de Bartole," in *Bartolo da Sassoferrato. Studi e documenti*, II, 199–216, has revived the sense of diffidence and limits with which the lawyers contested the idea of imperial sovereignty; see below n. 78.

57. *Die Konstitutionen Friedrichs II*, pp. 174–185 (Bk. II, rubs. 1–6); and Ficker, *Forschungen*, I, 223–225.

58. *De bannitis pro maleficio*, ed. Kantorowicz, in *Albertus Gandinus*, II, 131–132.

59. Ibid., pp. 133 ff., 137–140, 143 ff., 148–151.

60. Pertile, *Storia del diritto italiano*, V, 326, cites these and many other examples; see, too, Calvalca, *Il bando*, pp. 55–58.

61. *Statuti di Bologna dell'anno 1288*, Bk. V, rubs. 2, 66, ed. Gina Fasoli and Pietro Sella (Vatican City, 1937–1939), I, 285–290, 356–358; cf. the Florentine Ordinances of Justice (1293), rub. 52, in Gaetano Salvemini, *Magnati e popolani in Firenze dal 1280 al 1295*, 2nd ed. (Turin, 1960), p. 425.

62. *De regimine civitatum*, II, q. 19, in *Bartoli opera omnia*, X, fol. 153r.

63. Davidsohn, *Forschungen*, III, 300ff.; and Renato Piattoli, "I ghibellini del comune di Prato," p. 220.

64. *Cronica di Dino Compagni*, II, xxx–xxxi.

65. Mooney, "The Legal Ban," pp. 162–165.

66. *Codice dantesco*, pp. 153–157; and Davidsohn, *Geschichte*, III, 587ff.

67. Barbadoro, *Le finanze*, p. 219; and Del Lungo, "Una vendetta," pp. 393–396.

68. Mooney, "The Legal Ban," pp. 124–127.

69. *Super constitutionem "Qui sint rebelles,"* in *Bartoli opera omnia*, X, fol. 104v.

70. *Codice dantesco*, p. 154.

71. As cited, in *Alberici de Rosate dictionarium iuris tam civilis quam canonici* (Venice, 1573), s.v. "rebellis."

72. Ghisalberti, "Sulla teoria dei delitti di lesa maestà," pp. 171–177.

73. *Glossarium mediae et infimae latinitatis*, ed. Du Cange, s.v. "fellonia." Cf. Frederick Pollock and F. W. Maitland, *The History of English Law Before the Time of Edward I*, 2nd ed. (Cambridge, 1898–1899), II, 464ff.; and Heinrich Mitteis, *Politische Prozesse des frühen Mittelalters in Deutschland und Frankreich* (Heidelberg, 1927), p. 9.

74. See Ghisalberti, "Sulla teoria dei delitti di lesa maestà," pp. 113–124.

75. Walter Ullmann, "The Medieval Theory of Legal and Illegal Organizations," pp. 285–291.

76. *MGH, Constitutiones et acta publica*, IV.1, nos. 715–716; and *Bartoli opera omnia*, X, fol. 104v.

77. On these much-discussed developments, see Gaines Post, "Rex Imperator," in Post, *Studies in Medieval Legal Thought: Public Law and the State* (Princeton, 1964), esp. p. 455.

78. While scholars such as Francesco Ercole and Sergio Mochi Onory stressed the notion of civic independence, the classic works of Otto von Gierke and then studies by Francesco Calasso and C. N. S. Woolf emphasized the continuing de jure dependence of rulers subject to the emperor. Cf. David, "L'hégémonie impériale," pp. 199–216; and Quentin Skinner, *The Foundations of Modern Political Thought* (Cambridge, 1978), I, 3–22, for a valuable analysis stressing the "revolutionary" aspects of communal claims to liberty.

79. Post, "Rex Imperator," p. 441; and Ghisalberti, "Sulla teoria dei delitti di lesa maestà," pp. 146–150.

80. Michele Barbi, "Per un passo dell'epistola all'amico fiorentino," *Studi danteschi*, 2 (1920): 115–148. On pardoning powers, see Kirchheimer, *Political Justice*, p. 20; and Douglas Hay, "Property, Authority, and the Criminal Law," in *Albion's Fatal Tree: Crime and Society in Eighteenth-Century England* (New York, 1975), p. 48.

81. *Epistola*, XII, 4, in *Opere*, ed. Porena and Pazzaglia, p. 1382.

82. Elisabetta Cavallari, *La fortuna del Dante nel Trecento* (Florence, 1921); Konrad Eubel, "Zur Zaubereinwesen anfangs des 14. Jahrhunderts," *Historisches Jahrbuch*, 18 (1897): 621; and Corrado Ricci, *L'ultimo rifugio di Dante*, 2nd ed. (Milan, 1921), pp. 165–170, 182–189.

CHAPTER FOUR

1. Giovanni Soranzo, *La lega italica (1454–1455)* (Milan, n.d.), pp. 47–50, and the appendix of documents, pp. 191–213.

2. Ibid., p. 68.

3. Luigi Simeoni, *Le signorie*, 2 vols. (Milan, 1950); Nino Valeri, *L'Italia nell'età dei principati* (Milan, 1949); the chapter by Corrado Vivanti, in the Einaudi *Storia d'Italia*, II.1, 277–427; and now Martines, *Power and Imagination*, seem to me, in their very different ways, the most valuable general works on this period—and process.

4. Gustav Pirchan, *Italien und Kaiser Karl IV. in der Zeit seiner zweiten Romfahrt* (Prague, 1930), I, 121–122; C. C. Bayley, "Petrarch, Charles IV, and the 'Renovatio Imperii,' " *Speculum*, 17 (1942): 323–341. On Italian "national sentiment," see Francesco Ercole, *Dal comune al principato* (Florence, 1929), pp. 215–225.

5. Giovanni Soranzo, "Collegati, raccomandati, aderenti negli stati italiani dei secoli XIV e XV," *Archivio storico italiano*, 99 (1941): 3–35; and Valeri, *L'Italia*, pp. 261–264, 391.

6. Cf., in general, Guillaume Mollat, *The Popes of Avignon, 1305–1378*, trans. Janet Love (London/New York, 1963); and Peter Partner, *The Lands of St. Peter* (Berkeley/Los Angeles, 1972), pp. 327–446.

7. *Il principe*, XI, in *Tutte le opere*, p. 274.

8. Leon Mirot, *La politique française en Italie de 1380 à 1422* (Paris, 1934); and Georges Peyronnet, "I Durazzo e Renato d'Angiò, 1281–1442," in *Storia di Napoli* (Naples, 1969), III, 337–358.

9. "Io sono un povero re, amico delli saccomani, / Amatore delli populi e distruttore dei tiranni": Alessandro Cutolo, *Re Ladislao di Angiò Durazzo*, 2nd ed. (Naples, 1969), p. 416n.

10. Ronald G. Witt, *Coluccio Salutati and His Public Letters* (Geneva, 1976), p. 85. It is true that Charles of Durazzo aroused much Guelph enthusiasm among the Florentines in the 1380s; but on the good authority of Gene Brucker, *The Civic World of Early Renaissance Florence* (Princeton, 1977), pp. 76–77, it seems clear that the Florentine response was wishful thinking at best. For a contemporary account of Charles of Durazzo's abandonment of "the vile *usciti*, deserted despite all his promises, all the letters and the heavy seals," see *Annales senenses Nerio Donati filio*, in *RIS*, XV, 270.

11. Vivanti, in the Einaudi *Storia d'Italia*, II.1, 310–317, gives a crisp summary of development "verso gli stati regionali."

12. Quoted by Valeri, *L'Italia*, p. 418. Cf. Francesco Guicciardini's nostalgic backward glance from the perspective of the Italian wars after 1494: "essendo divisa Italia principalmente in cinque stati, papa, Napoli, Vinegia, Milano e Firenze, erano gli studi di ciascuno, per conservazione delle cose

proprie, vòlti a riguardare che nessuno occupasse di quello d'altri ed accrescessi tanto che tutti avessino a temere, e per questo tenendo conto di ogni piccolo movimento che si faceva e facendo romore eziando della alterazione di ogni minimo castelluzzo . . .": *Storie fiorentine dal 1378 al 1509*, ed. Roberto Palmarocchi (Bari, 1931), p. 92.

13. J. H. Hexter, *The Vision of Politics on the Eve of the Reformation: More, Machiavelli, and Seyssel* (New York, 1973), pp. 150–178.

14. Chittolini, "La crisi," p. 112; for an analogous situation in northern Italy, see the same author's "Infeudazioni e politica feudale nel ducato visconteo-sforzesco," *Quaderni storici*, 19 (1972): 104–121. Vivanti has surveyed the "presenza del feudo" and other limits to centralization especially emphasized by some recent historians in the Einaudi *Storia d'Italia*, II.1, 296–304.

15. See Larner, *Lords of the Romagna*; and P. J. Jones, *The Malatesta of Rimini and the Papal State* (Cambridge, 1974).

16. *Johannis Antonii Campani de vita et gestis Braccii*, ed. Roberto Valentini, in *RIS*, n.s., XIX.4, pp. 105–114; and Pompeo Pellini, *Dell'historia di Perugia* (Venice, 1664), II, 219–287, in *Historiae urbium et regionum Italiae rariores*, XV.2 (Bologna, 1968). Qualifying the old view of the condottieri as prime representatives of "Renaissance individualism," Michael Mallett emphasizes the constraints the Renaissance environment imposed on them in *Mercenaries and Their Masters*, pp. 107–145.

17. C. C. Bayley, *War and Society in Renaissance Florence* (Toronto, 1961), pp. 151–177.

18. Luigi Banchi, "La guerra de' Senesi col conte di Pitigliano (1454–1455)," *Archivio storico italiano*, ser. IV, 3 (1879): 181–197. Florentine *fuorusciti* found themselves similarly without allies in 1468: Giuseppe Nebbia, "La lega italica del 1455: sue vicende e sua rinnovazione nel 1470," *Archivio storico lombardo*, n.s., 4 (1939): 133.

19. Ester Pastorello, *Nuove ricerche sulla storia di Padova e dei principi di Carrara al tempo di Giangaleazzo Visconti* (Padua, 1908), pp. 26–28.

20. Garrett Mattingly, *Renaissance Diplomacy* (Boston, 1955), pp. 47–104; more recent work on questions of precedent has refined but generally confirmed Mattingly's account: Donald Queller, *The Office of Ambassador in the Middle Ages* (Princeton, 1967), esp. pp. 76–84.

21. V. E. Hrabar, *De legatis et legationibus varii* (Dorpat, 1906), p. 66.

22. Lydia Cerioni, "La politica italiana di Luigi XI e la missione di Filippo di Commines," *Archivio storico italiano*, ser. VII, 4 (1950): 148.

23. Hrabar, *De legatis*, p. 67.

24. Marzi, *La cancelleria della repubblica fiorentina*, p. 354.

25. Documents in Luigi Passerini, *Gli Alberti di Firenze* (Florence, 1870), I, 319.

26. *Discorsi sopra la prima deca di Tito Livio*, II, 31, in *Tutte le opere*, p. 192.

27. Laura De Feo Corso, "Il Filelfo in Siena," *Bullettino senese di storia patria*, 47 (1940): 306–307.

28. Niccolò d'Este to the Count of Modigliano (10 November 1385),

quoted by Brucker, *The Civic World*, p. 274; and *De principe*, in *Ioannis Ioviani Pontani opera* (Venice, 1501), fol. 32v.

29. See pp. 108–111 above.

30. Christine Meek, *Lucca, 1369–1404: Politics and Society in an Early Renaissance City-State* (Oxford, 1978), p. 272.

31. Pertile, *Storia del diritto italiano*, V, 304n.; Pompeo Molmenti, *I banditi della repubblica veneta* (Florence, 1896); for the Sforza case, see pp. 105–106 above.

32. A story, *ben trovato* at least, told by Baldassare Castiglione, *Book of the Courtier*, trans. Charles S. Singleton (Garden City, N.Y., 1959), p. 163.

33. *Epistulae ad familiares* IV, vii, 4, ed. W. G. Williams, Loeb Classical Library (Cambridge, Mass., 1952); and *Epistola Francisci Philelphi ad Honofrium et Ioannem Franciscum Strozzae*, in Angelo Fabroni, *Pallantis Stroctii vita* (Parma, 1802), pp. 41–50.

34. Jacob Burckhardt, *The Civilization of the Renaissance in Italy*, trans. S. G. C. Middlemore (Vienna/New York, n.d.), p. 72.

35. *Gualvanei de la Flamma, O. P., Opusculum de rebus gestis ab Azone, Luchino et Johanne Vicecomitibus*, ed. Carlo Castiglioni, in *RIS*, n.s., XII.4, 43–45.

36. *Ferreti Vicentini de Scaligerorum origine*, in *Le opere di Ferreto de' Ferreti*, ed. Carlo Cipolla (Rome, 1920), III, 31, 39.

37. *Leonardi Aretini historiarum Florentini populi libri*, Bk. III, ed. Emilio Santini, in *RIS*, n.s., XIX.3, 52; and Guicciardini, *Maxims and Reflections*, p. 97. For Ludovico Sforza's use of these tactics again in Milan, see *Diario ferrarese dall'anno 1409 sino al 1502*, in *RIS*, n.s., XXIV, cols. 306–309.

38. Nino Valeri, "L'insegnamento di Giangaleazzo Visconti e i consigli al principe di Carlo Malatesta," *Bollettino storico-bibliografico subalpino*, 36 (1934): 452–487; and Jones, *Malatesta*, pp. 321–322.

39. Simeoni, *Le signorie*, II, 18; and *Fr. Johannis Ferrarensis ex annalium libris marchionum Estensium excerpta*, ed. Luigi Simeoni, in *RIS*, n.s., XX.2, 37, 43.

40. Marvin B. Becker, *Florence in Transition* (Baltimore, 1967), I, 19–25, 207–211.

41. See the two articles by William M. Bowsky: "The Medieval Commune and Internal Violence: Police Power and Public Safety in Siena, 1287–1355," *American Historical Review*, 82 (1967): 13; and "The Anatomy of Rebellion in Fourteenth-Century Siena: From Commune to Signory?" in *Violence and Civil Disorder in Italian Cities, 1200–1500*, ed. Lauro Martines (Berkeley/Los Angeles, 1972), pp. 250–252. See also Guido Ruggiero, *Violence in Early Renaissance Venice* (New Brunswick, N.J., 1980), p. 45.

42. Cf. Alan Ryder, *The Kingdom of Naples Under Alfonso the Magnanimous: The Making of a Modern State* (Oxford, 1976), pp. 162, 167–168.

43. Nicolai Rubinstein, "Political Ideas in Sienese Art: The Frescoes by Ambrogio Lorenzetti and Taddeo di Bartolo in the Palazzo Pubblico," *Journal of the Warburg and Courtauld Institutes*, 12 (1958): 179–207; Helene Wieruszowski, "Ars Dictaminis in the Time of Dante," in Wieruszowski, *Politics and*

Culture in Medieval Spain and Italy (Rome, 1971), pp. 359–377; and Bowsky, "Police Power," p. 6 and n. 22.

44. See Martines, *Lawyers and Statecraft*, esp. pp. 397–404; and Sorbelli, "I teorici del reggimento comunale," p. 131.

45. Jones, *Malatesta*, pp. 321–322. For other examples, see Caterina Santoro, *Gli uffici del dominio sforzesco, 1450–1500* (Milan, 1948), pp. xix–xxii; Vincent Illardi, "The Visconti-Sforza Regime of Milan: Recently Published Sources," *Renaissance Quarterly*, 31 (1978): 331–342; Werner Gundersheimer, *Ferrara: The Style of a Renaissance Despotism* (Princeton, 1975), pp. 290–291; and Ryder, *The Kingdom of Naples*, pp. 91–124.

46. Anthony Molho, "The Florentine Oligarchy and the *Balìe* of the Late Trecento," *Speculum*, 43 (1968): 23–51; Brucker, *Civic World*, pp. 90ff.; and Dale Kent, *The Rise of the Medici: Faction in Florence, 1426–1434* (Oxford, 1978), pp. 295, 338–339.

47. The work of Nicolai Rubinstein has illuminated these themes in precise detail; see esp. his *The Government of Florence Under the Medici, 1434 to 1494* (Oxford, 1966); and his essay "Florentine Constitutionalism and Medici Ascendancy in the Fifteenth Century," in *Florentine Studies*, ed. Nicolai Rubinstein (London, 1968), pp. 443–462.

48. Marin Sanuto, *Cronachetta*, quoted by Gaetano Cozzi, "Authority and the Law in Renaissance Venice," in *Renaissance Venice*, ed. John R. Hale (London, 1973), p. 303. On the Ten, see Cozzi's discussion and bibliography; Stanley Chojnacki, "Crime, Punishment, and the Trecento Venetian State," in *Violence and Disorder in Italian Cities*, ed. L. Martines, esp. p. 220; and Ruggiero, *Violence in Early Renaissance Venice*, pp. 6–17.

49. Domenico Morosini, quoted from Sanuto's *Diarii* by Cozzi, "Authority and the Law," p. 306.

50. From the *Storia fiorentina*, quoted by G. Antonelli, "La magistratura degli Otto di Guardia a Firenze," *Archivio storico italiano*, 112 (1954): 5.

51. So, e.g., Carlo Calisse, *A History of Italian Law* (reprint New York, 1968), p. 175. For actual procedures of the Ten and the Eight, see Ruggiero, *Violence*, pp. 33–39; and Antonelli, "La magistratura degli Otto," pp. 5–8.

52. I follow the searching reading of the *Consulte e Pratiche* materials from the Archivio di Stato, Florence, in Brucker, *Civic World*, pp. 75–101, 325–328, 337–339, 488.

53. *Leonardi Aretini historiarum libri*, Bk. II, p. 264; cf. Donald J. Wilcox, *The Development of Florentine Humanist Historiography in the Fifteenth Century* (Cambridge, Mass., 1969), pp. 79–81.

54. See Brucker, *Civic World*, pp. 3–13, for a succinct guide to the controversies among historians over these developments; and John Najemy, "Guild Republicanism in Renaissance Florence: The Success and Ultimate Failure of Corporate Politics," *American Historical Review* 84 (1979): 53–71.

55. One letter (30 May 1396) exists in two manuscript copies in the Biblioteca Nazionale, Florence: *Ms. Palatino*, 545, fols. 24v–30v; and *Fondo Panciatichi* 158, fols. 183r–185r (I am grateful to Gene Brucker for allowing me to use his transcriptions). The other letter (10 November 1396) is printed in *I*

sermoni evangelici, le lettere ed altri scritti inediti e rari di F. Sacchetti, ed. O. Gigli (Florence, 1857), pp. 188–198.

56. *Ms. Palatino,* 545, fol. 26r.

57. Brucker, *Civic World,* pp. 96–101, gives a full analysis of this affair and of Acciaiuoli's responsibility.

58. *I sermoni evangelici,* p. 191.

59. Ibid., p. 192.

60. *Ms. Palatino,* 545, fols. 29r–29v.

61. Ibid., fol. 30r.

62. For the Velluti and the Strozzi petitions, see Brucker, *Civic World,* p. 259.

63. Ida Masetti-Bencini, "Note ed appunti . . . sulla vita politica di Neri Capponi," *Rivista delle biblioteche e degli archivi,* 20 (1909): 41–42.

64. Averardo de' Medici to Neri Capponi, Paolo Rucellai, and Bancho Sandrini (9 September 1433), in Ida Masetti-Bencini, "Neri Capponi: Note biografiche," *Rivista delle biblioteche e degli archivi,* 16 (1905): 59.

65. Dale Kent, "I Medici in esilio: Una vittoria di famiglia e una disfatta personale," *Archivio storico italiano,* 132 (1974–1976): 3–64, is a fascinating account, based on the letters of Averardo's grandson Francesco; see, too, Kent, *Rise of the Medici,* pp. 312–315.

66. From a letter of Francesco di Giuliano de' Medici (15 November 1433), quoted by Kent, "I Medici," p. 19; I draw on this article and *Rise of the Medici,* pp. 308ff., for the quotations from Francesco's correspondence and related documents which follow in the text.

67. Alessandra Macinghi negli Strozzi, *Lettere di una gentildonna ai figliuoli esuli,* ed. Cesare Guasti (Florence, 1877), pp. xxxiii, 143.

68. Vincent Illardi, "The Assassination of Galeazzo Maria Sforza and the Reaction of Italian Diplomacy," in *Violence and Disorder in Italian Cities,* ed. L. Martines, pp. 74–75; and Riccardo Fubini, "Osservazioni e documenti sulla crisi del ducato di Milano nel 1477 e sulla riforma del Consiglio Segreto ducale di Bona Sforza," *Essays Presented to Myron P. Gilmore,* ed. Sergio Bertelli and Gloria Ramakus (Florence, 1978), I, 45–75.

69. Alessandro Cutolo, "Documenti sull'esilio pisano di Ludovico il Moro e gli avvenimenti contemporanei," *Archivio storico lombardo,* n.s., 4 (1939): 131–161, from which I have taken the following account and quotations.

70. I quote the three letters (13, 23, and 24 March 1484) from Della Valle to Francesco Gaddi in *Nuovi documenti per la storia del Rinascimento,* ed. Tamaro De Marinis and Alessandro Perosa (Florence, 1970), pp. 30–36. On contemporary campaigns for law and order in Rome, see C. W. Westfall, *"In This Most Perfect Paradise": Alberti, Nicholas V, and the Invention of Conscious Urban Planning in Rome, 1447–1455* (University Park, Pa., 1975), pp. 19–21; and Egmont Lee, *Sixtus IV and Men of Letters* (Rome, 1978), pp. 132–134.

71. See Ludwig von Pastor, *History of the Popes,* trans. Frederick Antrobus (St. Louis, 1910), IV, 251, 264–269, 296.

72. Paolo Piccolomini, "Niccolò Vitelli esule in Castiglion Fiorentino

secondo la testimonianza di un contemporaneo," *Bollettino della Deputazione di Storia Patria per l'Umbria*, 8 (1902): 159–162.

73. *A. Rinuccini dialogus de libertate*, ed. Francesco Adorno, in *Atti e memorie dell'Accademia Toscana di Scienze et Lettere "La Colombaria,"* 22 (1957): 265–303.

74. *De libertate*, p. 298; cf. Francesco Adorno, "La crisi dell'umanesimo civile fiorentino da Alamanno Rinuccini al Machiavelli," *Rivista di storia della filosofia*, 7 (1952): 19–40.

75. See, e.g., Machiavelli's famous analysis of conspiracies in his *Discorsi*, III, 6, in *Tutte le opere*, pp. 200–211; Ferruccio Martini, *Lorenzino de' Medici e il tirannicidio nel Rinascimento* (Florence, 1882); and Lauro Martines, "The Gentleman in Renaissance Italy: Strains of Isolation in the Body Politic," in *The Darker Vision of the Renaissance*, ed. Robert S. Kinsman (Berkeley/Los Angeles, 1974), pp. 77–93.

76. ASF, *Balìe*, 17, fol. 62v; see Gene Brucker, "The Ciompi Revolution," in *Florentine Studies*, ed. Rubinstein, pp. 314–356; and Nicolai Rubinstein, "The Political Regime in Florence After the Tumulto dei Ciompi," *Journal of Italian History*, 2 (1979): 405–419.

77. ASF, *Balìe*, 17, fols. 62v, 67r–68v.

78. Ibid., 20, fols. 82ff., in Passerini, *Gli Alberti*, II, 238–240.

79. Ibid., 29, fol. 95r, in Passerini, II, 248–265.

80. Ibid., 39, fols. 5ff., in Passerini, II, 320–340.

81. Passerini, II, 47–49.

82. Kent, "Medici in esilio"; and Kent, *Rise of the Medici*, pp. 339–348.

83. ASF, *Otto di Guardia* (rep.), 224, fols. 71v, 21ff.

84. For details, see Rubinstein, *Government of Florence*, pp. 109–112, 164–166.

85. ASF, *Otto di Guardia* (rep.), 224 ("Banditi e Ribelli, 1434–1468") includes legislation, sentences, and declarations of the Eight, of the *balìe* and their captain, and of officials on rebels for the thirty-four-year period; cf. Antonelli, "La magistratura degli Otto."

86. ASF, *Capitani di Parte* (numeri rossi), 51 (1365–1376), 50 (1375–1431), 65 (1431–1509).

87. There is a compendium of legislation "De offitialibus turris," in ASF, *Capitani di Parte, Libro della Luna*, fols. 210ff.; cf. Barbadoro, *Le finanze della repubblica fiorentina*, pp. 218–238, 478–494.

88. ASF, *Capitani di Parte* (numeri rossi), 50, fols. 106r (Mariano di Benedetto), 109r (Cipriano), 133r–135r (Riccardo and Gherardo di Benedetto), 135v (Bernardo di Jacopo), 142v (Piero di Bartolomeo), 148r (Antonio), and 164v (Beltramo di Marco).

89. Ibid., 65, fols. 34r, 16r, 146r, 163v, 194v–195r, 201r.

90. These suggestions find some support in the figures on Florentine crimes and convictions for 1352–1355 and 1380–1383, as reported by Umberto Dorini, *Il diritto penale e la delinquenza in Firenze nel secolo XIV* (Lucca, 1923), and tabulated by Mooney, "The Legal Ban," pp. 85–87. The two sets of statistics show a decrease in crimes against persons (from 492 to 428) and

against property (from 226 to 116), the categories representing 40 percent of the total number of crimes reported to the courts. The conviction rate rose from 70 percent to 75 or 80 percent in both categories, respectively. It is true that the rate of contumacy remained high (often 50 percent or higher, especially in murder cases, where it reached 72 percent and 86 percent in the two periods); on the other hand, the corresponding figures in cases of armed assault indicate a sharp drop from 35 percent to 18 percent. Parallel conclusions have been reached by Marvin B. Becker, "Changing Patterns of Violence and Justice in Fourteenth- and Fifteenth-Century Florence," *Comparative Studies in Society and History*, 19 (1976): 281–296.

91. ASF, *Capitani di Parte* (numeri rossi), 50, fol. 148r.

92. See pp. 83–84 above; for the arguments actually employed, see Martines, *Lawyers*, pp. 119–129. Cf. the review of these developments by Skinner, *Foundations of Modern Political Thought*, I, 3–22; and the discussion of their eventual implications in political discourse by J. G. A. Pocock, *The Machiavellian Moment: Florentine Political Thought and the Atlantic Republican Tradition* (Princeton/ London, 1975), chaps. 2–3.

93. ASF, *Capitani di Parte* (numeri rossi), 65, fols. 86v–87v.

94. *Tractatus Universi Iuris* (Venice, 1584), XI.1, fol. 365r (*De bannitis*, II, 1, q. 3). Editions appeared in 1486 (Pescia), 1493 (Milan), 1498 (Venice), and 1550 (Lyons). See Mooney, "The Legal Ban," pp. 194–237.

95. *De bannitis*, II, 1, q. 4 (ed. cit., fol. 365r–365v).

96. Ibid., *Proemium*, fol. 357r.

97. Alessandra Macinghi negli Strozzi, *Lettere*, p. 300.

98. Raphael de Cerchiis, *Il Birraccino . . . in quo continentur omnes ordines et actus, quos iudices et eorum notarii, omnesque alii offitiales in officio constituti observare et facere debeant . . .* (Venice, 1542). Special help in making this book available was given to me by the late Charles McCurry of the Robbins Collection on Medieval Canon Law at the University of California, Berkeley, and I would like to acknowledge here that very characteristic kindness.

99. Ibid., fol. 5r.

100. Ibid., fol. 46r.

101. "Item ligatur statutis suae civitatis in sui odium disponentibus, sicut ligaretur non bannitus secundum ea quae habentur in 1. cunctos populos, de summa trinitate, et ideo omnia statuta privativa porrigentia effectum suum extra territorium secundum ibi notum per doctores locum habebunt in talibus bannitis quocunque vadant . . .": *De bannitis*, II, 1, q. 5, fol. 365v. Cf. Mooney, "The Legal Ban," pp. 218, 234n.; and, for earlier opinion, Ghisalberti, "La condanna al bando," pp. 41–46.

102. See Cavalca, *Il bando*, pp. 219, 225, and also, for parallel limitations on the punishment of families for their *banniti* members, pp. 114–115.

103. So, e.g., the term *relegati* applied to the anti-Medicean exiles of 1434 in ASF, *Otto di Guardia* (rep.), 224, fol. 1. For other examples, see Pertile, *Storia del diritto italiano*, V, 302n.

104. *Iulii Clarii sententiarum receptarum libri* (Venice, 1595), V, q. 71, 1.

105. Alison Brown, *Bartolomeo Scala, 1430–1494, Chancellor of Florence:*

The Humanist as Bureaucrat (Princeton, 1979), p. 296. Cf. Ghisalberti, "Sulla teoria dei delitti di lesa maestà," pp. 172–177; for historians' controversies over legal change during the Renaissance, see I. Mereu, *Storia del diritto penale nel '500. Studi e ricerche* (Naples, 1964).

106. Piero Pieri, *Il rinascimento e la crisi militare italiana* (Turin, 1952), remains the standard modern account and analysis of the Italian wars; for a good synthesis of more recent literature and for contemporary reactions, see Corrado Vivanti in the Einaudi *Storia d'Italia*, II.1, 346–385.

107. Cf. Michel François, "L'idée d'empire en France à l'époque de Charles Quint," in *Charles Quint et son temps* (Paris, 1959); Karl Brandi, *The Emperor Charles V*, trans. C. V. Wedgwood (London, 1939), pp. 112–114 *et passim*; and Loren Partridge and Randolph Starn, *A Renaissance Likeness: Art and Culture in Raphael's Julius II* (Berkeley/Los Angeles, 1980), pp. 42–74.

108. See, e.g., Alessandro D'Ancona, *La poesia popolare italiana*, 2nd ed. (Livorno, 1906), pp. 63–87.

109. See the Epilogue below.

110. Machiavelli's chapters (*Discorsi*, II, 31, and III, 6, in *Tutte le opere*, pp. 191–192, 200–211) on the dangers of trusting the representations of exiles and the futility of conspiracies might have served as texts for these developments; as Francesco Guicciardini put it in one of his *Ricordi* (*Maxims and Reflections*, p. 91), a prince could treat exiles "just as he pleases." For the specific case of the Florentine exiles of the 1530s, see my *Donato Giannotti and His Epistolae* (Geneva, 1968), pp. 41–48.

111. See, e.g., Federico Chabod, *Storia di Milano nell'epoca di Carlo V*, in Chabod, *Opere* (Turin, 1961), III, 412–442; and Giorgio Spini, *Cosimo de' Medici e l'indipendenza dello stato mediceo* (Florence, 1945).

112. Berengo, *Nobili e mercanti nella Lucca del Cinquecento*, pp. 157–159; and Rudolf von Albertini, *Das florentinische Staatsbewusstsein im Übergang von der Republik bis zum Prinzipat* (Bern, 1955), pp. 209–222.

113. I quote excerpts from the "Querele Pôrte da' fuorusciti a Cesare," in *Opere inedite di Francesco Guicciardini*, ed. Giuseppe Canestrini (Florence, 1866), IX, 357–358, 363, 368, 387.

CHAPTER FIVE

1. Exile-poets, far from being marginal in literature, are represented throughout the standard anthologies I have used for this chapter: *Poeti del Duecento*, ed. Gianfranco Contini, 2 vols. (Milan/Naples, 1960); *Poeti del dolce stil nuovo*, ed. Mario Marti (Florence, 1969); *Rimatori del '300*, ed. Giuseppe Corsi (Turin, 1969); and *Sonetti burleschi e realistici dei primi due secoli*, ed. Aldo Francesco Massèra and Luigi Russo (Bari, 1940). The following list gives the names of thirty-two poets who wrote in exile (or were *fuorusciti* at one time or another) in the thirteenth and fourteenth centuries; included are fifteen exiles from Florence, four from Perugia, two each from Siena, Lucca, Pistoia, and Venice, and one each from Arezzo, Bologna, Milan, Ferrara, and Padua:

Antonio degli Alberti (d. 1415)
Antonio da Ferrara (d. ca. 1374)
Gianni Alfani (d. after 1311?)
Dante Alighieri (d. 1321)
Pietro Alighieri (d. 1364)
Cecco Angiolieri (d. ca. 1312)
Cucco Baglioni (d. after 1333)
Sennuccio del Bene (d. 1349)
Guido Cavalcanti (d. 1301)
Cino da Pistoia (d. ca. 1337)
Maggiolo Cocciolo (d. after 1371)
Ser Pietro Faitinelli (d. 1349)
Francesco di Vanozzo (d. after 1389)
Matteo Frescobaldi (d. 1348)
Carnino Ghiberti (fl. 1260–1269)
Guido Guinizelli (d. ca. 1276)

Guittone d'Arezzo (d. ca. 1294)
Paolo Lanfranchi da Pistoia (fl. 1290)
Brunetto Latini (d. ca. 1295)
Ser Luporo da Lucca (d. after 1346?)
Monte Andrea da Firenze (fl. 1260)
Trebaldino Manfredini (d. after 1363)
Ser Cecco Nuccoli (fl. 1360)
Schiatta Pallavillani (fl. 1280)
Giovanni Quirini (d. after 1327)
Niccolò Quirini (d. 1328)
Giannozzo Sacchetti (d. 1379)
Niccolò Soldanieri (d. 1385?)
Pieraccio Tedaldi (d. ca. 1350)
Fazio degli Uberti (d. 1367)
Piero Asino degli Uberti (fl. 1260)
Brizio Visconti (d. 1357)

For orientation (and still other exile-authors), see Natalino Sapegno, *Il Trecento*, 3rd ed. (Milan, 1966).

2. Flaminio Pellegrini, "Il Serventese dei Lambertazzi e dei Geremei," in *Atti e memorie della R. Deputazione di Storia Patria per le Provincie di Romagna*, ser. III, 9 (1891): 206–211, esp. lines 92–138, 165–168.

3. "Provenzano, al tuo parere, / ke faranno li 'sciti? / Raveranno el loro avere, / k'al papa ne son giti, / [o] fieno sì arditi / k'a Siena fien guerrieri? / . . . / Ruggieri, al buon ver dire, / paion sì ismarriti! / meglio è kacciar ke fuggire": *Poeti del Duecento*, I, 908, lines 17–20. The *tenzone* between Ruggieri Apugliese the Guelph and Provenzano [Salvani?] the Ghibelline refers to the period when the Guelphs, defeated at Montaperti in 1260, were menacing Siena from the countryside around the (still) fortified village of Radicofani.

4. It was a fellow exile, Fazio degli Uberti, to whom Antonio sent the sonnet (ca. 1350) which begins: "Gran tempo ito son per questo mare / secondo che fortuna e 'l ciel m'ha scorto, / senz'ancora gittar in alcun porto / per metter fine al mio lungo affannare": *Rimatori del '300*, p. 348.

5. Brunetto was on his way as Florentine ambassador to the court of Alfonso of Castile when he met a traveler with news of Montaperti, "ch'i guelfi di Fiorenza / per mala providenza / e per forza di guerra / eran fuor de la terra / e 'l dannagio era forte / di pregioni e di morte / . . . / e io, in tal corotto / pensando a capo chino, / perdei il gran cammino, / e tenni a la traversa / d'una selva diversa": *Il tesoretto*, in *Poeti del Duecento*, I, 181–182, lines 157–162, 186–190. Like Dante in the *selva oscura*, Brunetto was soon confronted by an apparition promising him aid and instruction.

6. Cecco's sonnet *El mi rincresce sì lo star di fuore* (ca. 1360), one of the exiles' most irreverent, can be read in *Rimatori del '300*, p. 706; for the "amaro morsello" of Ser Pietro Faitinelli's exile, see n. 9 below.

7. "Io son fra gente barbare, crudeli / che senza legge vivon di rapina, / e pasce monti per neve e per brina / sentendo ad or ad or graviosi geli": Michele

Barbi and Vittorio Pernicone, "Sulla corrispondenza poetica tra Dante e Giovanni Quirini," *Studi danteschi*, 25 (1940): 91.

8. "Se Die m'aiuti, a le sante guagnèle, / s'i' veggio 'l dí, sia in Siena ribandito, / se data mi fosse in occhio col dito, / a sofferire mi parrá latt'e miele / ... / E parró un colombo senza fele / ... / E tutto questo mal mi parebb'oro": *Sonetti burleschi e realistici*, p. 111.

9. Ser Pietro's *S'io veggio in Lucca bella* is one of the most moving in all the exiles' poetry:

S'io veggio in Lucca bella mio ritorno,
che fi' quando la pera fie ben mezza, in nullo
cuore uman tant'allegrezza giá mai non fu, quant'io
avrò quel giorno.

Le mura andrò leccando d'ogn'intorno e gli
uomini, piangendo d'allegrezza; odio, rancore, guerra
ed ogni empiezza porrò giú contra quei, che mi
cacciorno.

E qui me'voglio 'l bretto castagniccio,
'nanzi ch'altrove pan di gran calvello; 'nanzi
ch'altrove piume, qui il graticcio.

Ch'i'ho provato sí amaro morsello, e provo
e proverò, stando esiticcio, che 'l bianco e 'l
ghibellin vo'per fratello. (*Sonetti burleschi e realistici*, p. 190)

10. Fazio gave up "l'acceso imaginare" of Florence in his didactic travel fantasy *Il Dittamondo* (III, 7, lines 98–102) with these parting words: "A la città, che dietro lasso, / avea il cuore con tutti i miei sensi;— / che io piangea fra me e dicea: lasso!, / ritornerò già mai a rivedere / questo caro piacer che ora lasso?": *Il Dittamondo e le rime*, I, 205. For Pieraccio's would-be return "nel dilettoso spazio de la nobil città gioiosa e magna": *Sonetti burleschi e realistici*, p. 295.

11. "O dolce terra aretina, / pianto m'aduce e dolore / ... / foll'è chi mal prova et torna a esso": *Poeti del Duecento*, I, 222, 226.

12. "Gente noiosa e villana / e malvagia e vil signoria / e giùdici pien' di falsia / e guerra perigliosa e strana / fanno me, lasso, la mia terra odiare / e l'altrui forte amare: / però me departut'ho / d'essa e qua [Bologna] venuto": ibid., 200. Cf. against the Florentines, more like dragons and bears within their walls than citizens, *Le lettere di fra Guittone d'Arezzo*, ed. Francesco Meriano (Bologna, 1922), pp. 177–187.

13. *Tre donne intorno al cor mi son venute*, in *Opere*, ed. Porena and Pazzaglia, p. 1068, lines 101–107. Patrick Boyde, *Dante's Style in His Lyric Poetry* (Cambridge, 1971), pp. 147–148, gives a good analysis of the way, "as so often in Dante, one notes a general resemblance to a traditional feature only in order to call attention to his individual handling of the convention."

14. "Vedove e pupilli e innocenti / del mio sangue miglior van per lo pane / per l'altrui terre strane / con gran vergogna e con mortale affanno": from the *Lamento di Firenze*, in *Rimatori del '300*, pp. 268–274, and *Il dittamondo e le rime*, II, 37–41.

15. *Rimatori del '300*, pp. 215–233.

16. Ibid., p. 90; cf. Messer Niccolò del Rosso's *Oi terra, ch'eri de delicie arca* and other poems with similar themes in *Sonetti burleschi e realistici*, pp. 226, 222–224. On Matteo's exile from Florence after a failed Frescobaldi-Bardi coup in 1340, see Luigi Debenedetti, "Matteo Frescobaldi e la sua famiglia," *Giornale storico della letteratura italiana*, 49 (1907): 324–325.

17. *Io veggo il tempo de la primavera*, in *Rimatori del '300*, pp. 103–105.

18. For the exile motif in pastoral poetry, see Paul Alpers, *The Singer of the Eclogues* (Berkeley/ Los Angeles, 1979), pp. 65–69, 139–140. The duke delivers the lines on the "uses of adversity" in *As You Like It*, II, i; the Pistoiese Black Guelphs, including the lineage of his Lady Selvaggia, are the "wild folk" in Cino da Pistoia's *Se m'ha conquiso la selvaggia gente*, in *Poeti del dolce stil nuovo*, p. 662.

19. *Rimatori del '300*, pp. 58, 62 (Quirini); p. 127 (Sennuccio).

20. "*Serventese*," p. 123; *Rimatori del '300*, p. 180 ("Ballata, io son come 'l porco ferito / sor cui amici son spasimati a doglia").

21. "Tu lascerai ogni cosa diletta / più caramente, e questo è quello strale / che l'arco de lo esilio pria saetta. / Tu proverai sì come sa di sale / lo pane altrui e come è duro calle / lo scendere e 'l salir per l'altrui scale": *Paradiso*, XVII, 55–60. I do not know any translation that does justice to these great lines; Charles S. Singleton's prose version (Princeton, 1975) reads: "You shall leave everything beloved most dearly; and this is the arrow which the bow of the exile shoots first. You shall come to know how salt is the taste of another's bread; and how hard the path to descend and mount by another man's stairs."

22. "Onde mi dée venir giuochi e sollazzi? / onde mi dée venir motti con risa? / onde, se non tormenti d'ogni guisa? / onde mi dee venir, se non ch'io impazzi?" Ser Pietro gives this answer: "E non mi par veder fronde né fiore / di far cosí per fretta la tornata: / ond'io porto asto grande a chi ci muore." See *Sonetti burleschi e realistici*, p. 190; and Egisto Gerunzi, "Piero de' Faytinelli detto 'Mugnone' e il moto di Uguccione della Faggiola in Toscana," *Propugnatore*, 17 (1884): 325–376.

23. Dante puts some of his most stinging indictments in the mouth of his ancestor Cacciaguida, in *Paradiso*, XV, 97–129, and XVI, 49–154; Ser Pietro lashes out at a whole list of characters, including "Nello, mercenai' popolaruccio," in verses that begin: "Io non vo' dir ch'io non viva turbato, / ch'io son di Lucca nato, / e tengo del taulier la man di fòre: / ma, quando mi rimetto ben per core / come 'l senno e'l valore / e'l nobil sangue v'era diventato . . .": *Sonetti burleschi e realistici*, p. 191.

24. "O biastemia di Dio con la qual nacqui / maledetto sia il dí che mi ci giunse / come figura mostruosa e strana! / . . . / Almen, da poi ch'uscito fui di fore, / perché non fui io dismembrato o storto, / e poi a' can dato a mangiare il core? / Maledetta la luce e lo splendore / che prima mai s'aggiunse a gli occhi mei, / e chi ne fu l'autore / co' denti 'l teness'io come vorrei!": *Rimatori del '300*, p. 596. Earlier examples of *maledizioni* that may have been written in exile include: *S'i fosse foco, arderei 'l mondo* by Cecco Angiolieri, in *Rimatori comico-realistici*, I, 400–401; the six-part *canzone maledicente* by Antonio da

Ferrara (e.g., "Quel punto novo ch'io scopersi tempo / e caldo e poggia e vento, / sia maladetto e chi me vide prima"), in *Rimatori del '300*, pp. 329–333; and *Perch'io son giunto in parte che 'l dolore* by Giannozzo Sacchetti, in *Rimatori del '300*, pp. 387–390.

25. "L'orgolio e la superbia ch'en vui regna, / signor' veniciani, for mesura, / aprestavi sentenza acerba e dura": *Rimatori del '300*, p. 61.

26. "Vedrai soffiar la fiamma / ed ir' di torre in torre, / vedrai rubare e torre, / e correr sangue ongni tua bella via, / e qual fuggir per via, / e padri abbandonar figliuoli e terra, qual morto in sulla terra": from the *frottola* to Alessio Rinucci, Florentine ambassador to Mastino della Scala at Verona in 1336, in *Il Dittamondo e le rime*, II, 49. The evidence on Fazio's life in exile (the Uberti had been *fuorusciti* since 1268) is pieced together in the second volume of *Liriche edite ed inedite di Fazio degli Uberti*, ed. Rodolfo Renier (Florence, 1883).

27. For these themes, see Guido Cavalcanti's *Perch'i' no spero di tornar giammai* and Gianni Alfani's *Ballatetta dolente*, in *Poeti del dolce stil nuovo*, pp. 211–213, 342–343. Other examples appear in *Le rime della Scuola Siciliana*, ed. Bruno Panvini (Florence, 1962), I, 530, lines 29–30; 567, lines 2–8; 568, line 37; and in *Poeti del Duecento*, I, 91, lines 1–3 (Tomaso di Sasso di Messina); 143, lines 45–46 (Jacopo Mostacci); 371–373; 385–387 (Bondie Dietiaiuti). Petrarch carried on this tradition in many sonnets; so, e.g., "Per consiglio di lui [Amore], donna, m'avete / Scacciato del mio dolce albergo fora: / Misero essilio! avegna ch' i' non fora / D'abitar degno ove voi sola siete": *Le rime*, XLV, 508, ed. Giosuè Carducci and Severino Ferrari (Florence, 1957), pp. 66–67. Eight other references are listed in Kenneth McKenzie, *Concordanza delle rime di Francesco Petrarca* (Oxford, 1912), s.v. "esilio."

28. *Opere*, pp. 996–998 (*La dispietata mente che pur mira*, esp. lines 5–9); p. 1005 (*Deh, ragioniamo insieme un poco, Amore*); p. 1082 (*Amor da che convien pur ch'io mi doglia*).

29. "S'io non m'agiungo a voi proprio incarnato, / non pos' durar che non pèra del tutto, / poi che sì grave fascio d'amor ag[g]io: / com'albore che troppo à caricato, / che frange e perde se e lo suo frutto, / simile, amore, io mi disperderag[g]io": *Luntan vi son ma presso è il cuore*, in *Poeti del Duecento*, I, 372, lines 25–30.

30. *Rimatori del '300*, p. 131 (Sennuccio); p. 706 (Cecco).

31. "Chi ragione o virtù contra gli [Amore] sprieme, / fa come que' che 'n la tempesta sona": *Opere*, p. 1078, from the exchange between Dante and Cino reproduced on pp. 1077–1081; cf. Guido Zaccagnini, *Cino da Pistoia* (Pistoia, 1918), pp. 137–144. For Love's gaze "per la rotta gonna" in *Tre donne* (lines 27–28), see *Opere*, p. 1066.

32. "Dunque, parte crudel, perché mi fai / pena sentir del mal ch'io non commetto?": *Poeti del Dolce stil nuovo*, p. 707, lines 13–14.

33. *Dominici de Gravina Notarii Chronicon de rebus in Apulia gestis*, ed. Albano Sorbelli, in *RIS*, n.s., XII.3, 19–20.

34. See Dante's letters (V, VI, VII) in *Opere*, pp. 1350, 1357, 1364; cf. Ovid's line on the expulsion of Hippolytus from Athens: "meritum nihil eiecit urbe."

35. "O furor infelix, o quanta licentia dici / Ausus es . . . / . . . Nam crimina clamant, / Murmura plura gemunt, violataque iura queruntur": *F. Stephanardi Liber*, pp. 38, 42.

36. *Epistola* VI, 3, in *Opere*, p. 1361.

37. See Guittone's *Ahi lasso, or è stagion de dolor tanto*, in *Poeti del Duecento*, I, 206–207, lines 16–34. Chiaro wrote *Ahi dolze e gaia terra fiorentina* just after the Ghibelline defeat at Benevento (1266); it was in the 1270s that Panuccio debated with himself over abandoning "la dolorosa noia" of Pisa since "giustisi' ha deserta, ond'è caduta / con ragion e perduta": *Poeti del Duecento*, I, 414–416, 304–308.

38. "Nel tempo ch'era Italia tutta d'oro, / e Saturno l'avía en un contesto, / sotto l'ombra di Zove, Enrico sesto / occupolla e spugliò d'ogni tesoro. / Allor sfrenò del laberinto il toro, / per cui fu il sisma ver'la Glesia desto; / e'l guelfo cum pacifico protesto / ebbe morte et exilio, angossia e ploro": *Sonetti burleschi e realistici*, p. 228.

39. See Marvin B. Becker, "Individualism in the Early Italian Renaissance: Burden and Blessing," *Studies in the Renaissance*, 19 (1972): 273–297; Charles T. Davis, "Il buon tempo antico," in *Florentine Studies*, ed. Rubinstein, pp. 45–70; and Nicolai Rubinstein, "Some Ideas on Municipal Progress and Decline in the Italy of the Communes," in *Fritz Saxl Memorial Essays*, ed. D. J. Gordon (London, 1957), pp. 165ff. Cf. my "Meaning-Levels in the Theme of Historical Decline," *History and Theory*, 14 (1975): 1–31.

40. *Sonetti burleschi e realistici*, pp. 40–56.

41. "A voi che siete ora in Fiorenza dico / . . . poi che li Alamanni in casa avete, / servite 'i bene, e faitevo mostrare / le spade lor, con che v'han fesso i visi, / padri e figliuoli aucisi; / e piacemi che lor dobiate dare, / perch'ebber en ciò far / fatica assai, de vostra gran monete": *Poeti del Duecento*, I, 208–209, lines 67–75.

42. *Sonetti burleschi e realistici*, pp. 40ff.

43. A. Thomas, "Lettres latines inédites de Francesco da Barberino," *Romania*, 16 (1887): 73–91; Rafaello Morghen, "Le lettere politiche di Dante," in Morghen's *La civiltà medioevale al tramonto* (Bari, 1971), pp. 65–80.

44. So, e.g., Dante in *Paradiso*, XVII, 70–72; Fazio degli Uberti on Mastino della Scala, *Il dittamondo e le rime*, II, 41; and, much later, Simone Serdini on the Visconti in *Rimatori del '300*, pp. 604–608.

45. *De proeliis Tusciae Poema Fratris Raynerii de Grancis*, I, 10–11, ed. C. Meliconi, in *RIS*, n.s., XI.2, 8.

46. "E questo vo' che parli / al popolo mio, che curin tal ferite / con far gieneral pace / . . . / Con pacie, dico, e con buona concordia, / con limosine e santi sacrificii, / con laude e beneficii, / con sostenere digiuni e penitenza, / con disprezzare la guerra e la discordia, / con disprezzare i maladetti vizi, / con disprezzare offizii / che fan tra cittadini mala semenza": *Il Dittamondo e le rime*, II, 39.

47. *F. Stephanardi Liber*, p. 90.

48. See Manilio Dazzi, "Il Mussato storico," *Atti della R. Deputazione di Storia Patria per le Venezie*, 6 (1929): 416–420; and Ezio Raimondi, "L'*Ecerinis*

di Albertino Mussato," in *Studi Ezzeliniani, Istituto Storico Italiano per il Medio Evo, Studi Storici*, 45–47 (1963): 189–203.

49. *Poeti del dolce stil nuovo*, p. 875, line 41.

50. "Da poi che la natura ha fine posto / al viver di colui, in cui Virtute / come'n su' proprio loco dimorava, / i'prego lei che'l mio finir sia tosto / . . . / In uno è morto 'l senno e la prodezza, / iustizia tutta e temperanza intera. / E' non e morto (lasso, c'ho detto?), / anzi vive beato in gran dolcezza": *Poeti del dolce stil nuovo*, pp. 857–860, lines 1–4, 10–13. Cf., similarly, the anonymous poet (ibid., pp. 880–885); Dante (*Paradiso*, XXV, 137); and Sennuccio del Bene (*Rimatori del '300*, pp. 128–130).

51. *Il dittamondo e le rime*, II, 29–32 (*Tanto son volti il ciel di parte in parte*; to Louis of Bavaria, ca. 1323); 34–36 (*Di quel possi tu ber che bevve Crasso*; against Charles IV after the failure of his first Italian mission in 1354).

52. See Ser Pietro's *Giá per minacce guerra non si vénze* and *Voi gite molto ardite a far la mostra*, in *Sonetti burleschi e realistici*, pp. 188–189. For another case of an exile's disillusionment, see Eugenia Levi, "Antonio e Niccolò da Ferrara, poeti e uomini da corte nel Trecento," *Atti e memorie della Deputazione Ferrarese di Storia Patria*, 19 (1909): 220–253.

53. *Il dittamondo e le rime*, II, 29–32; cf. Petrarch's high and then fallen hopes over the imperial cause as discussed by Bayley, "Petrarch, Charles IV, and the 'Renovatio Imperii,' " pp. 323–341.

54. I use the Venice edition of 1515, fols. 243v–245r.

55. For judgments on Petrarch and his *De remediis*, see F. N. M. Diekstra, *A Dialogue Between Reason and Adversity: A Late Middle English Version of Petrarch's De Remediis* (Assen, 1968); Klaus Heitmann, *Fortuna und Virtus: Eine Studie zu Petrarcas Lebensweisheit* (Cologne/Graz, 1958); Charles Trinkaus, *In Our Image and Likeness: Humanity and Divinity in Italian Humanist Thought* (Chicago, 1970), I, chap. 1; and my "Petrarch's Consolation on Exile: A Humanist Use of Adversity," in *Essays Presented to Myron P. Gilmore*, ed. Sergio Bertelli and Gloria Ramakus (Florence, 1978), I, 241–254.

56. Cf. *Ratio's* first question—"Quid tu igitur iusto pelli malles exilio?"—and *Tusculan Disputations* III, 34, 107: "Nam iure exulantem consolari non oportet." The Senecan parallel is in *Ad Helviam* VIII, 5: "Alacres itaque et erecti . . . emetiamur quascumque terras."

57. "Non habemus hic manentem civitatem, dixit Paulus [Heb. 13:14]. Omne solum forti patria est, inquit Naso [*Fasti* I, 493–494]. Omne homini natale solum ait Statius [*Thebais* VIII, 320]. His te vocibus armatum velim . . .": *De remediis*, 1515 ed., fol. 244r. The examples of Socrates, Camillus, Rutilius, Metellus, Marcellus, and Cicero are specifically commended to the exile.

58. Cf. *Ad Helviam* IX, 2: "Angustus animus est, quem terrena delectant." Petrarch's line on Socrates and Metellus clearly follows *Tusculan Disputations* III, 37, 108, and *Ad Helviam* IX, 4–5. On *exilium* as *peregrinatio*, see above, Chapter One, n. 12; and *Tusculan Disputations* III, 37, 107 ("Iam vero exsilium, si rerum naturam, non ignominiam nominis quaerimus, quantum tandem a perpetua peregrinatione differt?"); *De remediis fortuitorum* VIII, 2, ed. F. Haase, *L. Annaei Senecae Opera* (Leipzig, 1852), III ("si enim sapiens est, peregrinatur, si stultus, exulat"). For the false fatherland where the "good and wise" are

exiled, cf. "Quanti vero ista patria aestimanda est, ex quo boni sapientesque pelluntur?": *Tusculan Disputations* III, 37, 109.

59. Ibid., 34, 81.

60. Petrarch drew the analogy between his Azzo da Correggio and Seneca's Gallio in the preface to the first book of *De remediis*; for Seneca's view of the consoler's task, see *Epistulae morales* LXIV, 8.

61. See above, pp. 26–30, on the traditions of consolation.

62. William J. Bouwsma, *The Culture of Renaissance Humanism*, American Historical Association Pamphlet, 401 (Washington, D.C., 1973), esp. pp. 12–18, is a good guide to the interpretation of "humanism-as-rhetoric" developed in the works of Paul Oskar Kristeller, Hanna Gray, Jerrold Seigel, Nancy Struever, Charles Trinkaus, and others.

63. In his *Commentarium*, ed. V. Nannucci (Florence, 1845), p. 250, Dante's son Pietro already pointed out Aristotelian and Senecan precedents for the "tetragono ai colpi di ventura"; the letter "ad amicum Florentinum" is *Epistola* XII, in *Opere*, p. 1382.

64. Ser Bartolomeo di ser Gorello, *Cronica dei fatti d'Arezzo*, XX, 8, ed. Arturo Bini and Giovanni Grazzini, in *RIS*, n.s., XV.1, 192.

65. "Poi che la ruota v'ha volto nel basso, / messer Simone, abbiate franco cuore, / e non pigliate cruccio nè rancore, / e non usate dire:—Oimè lasso! / . . . / Se arete con ragion la sofferenza, / voi tornarete lieto entro in Fiorenza": *Sonetti burleschi e realistici*, p. 300. This rare vein for poetry can be found, too, in Brizio Visconti—e.g., in *Rimatori del '300*, pp. 176–180.

66. Georg Voigt, *Die Wiederbelebung des classischen Alterthums*, 3rd ed. (Berlin, 1893), II, 417–436, is still a valuable survey of the neglected subject of Renaissance epistolography; see C. H. Clough, "The Cult of Antiquity: Letters and Letter Collections," in *Cultural Aspects of the Italian Renaissance: Essays in Honour of Paul Oskar Kristeller*, ed. C. H. Clough (Manchester, 1976), pp. 33–67.

67. *Epistolae familiares*, II, iii, ed. V. Rossi, I, 66–74.

68. Ibid., iv, 74–80.

69. Ibid., v–viii, 80–89.

70. Ibid., viii, 88.

71. Poggius Bracciolini, *Opera omnia*, ed. Th. de Tonelli (reprint Turin, 1964), III, 37–46. During the decade of the 1430s, in his *Della vita civile*, Matteo Palmieri advised his fellow citizens of Florence to give their all for the sake of the republic and, should misfortune strike, to meditate on consolations that "largely mitigate our sorrows." Giovanni Cavalcanti says that two Florentines exiled during these years—namely, Neri Capponi and Giovanni Vespucci—were living exemplars of the ancient virtue of fortitude in the face of adversity. See Marcella Grendler, *The "Trattato Politico-Morale" of Giovanni Cavalcanti, 1381–c. 1451: A Critical Edition and Interpretation* (Geneva, 1973), pp. 82–83.

72. J. M. Filelfo, *Novum epistolarium* (Milan, 1484), fol. d iii.

73. Franciscus Niger, *De modo epistolandi* (Venice, 1490), fol. B iiir.

74. The manuscript is still unpublished in the Biblioteca Nazionale, Florence, II, II, 70; excerpts appear in *Prosatori latini del Quattrocento*, ed. Eugenio Garin (Milan/Naples, 1952), pp. 489–517. See Carlo Errera, "Le 'Commenta-

tiones Florentinae de exilio' di Francesco Filelfo," *Archivio storico italiano*, ser. V, 5 (1890): 193–227. Filelfo had himself been confined to Rome in March 1432 for exercising his sharp tongue against Florence's Venetian allies; declared a rebel within ten months and sentenced to lose his tongue after being implicated in various intrigues against the Medici, he also wrote letters, an oration, and satire on behalf of the anti-Mediceans, as discussed by Remigio Sabbadini, "Notizie di alcuni dotti umanisti del secolo XV," *Giornale storico della letteratura italiana*, 5 (1885): 162–169; and Laura De Feo Corso, "Il Filelfo in Siena," *Bullettino senese di storia patria*, 47 (1940): 306–307. Carlo De' Rosmini, *Vita di Francesco Filelfo*, 3 vols. (Milan, 1808), is still the only complete biography.

75. Biblioteca Nazionale, Florence, II, II, 70, fols. 1r–4v.

76. Ibid., fol. 4v.

77. Ibid., fol. 8r.

78. Ibid., fol. 46v; Poggio ("Bambalione") entered the dialogue, which had already enlisted Rinaldo degli Albizzi and Giannozzo Manetti, on fol. 27r. For Poggio's pamphlet (1435) defending Cosimo de' Medici as a modern Scipio, who, "lest he stand in the way of liberty in his country, went voluntarily into exile," see J. W. Oppel, "Peace vs. Liberty in the Quattrocento: Poggio, Guarino, and the Scipio-Caesar Controversy," *Journal of Medieval and Renaissance Studies*, 4 (1974): 237.

79. *I libri della famiglia*, ed. Cecil Grayson (Bari, 1960), p. 26.

80. Ibid., p. 180.

81. Ibid., pp. 26, 183.

82. Ibid., pp. 270–273.

83. Ibid., p. 184.

84. *P. Alcyonii Medices Legatus de exilio* (Venice, 1522); see Mario Rosa's careful sketch of Alcionio's career in *Dizionario biografico degli italiani*, II, 77–80.

85. *De exilio*, fols. B i–B iii.

86. Ibid., fols. C i, C vii, G iiii.

87. See *Lamenti storici dei secoli XIV, XV, e XVI*, ed. Antonio Medin and Carlo Frati (Bologna, 1887), pp. 47–53, 81–84.

88. *Vita Philippi Mariae tertij Ligurum ducis*, ed. Attilio Butti, Felice Fossati, and Giuseppe Petraglione, in *RIS*, n.s., XX.1, 65 and n. 2.

89. *De principe*, in *Ioannis Ioviani Pontani opera* (Venice, 1501), fol. 29v.

90. *Fr. Johannis Ferrarensis ex annalium libris marchionum Estensium excerpta*, ed. Luigi Simeoni, in *RIS*, n.s., XX.2, 37, 43.

91. E.g., *Leonardi Bruni historiarum libri*, Bk. II, pp. 33–34—Bruni's account, with an exile ambassador's speech to King Manfred, of the tactics of the Ghibelline *fuorusciti* in 1258.

92. Ibid., p. 50 (Bk. II, the recourse to exile as a greater "morbus quam ut ... medicamento sanitas illi posset afferri"); p. 120 (Bk. V, a speech against the duplicities of exiles from Arezzo in 1323).

93. "Nemo enim civis qui contra Patriam veniret laudandus sit": ibid., p. 193 (Bk. VIII); held captive as a boy in 1384 by exiles from Arezzo, Bruni probably had good personal reasons for skepticism. For Farinata's speech ("At

ego inimicos meos persecutus sum; patriam vero semper dilexi"), see ibid., pp. 41–42 (Bk. II). Mark Phillips has recently noted Bruni's suppression of violence in his sources in order "to protect the dignity of the Florentine republic": "Machiavelli, Guicciardini, and the Tradition of Vernacular Historiography in Florence," *American Historical Review*, 84 (1979): 93. Cf. *Mattei Palmerii liber de temporibus*, in *RIS*, n.s., XXVL.1, 138–140, where Palmieri passes over the exile of the Medici but celebrates their return to Florence in 1434.

94. Solerti, *Le vite di Dante, Petrarca, e Boccaccio*, pp. 13, 26.

95. Ibid., pp. 98, 103.

96. Quoted by Dionisotti, "Dante nel Quattrocento," p. 373.

97. "E se per sorte, de' mali ch'egli [Dante] li predisse le ne fusse accaduto alcuno, Firenze arebbe più da dolersi d'aver nutrito quell'uomo che d'alcuna altra rovina. Ma la fortuna, per farlo mendace e per ricoprire con la gloria sua la calunnia falsa di quello, l'ha continuamente prosperata e fatta celebre per tutte le provincie del mondo . . . che, se Dante la vedessi, o egli accuserebbe se stesso o, ripercosso dai colpi di quella sua innata invidia, vorebbe, essendo risuscitato, di nuovo morire": *Discorso o dialogo intorno alla nostra lingua*, in Machiavelli, *Tutte le opere*, p. 925. For the problem of attribution and the politics of linguistic hegemony in Florence, see Cecil Grayson, "Machiavelli and Dante," in *Renaissance Studies in Honor of Hans Baron*, ed. Anthony Molho and John A. Tedeschi (Dekalb, Ill., 1971), pp. 363–384; and Sergio Bertelli, "Egemonia linguistica come egemonia culturale e politica nella Firenze cosimiana," *Bibliothèque d'humanisme et Renaissance*, 38 (1976): 249–283.

98. Charles Trinkaus, *Adversity's Noblemen: The Humanists on Happiness* (New York, 1940), pp. 139, 189.

99. Machiavelli to Francesco Vettori, 10 December 1513, in *Tutte le opere*, p. 1159. In Machiavelli's *Istorie fiorentine*, V, 8–9, Rinaldo degli Albizzi calls for resistance against the Medici in 1435, but this was a case, the historian is quick to point out, of the usual "vane speranze de'fuori usciti": ibid., pp. 743–744.

100. On which, see Albertini, *Das florentinische Staatsbewusstsein*.

101. Heitmann, *Fortuna und Virtus*, p. 235n., cites Petrarch's references in many of his works to the "exile" of man from God and from himself in this life. For Marsiglio Ficino, "as if we were exiles, we fall into sadness, although we do not know the cause of our sadness or think of it" (quoted by Trinkaus, *Image and Likeness*, II, 494); Eugenio Garin, *Portraits from the Quattrocento* (New York, 1972), p. 180, quotes Angelo Poliziano along similar lines. See William J. Bouwsma, "Anxiety and the Formation of Early Modern Culture," in *After the Reformation: Essays in Honor of J. H. Hexter*, ed. Barbara C. Malament (Phila., Pa., 1980), pp. 215–246.

EPILOGUE

1. The most recent accounts are by Roberto Cantagalli, *La guerra di Siena (1552–1559)* (Siena, 1962); and Arnaldo D'Addario, *Il problema senese nella storia italiana della prima metà del Cinquecento (La guerra di Siena)* (Florence, 1958).

2. For especially stimulating reflections on these alternatives, see Frank Kermode, *The Sense of an Ending: Studies in the Theory of Fiction* (New York, 1967); and the special issue of *Nineteenth-Century Fiction*, 33 (1978), on "narrative endings."

3. See Lucien Romier, *Les origines politiques des guerres de religion* (Paris, 1913), I, 232.

4. Cantagalli, *La guerra de Siena*, p. xxii.

5. Ibid., pp. lxiii–lxiv, 527.

6. Northrop Frye, *Anatomy of Criticism, Four Essays* (Princeton, 1957), p. 41; on tragic and other "explanations by emplotment" in historical writing, cf. Hayden White, *Metahistory: The Historical Imagination in Nineteenth-Century Europe* (Baltimore/London, 1973), pp. 7–11.

7. D'Addario, *Il problema senese*, p. 58; Romier, *Les origines politiques*, I, 156–250, remains the best account of the international interests at stake.

8. For this and other administrative details, see Vilma Baccinetti, "La repubblica senese ritirata a Montalcino," *Bullettino senese di storia patria*, 47 (1940): 1–38, 97–116.

9. Romier, *Les origines politiques*, I, 221–240; a number of the more important exiles at Montalcino are discussed in the study by Emile Picot, *Les italiens en France au XVIe siècle* (Bordeaux, 1901).

10. Nicholas Throckmorton to William Cecil, from Paris, 6 June 1559; and Cosimo de' Medici to Bernardo Minerbetti, 27 July 1559, cited by Cantagalli, *La guerra di Siena*, pp. 527, 558n.

11. Giovan Battista Adriani wrote the most elaborate official account in his *Istoria dei suoi tempi dall'anno 1536 all'anno 1574* (Venice, 1587); cf. Michele Lupo Gentile, "Studi sulla storiografia alla corte di Cosimo de' Medici," *Annali della R. Scuola Normale Superiore di Pisa*, 19 (1905): 1–164; and Von Albertini, *Das florentinische Staatsbewusstsein*, pp. 299–341.

12. See Frye, *Anatomy of Criticism*, pp. 41–43; and Gilbert Highet, *The Anatomy of Satire* (Princeton, 1962), pp. 156–158.

13. On the case for Italy's sixteenth-century "retrogression," see, e.g., Armando Sapori, "Medioevo e Rinascimento, per una diversa periodizzazione," *Archivio storico italiano*, 115 (1955): 135–164; Roberto S. Lopez, *The Three Ages of the Italian Renaissance* (Charlottesville, Va., 1970), pp. 54–74; Luigi Bulferetti, "Il problema della 'decadenza' italiana," in *Nuove questioni di storia moderna* (Milan, 1964), pp. 803–845; and William J. Bouwsma, "Changing Assumptions in Later Renaissance Culture," *Viator*, 7 (1976): 421–440.

14. *Poetics* VII.3, ed. S. H. Butcher (London, 1911), pp. 30–31.

15. Cf., e.g., Barbara Herrnstein Smith, *Poetic Closure: A Study of How Poems End* (Chicago, 1968).

16. Cf. Armand Dubarry, *Le brigandage en Italie* (Paris, 1875), pp. 83–121; Jean Delumeau, *Vie économique et sociale de Rome dans la seconde moitié du siècle XVIe* (Paris, 1959), II, 543–566; and Fernand Braudel, *The Mediterranean*, II, 734–756.

17. Lorenzo Grottanelli, *Alfonso Piccolomini, storia del secolo XVI* (Florence, 1892).

18. Quoted by Eric Cochrane, *Florence in the Forgotten Centuries, 1527–1800* (Chicago/London, 1973), p. 180; I draw on Cochrane's vivid evocation of Scipione Ammirato's "perfect day" (27 June 1591) for what follows.

19. E.g., Riguccio Galluzzi, *Storia del granducato di Toscana* (Florence, 1822), IV, 122–125; V, 77–80, 86–89.

20. There is a fascinating account by a native of the region: Giacomo Barzellotti, *Monte Amiata e il suo profeta* (Milan, 1910). What was for him chiefly a religious movement has been reconsidered as a case of "primitive rebellion" by E. J. Hobsbawm, *Primitive Rebels: Studies in Archaic Forms of Social Movement in the 19th and 20th Centuries* (New York, 1959), pp. 65–73. I use both accounts and both perspectives in the following pages.

21. Quoted by Eugenio Lazzareschi, *Davide Lazzaretti* (Brescia, 1945), p. 238.

22. Quoted in Barzellotti's detailed description (*Monte Amiata*, pp. 256–257) of the descent and confrontation.

23. Hobsbawm, *Primitive Rebels*, p. 71, tells this story.

24. Richard Cobb, *The Police and the People: French Popular Protest, 1789–1820* (Oxford, 1970), p. 3.

25. Ibid., p. 81.

26. Grottanelli, *Alfonso Piccolomini*, pp. 5, 12, 41; and Hobsbawm, *Primitive Rebels*, pp. 66, 71.

27. Galuzzi, *Storia*, IV, 122–125; and Barzellotti, *Monte Amiata*, pp. 15, 68.

28. Allan Silver, "The Demand for Order in Civil Society: A Review of Some Themes in the History of Urban Crime, Police, and Riot," in *The Police: Six Sociological Essays*, ed. David Bordua (New York/London, 1967), pp. 2–21, is especially suggestive on these themes; so, too, is White, "The Forms of Wildness: Archeology of an Idea," in *The Wild Man Within*, ed. E. Dudley and M. Novak, pp. 4–31. Cf. Chapter One above.

29. As noted in Grand Duke Pietro Leopoldo's *Relazioni sul governo della Toscana*, ed. Arnaldo Salvestrini (Florence, 1969–1974), III, 612–613.

30. The fundamental text here is Foucault's *Discipline and Punish*. See, too, Georg Rusche and Otto Kirchheimer, *Punishment and Social Structure* (New York, 1939); Pierre Deyon, *Le temps des prisons: Essai sur l'histoire de la délinquance et les origines du système pénitentiaire* (Paris, 1974); and Dario Melossi and Massimo Pavarini, *Carcere e fabbrica: alle origini del sistema penitenziario* (Bologna, 1977).

31. Emilio Santini, "Il significato nazionale delle celebrazioni della caduta della repubblica di Siena ritirata a Montalcino," *Bullettino senese di storia patria*, 66 (1959): 36–48.

32. E.g., in the manner of twenty modern exile-authors in their essays on twenty exiles of the past in *The Torch of Freedom*, ed. Emil Ludwig and Henry B. Kranz (New York, 1943). Cf. White, *Metahistory*, pp. 8–9, for the "Romantic drama of redemption" and comedy's "reconciliations of men with men, of men with their world and their society" as plot structures in historical writing.

33. Solzhenitsyn, *The Gulag Archipelago*, III, Pt. 6 ("Exile"), 369–370.

34. Tabori, *Anatomy of Exile*, pp. 326–397.

35. Ibid., pp. 276–293.

36. Ibid., pp. 24–26, citing the statute of the United Nations Commissioner for Refugees; cf. Paul Weis, "The Concept of the Refugee in International Law," *Journal du droit internationale*, 87 (1960): 928–1001.

37. Tabori, *Anatomy of Exile*, pp. 26, 306, citing the 1967 protocol and the reservation of subversives adopted by the Organization of African Unity.

38. Sadruddin Aga Khan, "What Remains to Be Done to Further Refugees' Human Rights," *Migration News*, 15 (1968): 3–5.

39. Cassin's remarks are in Tabori, *Anatomy of Exile*, p. 312.

INDEX

Acciaiuoli: family, 103; Donato, 102–104
Accursius, 77, 79
Acton, Lord John E. D., xvii
Aeneid, 8
Agolanti, family, 112
Aguglione, Baldo d', 62, 64, 66, 76
Alberti: family, 95, 100–101, 103, 109–119 *passim*; Alberto di Bernardo, 109; Benedetto, 109; Cipriano, 109; Francesco di Bivigliano, 110; Giannozzo, 142; Giovanni, 109; Leandro, 5; Leon Battista, 141–142; Lionardo, 143; Lorenzo, 142; Nerozzo, 109; Piero, 143
Alberti of Mangona, family, 45
Albizzi, family: Maso, 102; Rinaldo, 92, 141
Albornoz, Egidio, cardinal, 89
Alcionio, Pietro, 141, 143–144
Alessandria, 98
Alfani, Vermiglio degli, 55, 58
Alfonso "The Magnanimous," king of Naples, 86, 90, 96, 99
Alighieri: family, 46, 75, 81; Francesco, 75; Gemma, 46, 75. *See also* Dante Alighieri
Altoviti, Palmiro, 55, 70, 72
Ammirato, Scipione, 154
Amnesty, 47, 84, 97–98, 120
Ancona, 92, 110
Andrea, Monte, 129
Angevins of Naples, 34, 36, 38–39, 54, 83, 89. *See also* Charles I, king of

Naples; Ladislaus, king of Naples; Robert "The Wise," king of Naples
Anghiari, battle of (1440), 92
Angiolieri, Cecco, 14, 123
Antella, Guido di Filippo dell', 55
Antonio da Ferrara, 87, 122
Appenincola, Severo, 138–139
Apugliese, Ruggieri, 122
Aquila, 16, 95
Aragon, house of, 34, 119. *See also* Alfonso "The Magnanimous," king of Naples
Arcidosso, 156
Arena, Jacopo d', 77–78, 116
Arezzo, 36, 41, 43, 44, 46, 90, 123, 129, 137, 145
Arezzo, Fra Guittone d', 123, 129
Aristotle, 154
Ascoli, 32
Asti, 55, 56
Astraea, 131
Asylum, 95
Augustine, Saint, 22, 29, 60
Augustus Caesar, 19, 26
Azzo da Correggio, 134

Baexe, Righetto da, 122
Bagno, Panuccio del, 129
Banchi, Bartolo, 70
Bandello, Matteo, xvi, 45
Banditori, 73
Banniti, 73, 75, 81, 154; defined, 2, 21, 23,

Designer:	Marion O'Brien
Compositor:	Heritage Printers, Inc.
Printer:	Heritage Printers, Inc.
Binder:	The Delmar Companies
Text:	Janson Linotype
Display:	Janson Monotype